Be My Disciples™

Second Edition

Charley Cook
Corporate Vice President
Kendall Hunt Publishing

Amy S. McEntee, MA, MS
Publisher

Michael P. Horan, PhD
Elizabeth Nagel, SSD
Program Advisors

GRADE FOUR
PARISH EDITION

RCL Benziger®
A Kendall Hunt Company

The Subcommittee on the Catechism, United States Conference of Catholic Bishops, has found this text, copyright 2023, to be in conformity with the *Catechism of the Catholic Church*.

IMPRIMATUR
Reverend Steve J. Angi
Chancellor
Vicar General
Archdiocese of Cincinnati
Cincinnati, Ohio
June 30, 2021

The *Imprimatur* is a declaration that a book or pamphlet is free of doctrinal or moral error. It is not implied that those who have granted the Imprimatur agree with the contents, opinions or statements expressed.

Acknowledgments

Excerpts are taken and adapted from the *New American Bible*, revised edition, © 1991, 1986, 1970, 2010 Confraternity of Christian Doctrine, Washington, D.C., and are used by permission of the copyright owner. All rights reserved. No part of the *New American Bible* may be reproduced in any form without permission in writing from the copyright owner.

Excerpts are taken and adapted from the English translation of the *Roman Missal*, © 2010, International Commission on English in the Liturgy, Inc. (ICEL). All rights reserved. No part of the *Roman Missal* may be reproduced in any form without permission in writing from the copyright owner.

Excerpts are taken and adapted from the English translation of the *Catechism of the Catholic Church* for use in the United States of America, second edition, © 1997, United States Catholic Conference, Inc.- Liberia Editrice Vaticana. All rights reserved. No part of the *Catechism of the Catholic Church* may be reproduced in any form without permission in writing from the copyright owner.

Excerpts and adaptations of prayers were taken from the book of *Catholic Household Blessings & Prayers*, Revised and Updated Edition, © 2007, 2020, United States Conference of Catholic Bishops, Washington, D.C. All rights reserved. No part of the book of *Catholic Household Blessings & Prayers* may be reproduced or transmitted in any form or by any means, electronic or mechanical, including photocopying, recording, or by any information storage and retrieval system, without permission in writing from the copyright holder.

Toll Free 877-275-4725
Fax 800-688-8356

Visit us at RCLBenziger.com and BeMyDisciples.com

452896 ISBN 978-1-7924-2896-8 (Student Edition)
452328 ISBN 978-1-7924-2328-4 (Catechist Edition)

1st Printing
May 2022

Additional materials are available on RCL Benziger's digital resource platform, Flourish. Log in at **BeMyDisciples.com** to access ideas on ways your family can live as disciples of Jesus and more. For credentials and assistance, contact your parish administrator or **Flourish@RCLBenziger.com**.

Family Life Connection

Letter to Parents/Families

Dear Parents/Families,

Your family is a gift from God! As a way to support you and the Church's teachings on family living, RCL Benziger is pleased to include the *Family Life Connection* pages in your child's religion book, *Be My Disciples*.

The *Family Life Connection* is a two-page insert in each chapter. It is easily used at home with your family. The only additional resource needed is the Holy Bible.

The *Family Life Connection* will help your family integrate Catholic values and virtues into everyday living. You will also find simple explanations of the Church's teachings as related to the lessons in *Be My Disciples*. As your family works through the *Family Life Connection* activities, you will have the opportunity to

- practice strategies for effective communication,
- address important cultural issues in age-appropriate ways,
- review important tips for maintaining a safe environment, and
- practice skills for healthy and holy family living.

Pope Saint John Paul II, in his Apostolic Exhortation *On the Family*, challenges families to become what they are: "a community of life and love." The pope invites you to wrap your child in the love of Christ, so that your son or daughter will become a follower of the Lord. Pope Francis builds on that message by encouraging families in his letter entitled *The Joy of Love*. Pope Francis writes about the mission of the family as being one of love and focuses on the strengths and gifts of families. He addresses the importance of good habits and ways to live a moral life in order to internalize the values that begin in childhood.

May your family enjoy these *Family Life Connection* pages as you learn and practice the skills to build healthy relationships. May you continue to grow as a family of faith.

From our family to yours,

RCL Benziger

For more tips on how your family can live as disciples of Jesus, visit **BeMyDisciples.com**

Family Life Connection

RCL Benziger invites your family to pray each time you participate in the Family Life Connection *activities. We offer this prayer as a suggestion.*

Prayer for Families

Kind and loving God, Father and Creator,
you have given us the special gift of life
and the great gift of belonging to your family of faith.

We want to discover ways to live our Christian faith in our everyday family life.
Please be with us as we participate in this formation.
We know that it is a great opportunity for us to learn and grow as a family.

We promise to share openly and to work together with the activities.
We will make every effort to spend time together as a family—working, playing,
and praying together.

Help us to realize that you are always the center of our family.
Help us to recognize your presence during times of tears and fears, anger and pain,
and laughter and joy.
Acknowledging your role in our family will help us to grow closer and stronger as a family.

Finally, help us to live the Gospel message of your Son and our Savior, Jesus Christ.
Inspire in us, through the presence of the Holy Spirit, the strength to follow the
teachings of our Catholic Church.

We ask this in Jesus' name.
Amen!

Contents

A Snapshot of Me

My name is ______________________.

A hero of mine is ______________________.

My favorite Bible story is ______________________.

My favorite book is ______________________.

Making Good Choices

We use the gift of our minds to discover good choices. This year, you will learn four ways the Church helps us. You will learn

- what Catholics believe about our relationship with God;
- how the sacraments help us celebrate our good choices;
- rules that guide us in making good decisions; and
- ways to pray when we need God's help and guidance.

Figure It Out!

Follow this path to make good choices. At each stop along the way, discover a way God helps us to make right decisions. A clue in each box will help you know the answer. Unscramble the letters and write the answer. Move along the path to the next choice box.

Unit 1: We Believe, Part One

God is the real author of this. The Holy Spirit inspired the human writers of the Bible to write God's Word for his people. Unscramble the words, and then check your answer on page 13. Tell a partner about your favorite Scripture story.

D S A R E C   T E R U C S R P I

____

Unit 2: We Believe, Part Two

Write who guides us to live as children of God. Tell a partner one other thing you know about this answer. Check your answer on page 65.

L H Y O   T S R I P I

____

Unit 3: We Worship, Part One

During this season of the liturgical year, we celebrate that Christ is risen. He is always with us, and he will come again in glory. After you unscramble the word, check your answer on page 95. Share with a partner how your family celebrates this season.

S E R A E T

____

Unit 4: We Worship, Part Two

Write the sacrament that helps us begin anew. Tell a partner one thing that happens at this celebration. Check your answer on page 130.

N O T E L R I C A I C N O I

____

Unit 5: We Live, Part One

Write the name of the eight guides to happiness Jesus gave us. Tell a partner one kind of person who is blessed by God. Check your answer on pages 166 and 167.

A S E U T D I B T E

____

Unit 6: We Live, Part Two

Write the name of the prayer that teaches us how Jesus tells us to live. Tell a partner one thing this prayer teaches. Check your answer on pages 218 and 219.

R U O   H F T R E A

____

Do Not Worry

Leader: O Lord, we gather to thank you for speaking to us through the Holy Bible.

All: **Your Word is truth and life.**

Leader: A reading from the holy Gospel according to Saint Matthew.

All: **Glory to you, O Lord.**

Leader: (Jesus said,) "Therefore I tell you, do not worry about your life, . . . Look at the birds in the sky; they do not sow or reap, they gather nothing into barns, yet your heavenly Father feeds them. Are you not more important than they?. . . Learn from the way the wild flowers grow. They do not work or spin. But I tell you that not even Solomon in all his splendor was clothed like one of them. If God so clothes the grass of the field, which grows today and is thrown into the oven tomorrow, will he not much more provide for you, O you of little faith?"

MATTHEW 6:25-30

The Gospel of the Lord.

All: **Praise to you, Lord Jesus Christ.**

Come and bow before the Bible.

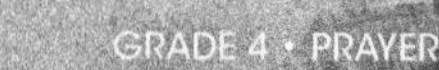

We Believe

UNIT 1

Part One

The Family of Jesus

Jesus has a family tree with very deep roots!

We call Jesus Christ the son of David and the son of Abraham.

Abraham became the father of Isaac, and Isaac the father of Jacob.

Many years later, Obed, who was descended from Jacob, became the father of Jesse. Jesse became the father of David the king.

Even later, another Jacob, who was descended from David, became the father of Joseph, the husband of Mary. Of her, Jesus the Messiah was born.

The total number of generations from Abraham to the Messiah is forty-two generations.

Based on Matthew 1:1-17

What I Have Learned

What is something you already know about these three faith terms?

faith

____

____

____

Divine Providence

____

____

____

Messiah

____

____

____

Faith Terms to Know

Put an X next to the faith terms you know. Put a ? next to faith terms you need to learn more about.

_______ Divine Revelation

_______ Sacred Scripture

_______ truthfulness

_______ YHWH

_______ Original Sin

_______ almighty

_______ Creator

The Bible

What do you know about how to find passages in the Bible?

____

____

____

The Church

What would you tell a friend about what the Church believes?

____

____

____

A Question I Have

What question would you like to ask about the mystery of God?

____

____

____

Our Lady of Subukia

A Devotion from Kenya

There is a towering white cross on a hill in the African nation of Kenya. It welcomes visitors of every faith to a shrine honoring the Mother of Jesus. The shrine stands on the equator. That is where the Northern and Southern Hemispheres meet. The shrine is called the Village of Mary, Mother of God. It is a place of prayer, peace, and penance.

The shrine welcomes thousands of visitors, called pilgrims, each year. There is a small chapel at the base of the hill. Pilgrims stop here to confess their sins. Then they walk up a steep and rocky path. Along the path are the Stations of the Cross. The difficult journey recalls Jesus' painful walk to his Crucifixion.

There is another chapel at the top of the hill. Near the chapel is a small spring of water. On December 7, 1991, a worker was clearing brush in the area. He found a damp patch of ground. The worker dug into the ground and water began to flow from the spot. Water has been flowing from the spring ever since that day. People believe the water helps bring about physical and spiritual refreshment. The water reminds visitors of their Baptisms.

? Why do you think the shrine has two chapels? Why do some visitors climb the steep and rocky path?

The shrine to Our Lady of Subukia was officially recognized by Pope John Paul II in 1999.

Popular Devotions

Our Lady of Subukia

The people of Kenya and other parts of Africa visit the shrine to remember Jesus' great love for them. They remember Jesus' great suffering and sacrifice. In each box, write the Station of the Cross indicated by the number. Then write a prayer to Jesus. Thank him for his great love.

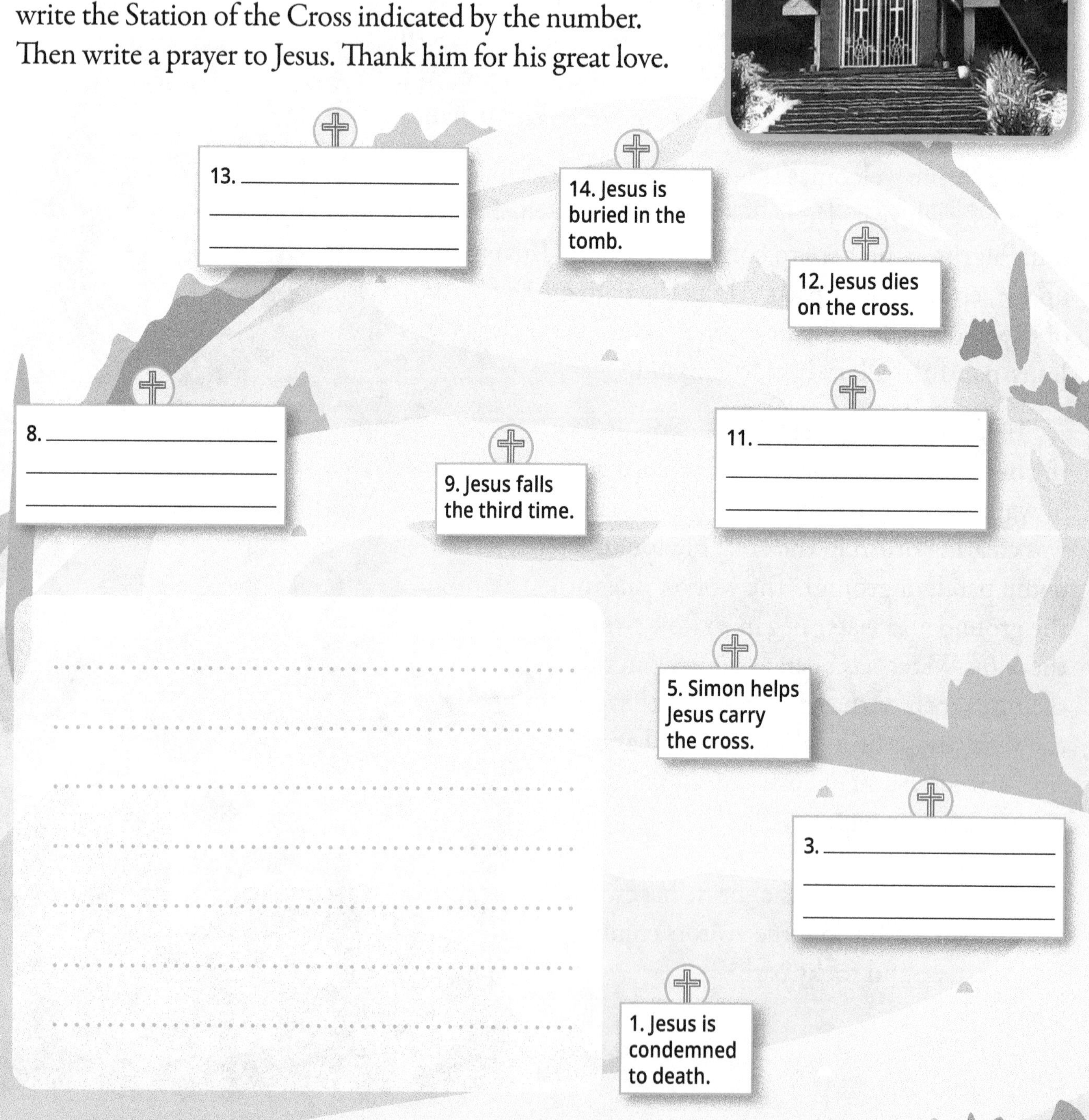

Looking Ahead

In this chapter, the Holy Spirit invites you to ▶

EXPLORE the Bible, God's Word for us.

DISCOVER how the Bible brings us closer to God.

DECIDE ways to live as a disciple of Jesus.

CHAPTER 1

God's Word to Us

? Is there a favorite story that your family enjoys telling? Why do you enjoy hearing this story?

The Bible is filled with stories about God's love. These words are from the first story in the Bible. Listen carefully to this part of the story of creation:

> Darkness was everywhere and a mighty wind filled the air. God said, "Let there be light," and there was light. God saw how good the light was. God separated the light from the darkness. God called the light "day," and he named the darkness "night." There was evening, and then came morning. It was the first day of creation. BASED ON GENESIS 1:1-3

? What else do you remember about the Bible story of creation?

Disciple Power

Truthfulness

God is the source of all truth. His Word is truth. God wants us to live in the truth. We do this when we let God's Word guide our words and actions. A person who is truthful does not tell lies. A truthful person admits mistakes. Love and trust grow when we practice truthfulness.

Reading the Bible

Megan's grandmother read her Bible early every morning before the rest of the family was awake. She told Megan that this was a special time of the day. Grandma said that she listened to and spoke to God during those quiet moments.

Many years later, after Grandma died, Megan's father gave the Bible to Megan. It was a very special gift. Megan was reminded of her grandmother when she turned the Bible's well-worn pages. It was a gift that she would always treasure.

God's people have always shared the stories found in the Bible. From the very first days of the Church, the followers of Jesus shared stories about Jesus and his teachings. About the year AD 50, the disciples of Jesus began writing down these stories. Today, these writings make up the New Testament, which was completed around the year AD 100.

Today the Bible is available in almost every language. It is one of the most widely read and studied books in the world.

Activity Look through this chapter and choose a Bible verse that has a message you would like people to know and believe. Write it on this card to pass on to someone.

____

____

____

____

The Faith Story of God's People

Sacred Scripture is the collection of holy writings found in the Bible. The words *sacred scripture* mean "holy writing." God is the real author of Sacred Scripture. The Holy Spirit inspired the human writers of the **Bible** to write God's Word for his people. This means that the human writers wrote down without error what God wanted to say to his people. The Church collected these holy writings of God's people and placed them in the Bible.

Here is part of one of the most important faith stories in the Bible. In it God reveals, or makes known, his name to Moses. God said,

> "Tell the Israelites: I AM sent me to you."
>
> Exodus 3:14

The English words *I am* are the same as the Hebrew word "YHWH." YHWH are four letters of the Hebrew alphabet. These letters represent the name for God that he revealed to Moses.

? Lord is another name the Bible uses for God. Do you know any other names that the Bible uses for God? What is your favorite name for God? What does that name tell you about him?

FAITH FOCUS
Why are the writings in the Bible holy?

FAITH VOCABULARY

Sacred Scripture
Sacred Scripture is the holy writings of the People of God, inspired by the Holy Spirit, and collected in the Bible.

Bible
The Bible is the Word of God. It was written by human writers who were inspired by the Holy Spirit.

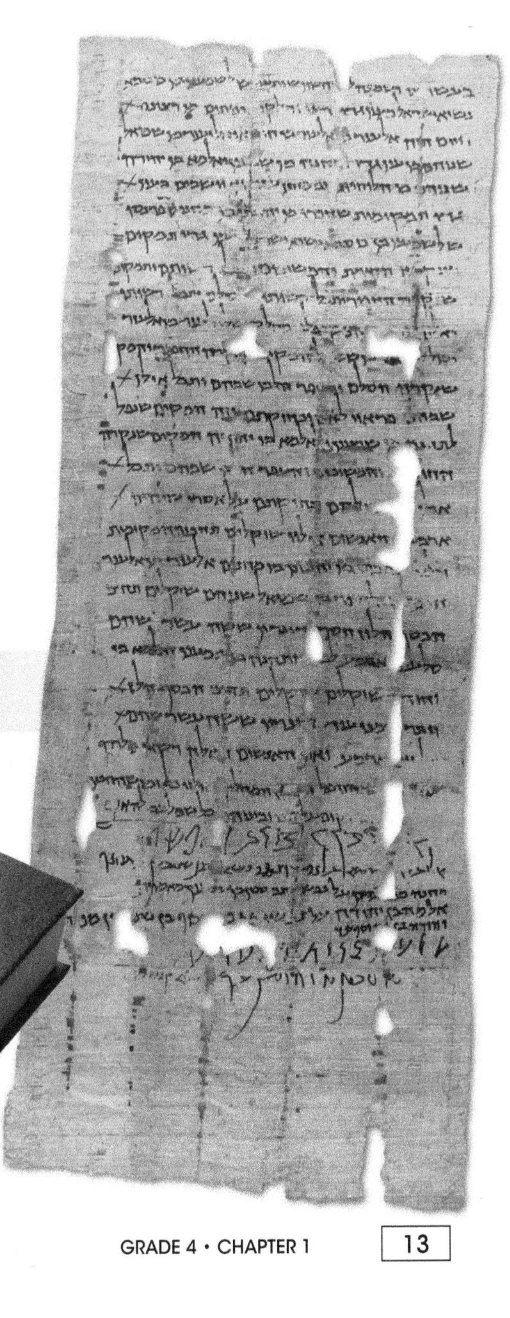

Dead Sea Scrolls

The Israelites

The Israelites were the people God first chose to be his people. The story of the Israelites begins with the Old Testament story of Abraham and Sarah.

The Old Testament

The Bible is divided into the Old Testament and the New Testament. The forty-six books of the Old Testament begin with the story of creation, Adam and Eve, and the Fall. We read that God created Adam and Eve to live in friendship with him, but then Adam and Eve turned away from God and his love.

God continued to love Adam and Eve, and he promised to send someone to renew that friendship. All the writings of the Bible after the story of creation and the Fall tell the story of God fulfilling that promise.

God's people, the Israelites, also made a promise to God. God and the Israelites entered into a sacred agreement, or Covenant. God promised that he alone would be their God. They promised to worship him alone and to obey the commands, or the laws, that he gave to Moses to give to them. These laws are summarized in the Ten Commandments. God's people promised,

"Everything the LORD has said, we will do." EXODUS 19:8

? What does God reveal to us in the Old Testament?

Moses Smashing the Tablets of the Law,
Rembrandt Harmensz van Rijn
1659 (oil on canvas)

The New Testament

The twenty-seven books of the New Testament tell about the fulfillment of God's promises in Jesus Christ. The Gospel is the heart of the New Testament. The word *gospel* means "good news."

There are four written accounts of the Gospel, or the Good News of Jesus Christ in the New Testament. They are named after four followers of Jesus: Matthew, Mark, Luke, and John. These four writers are called the Evangelists. The word *evangelist* means "writer of the Good News."

The Gospels pass on the Church's faith in Jesus. The center of the Gospels is the account of the Jesus' birth, life, suffering, Death, Resurrection, and Ascension. Through the Gospels and the other writings in the Bible, God speaks to us and invites us to believe and trust in him.

Catholics Believe

The Holy Spirit

The Holy Spirit inspired the human writers of the Bible. This means that they wrote down without error what God wanted to teach us.

Activity Here is a simple way to find any passage in the Bible.

LUKE 15:8-10

The word **Luke** refers to the name of the book. Check the table of contents in the front of the Bible to locate the page number where the book begins. The number 15 before the colon (:) refers to the chapter number. The numbers after the colon (8-10) refer to the verse numbers.

Find the passage in a Bible. Why do you think Jesus told this parable?

____

____

____

____

Luke

Chapter 15

Verses 8-10

LUKE 15 126

The Simile of Salt. "Salt is good, but if salt itself loses its taste, with what can its flavor be restored? It is fit neither for the soil nor for the manure pile; it is thrown out. Whoever has ears to hear ought to hear."

CHAPTER 15

The Parable of the Lost Sheep. The tax collectors and sinners were all drawing near to listen to him, but the Pharisees and scribes began to complain, saying, "This man welcomes sinners and eats with them." So to them he addressed this parable. "What man among you having a hundred sheep and losing one of them would not leave the ninety-nine in the desert and go after the lost one until he finds it? And when he does find it, he sets it on his shoulders with great joy and, upon his arrival home, he calls together his friends and neighbors and says to them, 'Rejoice with me because I have found my lost sheep.' I tell you, in just the same way there will be more joy in heaven over one sinner who repents than over ninety-nine righteous people who have no need of repentance.

The Parable of the Lost Coin. "Or what woman having ten coins and losing one would not light a lamp and sweep the house, searching carefully until she finds it? And when she does find it, she calls together her friends and neighbors and says to them, 'Rejoice with me because I have found the coin that I lost.' In just the same way, I tell you, there will be rejoicing among the angels of God over one sinner who repents."

The Parable of the Lost Son. Then he said, "A man had two sons, and the younger son said to his father, 'Father, give me the share of your estate that should come to me.' So the father divided the property between them. After a few days, the younger son collected all his belongings and

I FOLLOW JESUS

Remember that the Bible tells us that at creation, God brought light to the darkness. The image of light is used often in Scripture to describe God's presence with his people. Jesus uses the image of light too. Telling the truth is one way you can bring God's light to the world.

LIGHT OF THE WORLD

In this reading, Jesus is talking about what it means to be one of his disciples.

You are the light of the world. A city set on a mountain cannot be hidden. Nor do people light a lamp and then put it under a bushel basket in their home. They set it on a lampstand, where it gives light to all in the house. Just so, your light must shine before others, that they may see your good deeds and glorify your heavenly Father.

BASED ON MATTHEW 5:14-16

In this passage, Jesus tells us how God's love can shine through us by what we do and say. Discuss with a partner a time when telling the truth could share God's light with others. Describe your idea here.

Situation

____

____

____

____

Response

____

____

____

____

MY FAITH CHOICE

We grow in our love for God and others when we read and pray with Scripture. You can spend a few quiet moments each day listening to and speaking to God. Write when and where you will do this.

I will

______________________________.

Take a moment and ask God the Holy Spirit to help you let your light shine at home.

Chapter Review

Write a sentence about the Bible. Use three or more of these words.

YHWH	Jesus Christ	Covenant
Old Testament	New Testament	Gospel

____

____

____

____

____

TO HELP YOU REMEMBER

1. The Bible is the inspired, written Word of God.
2. The Holy Spirit inspired the human authors of the Bible.
3. The New Testament begins with the four Gospels, which tell us the Good News of Jesus Christ.

Lights in the World

Signing our foreheads, lips, and chests over our hearts is a gesture showing our faith in God. This gesture helps us to prepare to listen closely to God's Word.

Leader: Let us prepare ourselves to listen to God's Word by signing our foreheads, lips, and chests over our hearts with a small sign of the cross.

All: **Jesus, be in my mind, my lips, and my heart.**

Reader 1: Let us listen to God's Word. *Read aloud Genesis 1:1-3.*

All: **God, at creation you brought light to the darkness. May we bring your light to the world.**

Reader 2: *(Read aloud Matthew 5:14-16.)*

All: **Praise to you, Lord Jesus Christ.**

Leader: Listen quietly to God's Word in your heart. How can we be God's light for the world this week? Let us pray together.

All: **Lord, may your light shine in our lives. Amen.**

With My Family

This Week . . .

In Chapter 1, God's Word to Us, your child learned:

- ▶ The Bible is the inspired Word of God.
- ▶ The Holy Spirit inspired the human writers of the Bible to ensure that God's Word would be communicated faithfully and accurately.
- ▶ The two main parts of the Bible are the Old Testament and the New Testament.
- ▶ In the Gospels, we read how God has revealed himself fully in his Son, Jesus Christ.
- ▶ God is truth and the source of all truth.

For more about related teachings of the Church, see the *Catechism of the Catholic Church,* 101–133, and the *United States Catholic Catechism for Adults,* pages 23–33.

Sharing God's Word

Read and talk about a favorite Bible story. Tell about where you first heard the story. Remember that the Bible is God's Word to us.

We Live as Disciples

The Christian family is a school of discipleship. Choose one of the following activities to do as a family, or design a similar activity of your own:

- ▶ Create and decorate a special place for the Bible in your home. Open the Bible to a favorite story. Read the story and talk about it.
- ▶ Be on the lookout for family members practicing truthfulness during the week. Challenge each other to practice this virtue every day.

Our Spiritual Journey

We are a "pilgrim people." There are a variety of sacred gestures that Christians use to remind themselves that life as disciples of Christ is a spiritual journey, or pilgrimage. In this chapter, your child learned to pray with gestures. These are the same gestures that we use before we listen to the Gospel at Mass. Read and pray together the prayer on page 17.

Faith-Filled People

The Israelites
The Israelites were the first and only to be named as God's Chosen People. The story of the Israelites begins in the Old Testament.

For more ideas on ways your family can live as disciples of Jesus, visit BeMyDisciples.com

Choosing Good Habits

We always have a choice to act in a healthy and holy way. We can make healthy choices. We can say "no" to things that will harm us. We can say "no" to habits that are bad for us. For example, we do not have to lie to a friend. We do not have to cheat on a test. We do not have to do anything that we know is harmful to us. It can be difficult to say "no," especially to something we want or to someone we like. But we have choices. We do have control over our actions.

We can say "yes" to habits that are good for us. We can brush our teeth after meals. We can wash our clothes. We can keep our bodies clean. We can exercise to stay fit. We can pray for God's grace to give us strength. We can choose to do good. God loves us, and we can love others and ourselves.

Jesus taught us many ways to live healthy and holy lives. We call some of these the Works of Mercy. These disciplined actions provide us with ways to love others as God wants us to love them. Each of these actions allows us to be a gift to another person in a loving way.

Catholics Believe

The Great Commandment teaches us to love God and to love everyone as we love ourselves. We live the Great Commandment when we take good care of our minds, bodies, and spirits.

Activity Choose one of the Works of Mercy. Then tell how you will put it into action.

A Work of Mercy	I will

Faith Focus

We follow the Great Commandment by taking care of others and ourselves.

Healthy Habits @ Home

As a family, decide on one healthy habit to start, and one unhealthy habit to stop.

Healthy habit to start:

....

Unhealthy habit to stop:

....

Family Time

Cut out and hang at home

As a family, talk about forming habits. To help the conversation, consider these points:

- A habit is caused by repetition, not reward.
- Habits can be created in as few as ten days.
- Good habits are usually learned intentionally: we want to become better.

Family in Action

As a family, determine how you can show concern for others using all of the Works of Mercy. For example, "What can we do to provide drink to those who are thirsty?"

Participate in a parish-sponsored outreach event to serve those in need. After the event, share as a family how the experience helped family members better understand God's mercy.

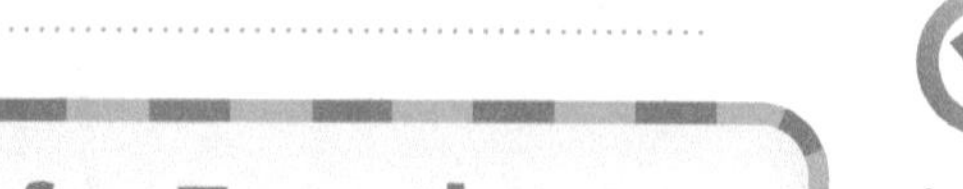

Safer Together

Families are safer together when they are aware of common risks at home. Review these tips for keeping your family safe.

- Educate your children about the dangers of household chemicals, sharp objects, and weapons.
- Read and follow safety warnings. Safety equipment should be used when appropriate.
- Set restrictions on your technology and media devices to avoid having your children accidentally exposed to inappropriate images.

Looking Ahead

In this chapter, the Holy Spirit invites you to ▸

EXPLORE what the creeds of the Church tell us.

DISCOVER how God has revealed himself.

DECIDE ways to live and share faith in God.

CHAPTER 2

I Will Be Your God

? How can you get to know your friends better? What are some of the ways that you come to know God? Who has helped you come to know God?

The Bible helps us to know God better. Imagine that you could go back to the time of Moses in the Old Testament. Listen as God speaks to Moses about his very special friendship with the people of Israel:

> Therefore, say to the Israelites: I am the LORD. I will free you from your slavery in Egypt. I will rescue you. I will be your God. BASED ON EXODUS 6:6-7

? What do you hear God telling you about himself in this passage?

Disciple Power

Faith

Faith is a gift from God. It is the Theological Virtue that helps us know God and believe in him and in all that he has revealed.

THE CHURCH FOLLOWS JESUS

The Creeds of the Church

A friend of yours, who is not Catholic, asks you, "What do you know and believe about God?" How would you respond?

We belong to the Catholic Church, and each Sunday we respond to this question and profess our faith by praying the Nicene Creed. We profess our faith in God and in all that he has revealed. The creeds of the Church are statements and symbols about what we believe. They are brief summaries and signs of the faith of the Church.

The creeds of the Church are also called professions of faith. We profess, or publicly announce and accept, faith in One God in Three Divine Persons—God the Father, God the Son, and God the Holy Spirit. We profess the faith of the Church in God the Holy Trinity.

Praying the creeds of the Church reminds us of what we believe. The creeds also remind us of who we are. We are followers and disciples of Jesus Christ. We are members of his Church.

We also profess our faith by living our faith. We are to love God and others as Jesus taught. We make a difference in the world by putting our faith into action. We live and grow in faith with other disciples of Jesus.

Activity Look at the pictures on this page. How are the young people professing and living their faith in God? What are they telling others about God through their actions? Which of these things do you do? Tell a partner.

God's Revelation

FAITH FOCUS

How does God make himself known to us?

FAITH VOCABULARY

Divine Revelation

Divine Revelation is God making known both himself and his plan of creation and Salvation for the world and all people.

God created us in his image and likeness. He created us to know, love, and serve him. He invites us to live in friendship with him. God wants everyone to be happy with him on Earth and in Heaven.

God has revealed, or made known, both himself and his plan of creation and Salvation for the world and all people. He invites all people to know and believe in him. We call this **Divine Revelation.** We can never fully know God or explain the mystery of God in words.

God's Promise to Love

Little by little and over a long time, God has revealed himself and his plan of creation and Salvation. The story of God's revelation was first written down in the Old Testament. There we read the story of creation and God's first promise to love people always.

After the story of creation, we read about God's Covenant with Noah and with Abraham. We then read about God's promises to Moses and David and to the other great leaders of God's people.

? Why did God reveal himself to us?

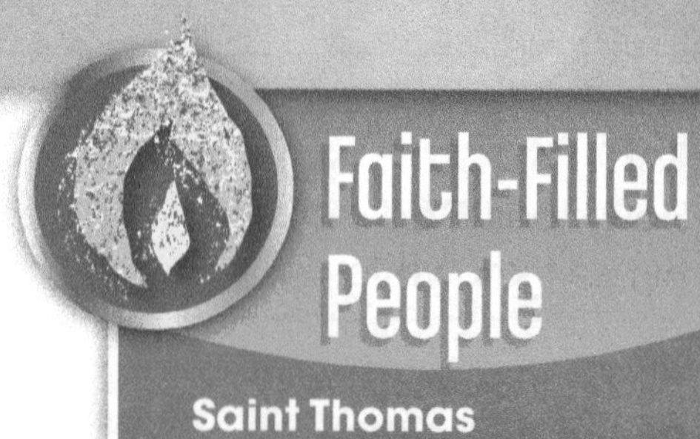

Faith-Filled People

Saint Thomas the Apostle

Thomas was one of the original Twelve Apostles. Thomas told Jesus that he was willing to die with him. Tradition tells us that Thomas was a house-builder.

Jesus Most Fully Reveals God

God has revealed himself most fully in Jesus Christ. There will be no further Revelation after Jesus. Everything that Jesus said and did on Earth tells us about God. Everything Jesus said and did invites us to believe in God, to place our trust in him, and to love God with all our hearts. This is what Jesus did. This is what Jesus' disciples are called to do.

Jesus is at the center of God's plan of creation and Salvation. He is the center of our lives. He is the center of the Covenant binding God and his people. Jesus Christ is the new and everlasting Covenant that God has made with people.

The New Testament tells the story of the new Covenant that God made in Jesus Christ. Jesus is the Son of God. He is true God and true man. We believe in Jesus Christ and in everything that he has revealed about God.

We live and deepen our friendship with God the Father and with Jesus Christ, who is God the Son, with the help of God the Holy Spirit.

? What are Jesus' disciples called to do? How do you do these things?

God's Gift of Faith

Faith is a gift from God. It is one of the three Theological Virtues. The Theological Virtues are faith, hope, and love. Faith is not something we can earn. The gift of faith helps us come to know and believe in God and in all that he has revealed. It is both God's invitation to believe in him and our acceptance of that invitation.

The Bible has many stories about people of faith. One of these stories tells about the faith of Thomas the Apostle:

> Jesus appeared to the disciples after he was raised from the dead. When the disciples told him that they had seen the Risen Jesus, Thomas refused to believe. A week later the Risen Jesus again appeared to the disciples. This time Thomas was there. He saw Jesus and believed. Jesus said, "Have you come to believe because you have seen me? Blessed are those who have not seen and have believed."
>
> Based on John 20:24-26, 28-29

Faith includes responding to God's wonderful invitation. Faith gives us the power to give ourselves to God, whom we do not see. Faith is believing in God simply because he is God and has revealed himself.

Catholics Believe

The Apostles' Creed

The Apostles' Creed is one of the earliest summaries of the faith of the Church. We call it the Apostles' Creed because it tells the main beliefs that the Church has professed from the time of the Apostles, about 2,000 years ago.

Activity **God's Overjoyed, Outspoken Disciples (GOOD).**

The name of your club is God's Overjoyed, Outspoken Disciples (GOOD). Members of GOOD help one another to live as faithful followers of Jesus. Write a want ad for finding people to join your club. In your ad, list the qualities that members need to have.

GOOD CLUB

____

____

____

____

I FOLLOW JESUS

FAITH INVITATION

God is always inviting us to know and believe in him. Read the "Faith Invitation" below. Choose one way that you can accept God's invitation. Tell how you will live as a person of faith and as a disciple of Jesus. Write one idea in the space provided.

Welcome!

I invite you to be a person of faith.
Come share friendship with me.
Experience my wonders in creation.
Read the Bible.
Talk with me in prayer each day.
Be a disciple of Jesus.
Live what he told you to do.
Reach out to others with love and kindness.
Honor and respect all of my gifts.
Celebrate my love in your life with me
and with others.

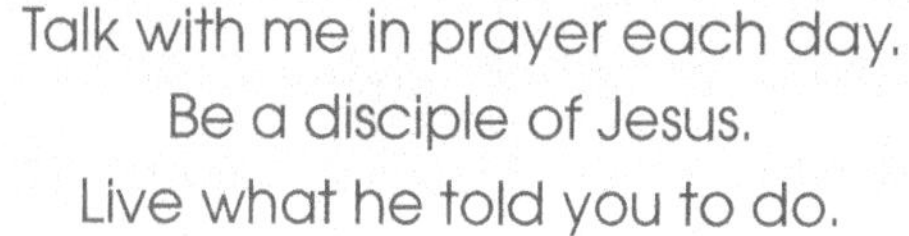

Please respond today!

____

____

____

MY FAITH CHOICE

God invites you to a life of faith in him. How can your words and actions show that you have faith in God? This week I will try to know God better. I will ____

____

____.

Take a moment today and every day to ask the Holy Spirit to deepen your gift of faith.

Chapter Review

Write the term on the line that best completes each statement.

creed revealed Revelation faith Covenant

1. God has ______________ his love for us in many ways.
2. The special friendship between God and the Israelites is called the ______________.
3. ______________ is both God's invitation to believe in him and also our acceptance of that invitation.
4. A ______________ is a brief summary of what the Church believes.
5. God making known his plan for us is called Divine ______________.

TO HELP YOU REMEMBER

1. God gives us the gift of faith to help us know and believe in him.
2. God has revealed, or made known, himself and his plan of creation and Salvation.
3. God has revealed himself most fully in his own Son, Jesus Christ. Jesus Christ is the fullness of Revelation.

We Profess Our Faith

At Baptism, we first profess our faith in God and what he has revealed. Pray this creed. It is part of the creed prayed at Baptism.

Leader: Let us profess our faith.
Do you believe in God, the Father almighty, creator of heaven and earth?

All: **I do.**

Leader: Do you believe in Jesus Christ, his only Son, our Lord?

All: **I do.**

Leader: Do you believe in the Holy Spirit?

All: **I do.**

Leader: This is the faith of our Church. We are proud to profess it in Jesus' name.

All: **Amen.**

Leader: Come forward and bless yourself with holy water. Make the Sign of the Cross.

Based on the *Order of Baptism*

With My Family

This Week . . .

In Chapter 2, I Will Be Your God, your child learned:

- ▶ God created us to know, love, and serve him, and to be happy with him on Earth and in Heaven.
- ▶ God has revealed himself most fully in his Son, Jesus Christ. We call this Divine Revelation.
- ▶ We can never fully comprehend the mystery of God.
- ▶ God gives us the virtue of faith to help us come to know and believe in him and in all that he has revealed. People of faith strive to come to know God and respond to him.

For more about related teachings of the Church, see the *Catechism of the Catholic Church*, 27–43, 50–67, and 142–197, and the *United States Catholic Catechism for Adults*, pages 12–18.

Sharing God's Word

Read together the Bible story about Jesus appearing to Thomas the Apostle and the other disciples after Jesus was raised from the dead. You can read this Gospel story in John 20:24-29 or read an adaptation of the story on page 23. Emphasize that faith includes believing in God even though we do not see God.

We Live as Disciples

The Christian home and family is a school of discipleship. Choose one of the following activities to do as a family, or design a similar activity of your own:

- ▶ Share stories of the Baptism of each family member. Look through a photo album; watch the videos; and show your child his or her baptismal gown, candle, and certificate. Share what his or her Baptism day was like.
- ▶ Read Jeremiah 7:23. Then pray together, asking God to strengthen your faith.

Our Spiritual Journey

Christians profess their faith in both words and actions. In this chapter, your child prayed a profession of faith that is based on the Order of Baptism. Read and pray together the baptismal profession of faith on page 25. Then talk about ways that you can join others in your parish to put your words of faith into action. Make a family decision and put it into action.

Faith-Filled People

Saint Thomas the Apostle
Feast Day: July 3
Thomas did not believe that Jesus was alive. When Thomas touched Jesus' wounds, he never doubted his faith again.

For more ideas on ways your family can live as disciples of Jesus, visit BeMyDisciples.com

Building a Culture of Life

Every person at every age is God's special creation. God is the author of all life. Every person gives us a glimpse of what God is like. Every human being at every stage of life is sacred, or holy. When a human life ends on Earth, even though the body dies, the soul still lives. Jesus' Resurrection shows us we will live forever. God wants us to live with him, along with Mary and all the saints, in Heaven.

In the Dr. Seuss story *Horton Hears a Who*, Horton the elephant becomes a hero. He responds to a cry for help from a tiny little person called a Who. Horton listens to the Who when no one else will. "Don't give up," he tells the Who. "I believe in you all! A person's a person no matter how small!" We too are to respect all human life, no matter how small.

Every person should be cared for and protected. When we care for and protect human life, we are building a culture of life. Every day we can do more to show respect for every person. We can show respect for human life through our good words and just actions.

Catholics Believe

All human life is sacred and a gift from God. Every person is to be respected not because of what he or she has or can do but because we all are children of God.

Activity

Who are the people you know who are like the "Who"? Draw and label some of them.

Family Life Connection

Healthy Habits @ Home

Pope Francis tells us that there are three phrases that every family needs to use at home. As a family, talk about how you can use these words more often in your own home.

Please ....

Thank you ....

Sorry ....

Family Time

Every stage of life offers opportunities to teach and to learn about life and about God. Have each family member complete these sentences:

- I could teach a teenager to . . .
- A teenager could teach me to . . .
- I could teach a grandparent to . . .
- A grandparent could teach me to . . .

Faith Focus

Human life is sacred and a gift from God.

Family in Action

During family mealtime this week, devote prayer to thanking God for the gift of life. Ask that all people respect and protect human life at every stage.

Write your prayer here

....

....

Safer Together

Your family can be safer together if you learn and practice the 3 R's of Safety: **Recognize**, **Respond**, and **Report**. Review the following together:

1. **Recognize** where you are and what is going on around you. Are the actions of those around you appropriate?
2. **Respond** if you are feeling uneasy or if someone is in danger. Be careful as you seek help.
3. **Report** the situation to a trusted adult. Be strong and tell the truth to an adult whom you trust.

Looking Ahead

In this chapter, the Holy Spirit invites you to ▶

EXPLORE how Isidore and Maria were stewards of God's creation.

DISCOVER what God tells us about himself and about who we are.

DECIDE ways to praise God by being a good steward.

CHAPTER 3

The Mystery of God

? What is your favorite song about God? When do you sing it? Why do you like singing it?

The People of God have written and sung many songs about God. Imagine that you and all of creation have come together to praise God. The writer of Psalm 148 looked at creation, and his heart burst into song:

> Praise the LORD from the heavens, Praise him, sun and moon; praise him, all you shining stars, Praise the LORD from the earth; Let all peoples praise the name of the LORD, for his name alone is greater than any other name. BASED ON PSALM 148:1, 3, 11, 13

? When have you and your family admired God's creation?

Disciple Power

Trust

To trust in someone is to count on them to care for our well-being and respect us. To say "I trust in God" means that we know that we can count on him to be true to his word.

Saint Isidore and Saint Maria

Isidore and his wife, Maria de la Cabeza, were farmers. They worked for a wealthy landowner in Spain many years ago. Isidore and Maria loved the land. They cared for the land because they believed it was God's gift to them. Today they are honored by the Church as saints. Isidore and his holy wife, Saint Maria, are examples of a married couple who placed God at the center of their lives.

Isidore and Maria were good stewards. Stewards faithfully care for someone or something that belongs to someone else. Have you ever planted a garden? If you have, you know that plants and trees need special care to grow and produce fruits, flowers, and vegetables.

God asks us to care for creation with the same special care we would use in a garden. When we are good stewards, as Saint Isidore and Saint Maria were, we care for God's creation and share its gifts with others, especially those in need.

Activity **Creation Caretakers**

God's creation needs many caretakers. What would a creation caretaker do? Write a job description here.

JOB SUMMARY:______________________________

____

SPECIAL TALENTS NEEDED:______________________________

____

BENEFITS:______________________________

HOURS:______________________________

God the Father

God tells us about himself in many ways. Just by looking at and thinking about creation, we can come to know something about God.

Here are some of the qualities, or attributes, that God tells us about himself in the Bible:

FAITH FOCUS
What does it mean to call God, the Creator?

FAITH VOCABULARY

Almighty
God's power to do everything and anything good.

Creator
God, who created everything and everyone, seen and unseen, out of love and without help.

Divine Providence
God's caring love for us.

1. God is the Father, the **Almighty**. God has the power to do everything and anything good. Every Sunday at Mass, we stand and profess our faith in One God who is the Father, the Almighty.

2. God is the **Creator**. There was nothing besides God before God created. God made everyone and everything, visible and invisible, out of love and without any help.

3. God is **all-present**. He is always with us. More than anyone else, God is always there for us. Placing our trust in God is the best thing we can ever do.

4. God is **all-knowing** and **all-loving**. God knows us by name and always loves us.

5. God is **truthful** and **faithful**. God's Word is always true. He always keeps his promises. He is always faithful. Like King David, we say,

   "[Y]ou, Lord God, are truly God and your words are truth. . ."
   2 Samuel 7:28

What do these attributes tell you about God? What else have you come to know about God from the Bible?

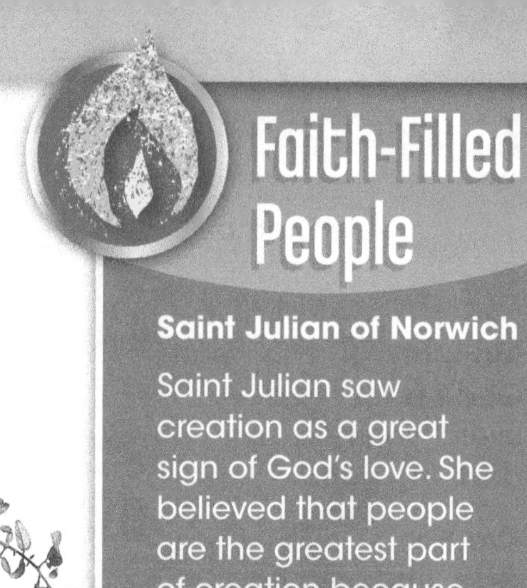

Saint Julian of Norwich

Saint Julian saw creation as a great sign of God's love. She believed that people are the greatest part of creation because Jesus, the Son of God, became a man. Because of Jesus, people are the heart of the universe. People are the greatest sign of God's love.

God Cares for All Creation

Best of all, God told us about himself through Jesus Christ. Jesus called his Father "Abba." The word *abba* means "father." This shows us Jesus' love for and trust in his Father.

Jesus showed his trust in the Father in everything he said and did. He invites us to trust God the Father as he did. One day he told his disciples,

> Look at the birds in the sky and the wild flowers. Your heavenly Father takes care of them. You are more important to God than they are. God will provide much more for you.
>
> Based on Matthew 6:26, 28, 30

Jesus invited his listeners to trust that God has great joy in providing for us. Every moment of every day of our lives, God, our Almighty Father, cares for us and his creation. We call this truth about God **Divine Providence.**

God asks us to share in his Divine Providence by taking care of his creation. Good stewards help to complete the work of creation. They look for people, places, or things that are in need and find ways to help.

? What are you doing right now to care for God's creation?

God Our Creator

In the Nicene Creed, we profess our faith in God, who is the Creator of all that is, visible and invisible. God is the Creator of all living creatures. He is the Creator of people and angels. Angels are spiritual creatures who do not have bodies as humans do. They endlessly give glory to God.

All of God's creation is good, but people are the greatest of all God's creations. God tells us the reason in the Bible:

> *God created mankind in his image; . . .*
> *male and female he created them.*
>
> Genesis 1:27

God created people to share in the life of the Holy Trinity now on Earth and forever in Heaven. The Holy Trinity is the mystery of One God in Three Divine Persons—God the Father, God the Son, and God the Holy Spirit.

Catholics Believe

Catholic Social Teaching

The Catholic Church has named certain principles to guide us in all our human relationships. These principles are called Catholic Social Teaching. Care for God's creation is one of these principles. It is part of God's plan for us to live in harmony with him, with others, and with nature.

Activity **In God's Image**

Look in a mirror. Remember that person staring back at you is created in God's image! Decorate this prayer card. Bless and thank God for creating you in his image.

I FOLLOW JESUS

A good steward can be counted on, or trusted, to take good care of things. God wants us to be good stewards of his creation. He trusts that each of us can be counted on to make a difference in caring for his creation. When we work together, we can do a better job of caring for God's creation.

GOOD STEWARDS

Pretend that your parish is planning a "Good Stewards" project to help others. Create an announcement for the home page of your parish's website.

Good Stewards of Creation

____

____

____

____

____

____

____

____

____

____

____

MY FAITH CHOICE

What is one way you can be a good steward at home? At school? In your neighborhood? This week I will

____

____

___________________________________.

Ask the Holy Spirit to help you return God's trust in you by taking care of the gifts God has given us.

Chapter Review

Complete the sentences. Use the words in the word bank.

Creator	**Abba**	**likeness**
Divine Providence		**Holy Trinity**

1. Jesus called God the Father ____________________.
2. God the Father is the First Person of the ____________________.
3. God the Father is the ____________________ of all that is, both visible and invisible.
4. God always loves us and provides for us. We call this truth about God ____________________.
5. God created us in his image and ________________.

TO HELP YOU REMEMBER

1. God is our Father, the Almighty, who is all-knowing, all-loving, all-present, truthful, and faithful.
2. God is the Creator of all that is. God always cares and provides for creation.
3. All people are created in the image and likeness of God.

Great Is Your Name

Psalms are prayerful songs to God. The Church prays the psalms every day. One way we pray the psalms is by alternately praying the verses aloud.

Leader: God, the Creator, how great is your name.

All: **God, the Creator, how great is your name.**

Group 1: Your love for us is so great.

Group 2: You always care for us.

All: **God, the Creator, how great is your name.**

Group 1: You have made us your greatest creation.

Group 2: You have given us the responsibility to be good stewards of your creation.

All: **God, the Creator, how great is your name.**

BASED ON PSALM 8:2, 5-7, 10

With My Family

This Week . . .

In Chapter 3, The Mystery of God, your child learned:

- We profess our faith in God, the Father, the Almighty, the Creator of all that is visible and invisible.
- God is love, truth, faithful, all-knowing, and all-good.
- We respond to God's loving care, or Divine Providence, by caring for creation and sharing the gifts of creation with those in need.
- When we practice the virtue of trust, we trust God and are trusted by him.

For more about related teachings of the Church, see the *Catechism of the Catholic Church*, 199–379, and the *United States Catholic Catechism for Adults*, pages 53–55.

Sharing God's Word

Read together the Bible story in Matthew 6:26-31, or read the adaptation of the story on page 30. Talk about how God cares for all creation.

We Live as Disciples

The Christian home and family is a school of discipleship. Choose one of the following activities to do as a family, or design a similar activity of your own:

- Invite your child to help you prepare a family meal. Talk about how your family can care for God's creation. Then choose one thing you will do this week together to care for creation.
- Invite your child to go food shopping with you. As you shop, talk about your family's blessings and how you might share those blessings with others.

Our Spiritual Journey

The psalms in the Bible reflect the ups and downs of the daily journey of God's people. Learn several psalm verses and pray them at appropriate times as a family. In this chapter, your child prayed verses of Psalm 8. Read and pray together Psalm 8 on page 33 or from your Bible.

Faith-Filled People

Saint Julian of Norwich
Feast Day: May 13
Saint Julian's deep faith was rooted in the idea of God's great love for all people.

For more ideas on ways your family can live as disciples of Jesus, visit BeMyDisciples.com

I Depend on You

"I need your help." Every family uses these words. Husbands and wives say them to each other. Children say them to their parents, and parents say them to their children. We depend on one another.

There are many things children need that they cannot provide for themselves, such as food, clothing, and a place to live. We depend upon others for things that money cannot buy. Our families help us fulfill these needs. Family members give us love. They encourage us when we try to do difficult things. Families help us when they pray for us.

Loving family members also provide guidance. That means that they give us good advice when we are not sure what to do. Sometimes we are faced with difficult decisions. When this happens, family members can give us guidance to help us make the right choices.

Catholics Believe

God created us in his image and likeness. He created us to live in communion with him and with one another.

Activity

Complete the chart by naming ways you can show each group how you depend on them and how they can depend on you. Share what you have written with your family.

	Family Members	My Friends	My Parish
How I depend on them			
How they depend on me			

Faith Focus

God created us to live in communion with him and with one another.

Healthy Habits @ Home

Read and think about the traits of a holy and healthy family. Choose one of these traits and work on it this week.

A healthy and holy family . . .

1. develops a sense of trust.
2. laughs and has a sense of play.
3. shares responsibilities.
4. teaches a sense of right and wrong.
5. has faith in God.
6. prays together.

Safer Together

Children may feel guilt or shame for their own actions and the actions of others. Your family will be safer together when you follow these tips:

- Reassure your child that sometimes it is difficult to talk about feelings. Explain that it is important to share his or her feelings with you.
- Make sure your child understands that we should never feel bad when telling the truth or reporting when someone does something harmful.
- Be sure to reinforce that your child is not responsible for what others do.

Family Time

Cut out and hang at home

Family members show one another love and respect by helping each other. Spend time as a family sharing responses to these questions:

- In what ways does my family depend on me?
- In what ways do we show appreciation for what we do for one another?

Family in Action

God created us to live in communion with him and with others. One way family members live in communion with each other is by depending on one another. Tell how by completing the following sentence. Share your ideas with each other.

When someone in our family needs

....,

I will

....

Looking Ahead

In this chapter, the Holy Spirit invites you to

EXPLORE how Dorothy Day gave hope to the poor.

DISCOVER God's plan of Salvation and the promise of the Messiah.

DECIDE how to be a messenger of hope.

CHAPTER 4

God's Promise

? Think about a promise that you have made. Why was it difficult or easy for you to keep your promise?

God promised to send a savior to his Chosen People, the Israelites. About thirty years after Jesus was born, some people believed that John the Baptist was this person. Imagine yourself in the desert, listening to John the Baptist's message of hope:

> "One mightier than I is coming after me. I am not worthy to stoop and loosen the thongs of his sandals. I have baptized you with water; he will baptize you with the holy Spirit."
> MARK 1:7-8

? What sort of person would John's words have led you to expect?

Disciple Power

Hope

Hope is a gift from God. The Theological Virtue of hope enables us to trust in God and in his promises. It helps us trust that God is always with us, in good times and difficult times.

THE CHURCH FOLLOWS JESUS

Building a Just World

Dorothy Day shared God's message of hope with people. Dorothy was a writer during the 20th century who reported on the sufferings of people who were living in poverty.

Dorothy prayed that she could find a way to change things for people who were poor. She wanted to do more than just write about them. Dorothy believed that the Holy Spirit was calling her to do this new kind of work.

Dorothy Day told her friend Peter Maurin about her new work. They chose to live among the poor. They began the Catholic Worker movement. They brought God's gift of hope to people in many ways. They set up Catholic Worker houses, where people who were homeless could live.

The Catholic Church has named Dorothy a Servant of God. This is part of the process in naming a person a saint. We honor Dorothy best when we live as she did, as disciples of Jesus. When we do, we are God's messengers of hope in our world. We work to build a just world as Jesus taught us to do.

Activity Find out more about the work that your parish does for people who are suffering. Start by writing three ways that you already know.

____

____

____

God's Plan of Salvation

God created us to be happy with him here on Earth and forever in Heaven, yet we know that people suffer. Many people are treated unjustly. Many children go hungry each day. When we see and hear about people who suffer, we wonder how people who suffer can be happy at all.

The people in the Old Testament asked God questions like that. They wrote the answer that God revealed to them in the Book of Genesis.

Adam and Eve, the names that the Bible gives to the first humans, rejected God's original plan of happiness. They freely chose to turn away from God. They rejected his plan of happiness for people and for all creation. The Church calls this choice made by Adam and Eve and its effect on all people **Original Sin**.

By this sin, Adam and Eve lost the gift of original holiness, or friendship with God. They not only lost this gift for themselves but for all human beings. Because of Original Sin, suffering, unhappiness, sin, and evil of all kinds came into the world. Because of Original Sin, we too suffer.

God's love refused to let evil and suffering destroy his original plan. He set a new plan in motion—God's plan of Salvation. God would send a savior. He promised to send someone who would free all people from sin and suffering.

? How can God's promise give people hope today?

FAITH FOCUS
What is God's plan of Salvation?

FAITH VOCABULARY

Original Sin
Original Sin is the sin committed by the first humans who lost original holiness not only for themselves but for all human beings.

Messiah
Jesus Christ is the Messiah, the person whom God promised to send to save people from sin.

Faith-Filled People

Isaiah the Prophet

Isaiah lived and worked in the city of Jerusalem about eight hunded years before the birth of Jesus. The name *Isaiah,* which means "God is Salvation," summarizes the message of hope that he announced to God's people.

The New Leader Promised by God

About six hundred years before the birth of Jesus, God's people, the Israelites, were suffering in many ways. Many of their kings and other leaders were treating them unjustly. Things became especially bad when many of the Israelites were forced to move out of their homeland and live in another country called Babylon. This period of suffering is known as the Exile.

God's people prayed for the savior God had promised. God sent the prophet Isaiah to speak to the Israelites. A prophet is someone whom God chooses to speak to people in his name. In the Book of the Prophet Isaiah, we read,

> Upon those who dwelt in the land of gloom
> a light has shone.
> For a child is born to us, a son is given us; . . .
> They name him Wonder-Counselor, God-Hero, . . .
> Prince of Peace.
>
> ISAIAH 9:1, 5

These words filled the hearts of the Israelites with hope. They trusted that God would one day send to them the savior he had promised. This Savior came to be called the **Messiah**, or God's Anointed One. The Israelites kept trusting that God's promise would come true.

? When did God's promise to the Israelites come true?

Jesus Christ Is the Messiah

Each year at Christmas, Catholics listen to the message of hope that Isaiah spoke to God's people. We hear the names, or titles, that Isaiah used to describe this promised savior, or messiah.

Wonder-Counselor
He is wise and clearly knows God's plan for all people.

God-Hero
He brings blessings to people because he follows God's commands.

Prince of Peace
He establishes the peace that God had always promised to his people.

These titles that Isaiah gave to the messiah help Christians understand who Jesus Christ is. They also help us understand the work that Jesus did among us.

The name *Christ* means "Anointed One." Jesus' birth and life, his suffering and Death, his Resurrection and Ascension brought the gift of Salvation to all people. Jesus established the beginning of the Kingdom of God. The Kingdom of God is a kingdom of mercy, love, peace, and justice that will last forever. It will finally come about when Jesus Christ returns in glory at the end of time.

Catholics Believe

Works of Mercy

The Corporal Works of Mercy and the Spiritual Works of Mercy are works of hope. They help prepare for the coming of the Kingdom that Jesus, the Messiah and Savior, began to build. When we live the Works of Mercy, we share the gift of hope with people.

Activity When you see people around you acting with mercy, love, peace, and justice, you are catching a glimpse of the Kingdom of God!

With your friends, plan a Kingdom of God collage of pictures and symbols that shows what God's kingdom is like. List the kinds of images you will include.

____

____

____

I FOLLOW JESUS

Disciples of Jesus are messengers of hope. You can see and hear Jesus' messengers of hope all around you. They are in your family, in your parish, and in your neighborhood. As Dorothy Day did, they bring God's message of hope to people who suffer.

MESSENGERS OF HOPE

Interview two or three members of your class and members of your family. Use the questions below. Find out what they know about people who bring hope to those who suffer. Write what you find out.

1. Who are people you know who bring hope to other people?

____

____

2. What are they doing for others?

____

____

3. How does their work bring hope to those whom they serve?

____

____

MY FAITH CHOICE

The Holy Spirit helps you be a messenger of hope. Choose one way that you will bring the message of God's hope to someone. This week, I will bring hope to someone. I will

____

______________________________.

Pray, "Come, Holy Spirit, fill my heart with the power of your love. Help me bring a message of hope to someone who is suffering. Amen."

Chapter Review

Complete this crossword puzzle.

Across

1. A prophet speaks in the name of ______________.

3. ______________ was a prophet.

5. The ______________ is the Anointed One, the Savior, promised by God.

Down

2. ______________ Sin is the name we give to the first sin committed by Adam and Eve.

4. ______________ is the Savior promised by God.

TO HELP YOU REMEMBER

1. God created all people to be happy with him now on Earth and forever in Heaven.
2. God promised to send someone who would save all people from sin.
3. Jesus is the Savior God promised to send.

Praise the Lord

Prayers of praise give glory to God. Pray this prayer to praise God the Father. Praise him for keeping his promise and sending us Jesus, the Savior of the world.

All: **Lord Jesus, you are the Savior. We praise you.**

Group 1: Lord Jesus, you bring hope to people who suffer from fighting and war.

Group 2: Lord Jesus, you bring hope to people who suffer from injustice.

Group 1: Lord Jesus, you bring hope to people who suffer from hunger.

Group 2: Lord Jesus, you bring the Good News of hope to the poor and to all people who suffer from want.

All: **Lord Jesus, you are the Savior. We praise you!**

With My Family

This Week . . .

In Chapter 4, God's Promise, your child learned:

- God promised to send the world a savior and messiah.
- Suffering, evil, sin, and death entered the world as a result of Original Sin.
- Isaiah the Prophet brought a message of hope to God's people, the Israelites.
- Jesus is the Messiah, God's Promised One, the Savior and Redeemer.
- Hope is a Theological Virtue; hopeful people know that God cares for them and is always with them.

For more about related teachings of the Catholic Church, see the *Catechism of the Catholic Church,* 385–412, and the *United States Catholic Catechism for Adults,* pages 18, 56–57.

Sharing God's Word

Read together the Bible story in Isaiah 9:1, 5 about Isaiah's message to the Israelites, or read the adaptation of the story on page 38. Emphasize that Jesus is the Messiah whom God promised to send.

We Live as Disciples

The Christian home and family is a school of discipleship. Choose one of the following activities to do as a family, or design a similar activity of your own:

- Ask family members to share stories about times when they were hurting or sad. Invite each to describe a person who helped and what that person did to help. How did this person bring hope?
- Use the internet to learn more about the Catholic Worker community closest to where you live. Choose a way to support this community.

Our Spiritual Journey

Almsgiving is one of the spiritual disciplines of the Church. We give alms when we share our material and spiritual blessings with people in need. In this chapter, your child learned about Dorothy Day. She said that each person must experience a "revolution of the heart" in order to work for justice. Pray together at mealtime this week: "Holy Spirit, set our hearts on fire with your love so we can work for justice in large and small ways. Amen."

Faith-Filled People

Isaiah the Prophet

Isaiah was a prophet in the Old Testament. His name, meaning "God is Salvation," summarizes the message of hope that Isaiah announced to God's people.

For more ideas on ways your family can live as disciples of Jesus, visit BeMyDisciples.com

Making New Friends

Catholics Believe

Through our loving actions, we choose to do good and love others as God has directed.

School has just started after summer break. You are excited to see your friends again. At dinner one night, your parents mention that a new family has moved into the neighborhood. There are two children. One is your age. They will be attending your school. Your mother has spoken to their parents. The children are scared and anxious about going to a new school where they do not know anyone.

We can show that we follow God's commandment to love others. Our actions can be a gift that we give another person. What could you do to help your new neighbors feel less scared about the start of the school year?

Activity

Here are two ways you could care for your new neighbors. Decide on two more things you can do.

1 Arrange with a parent or trusted adult to meet the new neighbors at the park to play. Invite several of your friends to meet their new classmates.

2 Meet the new neighbors at school on their first day to show them where to go.

3 ....

4 ....

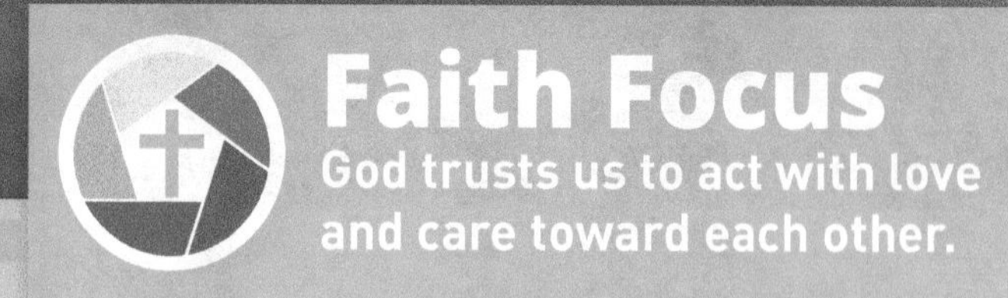

Faith Focus

God trusts us to act with love and care toward each other.

Healthy Habits @ Home

One way to be more loving and caring toward others is to try to understand their situation. What might they be thinking and feeling? When we take the time to understand what other people are experiencing, it is easier to help them. Talk about how other people feel in different situations. Remind your children that God trusts us to act with love and care toward each other.

Safer Together

Use these tips to keep your child safe when meeting and making new friends.

1. Introduce yourself to the parents of new friends your child meets.
2. Make sure that your families are in agreement about safety issues, such as adult supervision when the children are in the other family's home, monitoring of media and online activities, guidelines for acceptable and unacceptable behavior, and so forth.
3. Set boundaries regarding places your children may go, whose houses they may visit, people they may see, and things they may do with their friends.
4. Reinforce the importance of the buddy system.
5. Know where your children are at all times. Your children should never go anywhere with anyone without your permission.

Family Time

Cut out and hang at home

Use the story as an opportunity to help your child understand how we depend on each other to get through difficult times.

1. Talk about what it would be like if your child were going to a new school. Ask, "How would you feel?" "What would you need?" "How could other children help you be more comfortable?" Identify actions that offer encouragement and support.
2. Invite your child to put him- or herself in the shoes of the classmate. Ask questions to identify how the classmate might feel. These might include: "How would you feel?" "What would you be scared of?" "What would you want your new neighbors or classmates to do for you or say to you?" "How could your new classmates help you?"
3. Revisit the list of two things you can do. Encourage your child to add one more thing that he or she can say or do for the classmate, such as praying for the new student.

Unit 1 **Review**

Name ______________________

A. Choose the Best Word

Fill in the blanks using the words from the word bank.

Divine Revelation	Wonder-Counselor	Original Sin
Sacred Scripture	God's Anointed One	Faith

1. ______________ is God making himself and his plan for creation known over a long period of time.

2. ______________ is both a gift from God to know and believe in him and our acceptance of that gift.

3. Jesus is named ______________ because he is wise and knows God's plan for all people.

4. ______________ is the choice that Adam and Eve freely made to turn away from God.

5. Jesus came to be called the Messiah, or ______________.

B. Show What You Know

Match the words or phrases in Column A with the words or phrases in Column B.

Column A	**Column B**
1. Writers of the Bible	____ **a.** feed the hungry; visit the sick
2. The Israelites	____ **b.** Isaiah's description of the savior
3. Prince of Peace	____ **c.** the Kingdom of God
4. Corporal Works of Mercy	____ **d.** inspired by the Holy Spirit
5. Place and time of lasting love and justice	____ **e.** God's Chosen People

C. Connect with Scripture

Reread the Scripture passage on page 9.
What connection do you see between this passage and what you learned in this unit?

D. Be a Disciple

1. *Review the four pages in this unit titled The Church Follows Jesus. What person or ministry of the Church on these pages will inspire you to be a better disciple of Jesus? Explain your answer.*

---

2. *Work with a group. Review the four Disciple Power virtues, or gifts, you have learned about in this unit. After writing your own ideas, share with the group practical ways that you will live these virtues day by day.*

We Believe

UNIT 2

Part Two

Who Is the Greatest?

During the Last Supper, while they were at the table with Jesus, the disciples started talking about who was the greatest among them.

Jesus asked them a question: "Who is greater: the one who sits at the table and is served, or the one who serves? Most people think it is the one seated at the table. Yet I am among you as the one who serves.

"The kings of this world lord it over others and their authority is honored. That is not for you. The kingdom I want to give you is the one my Father gave me. You will eat and drink at my table in my kingdom. There you will have true greatness."

Based on Luke 22:24-30

What I Have Learned

What is something you already know about these three faith terms?

love

____

____

____

Last Supper

____

____

____

Pentecost

____

____

____

Faith Terms to Know

Put an X next to the faith terms you know. Put a ? next to faith terms you need to learn more about.

_______ miracle

_______ public ministry of Jesus

_______ Incarnation

_______ priest, prophet, king

_______ Body of Christ

_______ Advocate

_______ Resurrection

The Bible

What do you know about the work God the Father sent Jesus to do?

____

____

____

The Church

What do you know about how the people of the Church are signs of God's love?

____

____

____

A Question I Have

What question would you like to ask about being a disciple?

____

____

____

Day of the Dead

A Devotion from Mexico

This celebration usually takes place at the beginning of November in connection with the feasts of All Saints and All Souls' Day.

The Day of the Dead, or *Día de los Muertos*, is celebrated at the beginning of November. It is celebrated in Mexico and Central America. On this day, people remember loved ones who have died. They create *ofrendas* in their homes. *Ofrenda* means "offering." The *ofrendas* are decorated with pictures and objects that remind them of their ancestors. They may also attend celebrations at night. They visit the graves of their loved ones. They light candles and pray.

The Day of the Dead is a celebration to remember and honor the dead. The living speak with their loved ones in their hearts. They pray for them and remember stories about them. Families prepare special foods in the shape of skulls and skeletons made from chocolate or sugar.

Catholics attend special church ceremonies on this day. The churches may build special shrines. Relatives may light candles and leave prayers for their ancestors. They remember that God created us to live forever with him in Heaven.

Who are some of your ancestors you could honor on the Day of the Dead? If you could make an *ofrenda* to remember them, what would you place on it?

Day of the Dead

For people of faith, death is the end of earthly life and the beginning of eternal life. We are still connected to our loved ones in the Communion of Saints. Think of a loved one you would like to honor. Draw the items that help you to remember this person. Be sure to include a crucifix, a Bible, or another symbol of faith as a reminder that we are united in Christ.

Looking Ahead

In this chapter, the Holy Spirit invites you to

EXPLORE how Saint Anthony of Padua is a role model.

DISCOVER that God's promise to love us is fulfilled in Jesus.

DECIDE ways to be a sign of God's love.

CHAPTER 5

The Son of God

How do your parents and your teachers help you and guide you? How do they show you that they love and care for you?

Once, Jesus was teaching his disciples. He wanted them to know that he would always love them and care for them. Jesus told them,

"I know my sheep, and my sheep know me.
I will give up my life for my sheep." Based on John 10:14-15

Why did Jesus call himself the Good Shepherd? What did he want his disciples to know about him?

Disciple Power

Love

Love is the greatest of all the virtues. Jesus commanded his disciples, "Love one another, as I love you" (John 15:12). Jesus loves us so much that he died on the Cross for us. Read what Saint Paul tells us about love in 1 Corinthians 13:4-7.

THE CHURCH FOLLOWS JESUS

Saint Anthony of Padua

Some members of the Church set a good example for us. They show us how to live as disciples of Jesus. They are kind, helpful, and loving as Jesus, the Good Shepherd, was. The Church names these people *saints*. Saint Anthony of Padua is one of the saints of the Church.

Anthony of Padua was born in Portugal in 1195. He had a great love for the child Jesus. He was a great preacher and missionary. A missionary travels to tell others about Jesus Christ.

Anthony heard about four Franciscan missionaries who were martyrs. Christian martyrs are people who give up their lives for Jesus. Anthony loved Jesus so much. He, too, was willing to give up his life for Jesus.

Anthony joined the Franciscans. Franciscans join together to follow Jesus as Saint Francis of Assisi did. They give up all their possessions. They pray together. They sometimes travel to faraway places to tell others about Jesus.

Anthony of Padua has been named a saint of the Church. Saints faithfully put into practice the values Jesus lived while he was on Earth. We remember and celebrate the life of Saint Anthony of Padua each year on his feast day, June 13.

? Which saint are you or your parish church named after? Find out more about that saint. How is this person a role model for you and for the people in your parish?

The Incarnation

The birth of the Savior promised by God is one of the greatest revelations of his love for people. The angel Gabriel announced to the Blessed Virgin Mary,

> "[Mary,] the holy Spirit will come upon you, . . . [Your child] will be called holy, the Son of God."
>
> Luke 1:35

Mary's son, Jesus, is the only Son of God.

An angel also told Joseph, the husband of Mary, that the Virgin Mary would give birth to a son. The angel said,

> "You are to name him Jesus, because he will save his people from their sins." Matthew 1:21

Jesus is a Hebrew name that means "God saves."

The only Son of God the Father took on flesh. This means that the Son of God became truly human without giving up being God and lived among us. We call this mystery of faith the **Incarnation.** The word *incarnation* means "putting on flesh." Jesus is true God and true man.

Jesus, the only Son of God, is the Savior of the world. Because Mary is the Mother of Jesus, who is truly God, Mary is truly the Mother of God.

FAITH FOCUS
What did Jesus do to reveal God to us?

FAITH VOCABULARY

Incarnation
The Incarnation is the mystery of the Son of God, the Second Divine Person of the Trinity, becoming truly human while not giving up being God.

public ministry of Jesus
This is the saving work that God the Father sent his Son, Jesus, to do, beginning with the baptism of Jesus and his announcement of that work in the synagogue in Nazareth.

Activity The Church celebrates the birth of Jesus on Christmas. Write a sentence below telling why Christmas is a sign of God's love. Share your message with your family and friends.

____

____

____

____

Faith-Filled People

Patron Saints

Saint Anthony of Padua and other saints are also patron saints. Patron saints are role models for groups of people, such as lawyers, students, parishes, and nations. Their lives show us ways to continue the work that Jesus began on Earth.

Jesus Begins His Ministry

Jesus grew up in the town of Nazareth in Galilee. A short time after his baptism in the Jordan River, it became time for Jesus to begin the work that the Father sent him to do. We call this work the **public ministry of Jesus.**

Jesus went to the synagogue in Nazareth. He took a scroll containing the writings of the prophet Isaiah. He unrolled it, stood up, and read aloud:

The Spirit of the Lord is upon me,
because he has anointed me
to bring glad tidings to the poor.

He has sent me to proclaim liberty
to captives
and recovery of sight to the blind,
to let the oppressed go free,
and to proclaim a year acceptable
to the Lord.

LUKE 4:18-19

With these words, Jesus described the work the Father sent him to do. He is the Messiah, the Promised One, who had been sent to them by God.

? Describe one person whom you have read about or know who has continued the work of Jesus.

Signs of God's Love

Jesus' whole life on Earth revealed his Father's love for all people. Miracles were some of the most amazing things Jesus did. The word *miracle* means "wonder, something amazing and marvelous." The miracles of Jesus were amazing signs of God's love at work in the world.

The Gospels tell us about many miracles that Jesus performed during his public ministry. Read about the miracle of Jesus giving sight to two blind men in Matthew 9:27-31. See how Jesus changed their lives. Through this miracle, Jesus invited the two blind men and the other people who were there to believe and trust in God. The two blind men believed. They began to see not only with their eyes but also with "eyes of faith."

Jesus calls us to be people of faith. He calls us to see with eyes of faith and to live our faith. We are to be signs of God's love for others to see.

Catholics Believe

Signs of God's Love

The people of the Church are called to be signs of God's love. People in your parish do this in many ways. Priests and deacons, laypeople and religious, married and single people all work together to put into practice the values that Jesus lived while on Earth.

Activity Use the Faith Planner to write the things that you do during the day to be a sign of God's love.

Faith Planner

	Saturday	Sunday	Weekdays
Morning			
Noon			
Evening			

I FOLLOW JESUS

Followers of Jesus Christ do amazing things. They love, forgive, and show kindness to people as Jesus did. Saint Paul wanted to help the first Christians be like Jesus. He wanted them to imitate Jesus in what they did and said.

BE IMITATORS OF CHRIST

Imagine that you are sitting in a crowded room. You are listening to Saint Paul. Paul says,

> "So be imitators of God, as beloved children, and live in love, as Christ loved us . . . Live as children of light, for light produces every kind of goodness and righteousness and truth. Try to learn what is pleasing to the Lord."
>
> EPHESIANS 5:1-2, 8-10

Remember what you wrote in your Faith Planner. Write down three things that you can do to be an imitator of Christ.

____

____

____

____

____

____

MY FAITH CHOICE

This week, I will be an imitator of Christ. I will be a sign of God's love in the world. I will

____

____.

Talk with Jesus in prayer. Pray, "Jesus, help me come to know and follow you better. Amen."

Chapter Review

Circle the four faith words hidden in the puzzle. Share the meaning of each word with a partner.

P	T	B	I	M	T	U	A	M	I	M	K	I	T
K	U	N	A	Z	A	R	E	T	H	I	M	J	U
C	J	B	J	J	W	K	B	R	B	R	R	G	Y
T	K	U	L	I	I	D	G	E	D	A	S	F	E
J	A	H	R	I	N	J	D	T	R	C	T	D	I
D	W	J	N	O	C	I	Y	U	N	L	I	S	J
S	I	Q	O	K	A	M	T	W	Y	E	Q	R	L
Y	L	O	P	G	R	W	I	P	W	S	W	P	M
U	O	S	X	T	N	T	O	N	O	T	I	W	K
I	P	A	J	R	A	Y	D	F	I	Q	P	F	G
P	V	I	F	O	T	U	S	J	L	S	A	Q	T
Q	C	J	J	M	I	I	A	G	B	I	T	O	U
F	X	T	H	F	O	Q	V	K	C	R	D	R	R
G	A	Z	I	V	N	T	Z	R	Z	C	J	W	Y

TO HELP YOU REMEMBER

1. Jesus is the only Son of God, who became one of us and did not give up being God.
2. When Jesus began his public ministry, he announced that he is the Promised One of God.
3. Everything Jesus said and did was a sign of God's love for people.

WORD BANK

public ministry
Incarnation
Nazareth
miracles

We Believe

We profess our faith in Jesus Christ when we pray the creeds of the Church. We pray the Nicene Creed each Sunday at Mass. Pray this part of the Nicene Creed:

Group 1: I believe in one Lord Jesus Christ,
the Only Begotten Son of God,

Group 2: born of the Father before all ages.
God from God, Light from Light,

Group 1: true God from true God,
begotten, not made,
consubstantial with the Father;

Group 2: through him all things were made.

Group 1: For us men and for our salvation
he came down from heaven,

Group 2: and by the Holy Spirit was incarnate
of the Virgin Mary,
and became man.

With My Family

This Week . . .

In Chapter 5, The Son of God, your child learned:

- God fulfilled his promise to send the Messiah, the Savior and Redeemer of the world.
- The angel Gabriel announced to the Blessed Virgin Mary that she would give birth to the Son of God and name him Jesus.
- The Son of God became man without giving up being God. This mystery of faith is called the Incarnation. Jesus is true God and true man.
- The miracles of Jesus were unique signs of God's saving presence in the world, inviting people to faith in God.
- Jesus' whole life was a sign of God's saving love for all people. Love is the greatest of all the virtues.

For more about related teachings of the Church, see the *Catechism of the Catholic Church*, 422–507 and 512–560, and the *United States Catholic Catechism for Adults*, pages 79–87.

Sharing God's Word

Read together Luke 4:18-19, Jesus announcing the work that his Father had sent him to do, or read the adaptation of the story on page 50. Discuss how you see your parish continuing the work of Jesus.

We Live as Disciples

The Christian home and family is a school of discipleship. Choose one of the following activities to do as a family, or design a similar activity of your own:

- Read the story of Jesus' baptism in Matthew 3:13-17. Name some of the things that your family does or can do to tell others about Jesus.
- Name some of the people in your parish who are continuing the work of Jesus. Then choose one thing to do as a family this week to continue the work of Jesus.
- Make a "Top Ten" list of loving things that your family does for others. Post the list on your refrigerator as a reminder that your family practices the virtue of love and is a sign of God's love.

Our Spiritual Journey

Saint Paul teaches that love is the greatest of all the virtues. Love is the driving power of living our faith. In this chapter, your child professed his or her faith in God. Read and pray together the prayer on page 53. Then discuss how your love for God drives you to live your faith.

Faith-Filled People

Patron Saints

Patron saints are associated with specific causes. They pray for us when we need help and guidance.

For more ideas on ways your family can live as disciples of Jesus, visit **BeMyDisciples.com**

Feelings

Our emotions are God-given gifts within us that help us make decisions. They help us respond to the events in our lives in different ways. We might feel excited when we get presents for our birthdays. We could wake up startled during a terrible thunderstorm. We might feel restless or cranky during a long car ride.

Jesus had feelings just as we do. He did not hide his feelings. Sometimes Jesus was very happy. Jesus also felt sad when he saw people suffer. Imagine walking with Jesus through a dusty village. Imagine how Jesus felt when he reached out to help someone in need.

When we spend time with Jesus in prayer and by reading the Gospels, we can see how he expressed his feelings. We can see how his feelings helped him do the work his Father sent him to do. Jesus helps us listen to, understand, and respond to our own feelings.

Catholics Believe

God gave us many kinds of emotions. Jesus had emotions, too. He is divine, but he is also human. Jesus helps us learn from our feelings. He also shows us the best ways to share our feelings with others.

Activity

Draw and color a rainbow. On each color, write a feeling you think the color might symbolize. Share your work with your family.

Family Life Connection

Healthy Habits @ Home

With your family, read aloud Mark 1:35-45 from a Bible. Then think what it would be like if your family was with Jesus that day.

- Talk about your time with Jesus, especially during Mass.
- Share a way that Jesus helps you best respond to your feelings.

Family Time

Cut out and hang at home

With your family, imagine walking with Jesus through a dusty village. What do you feel as Jesus reaches out to help someone who is sick? Write what family members feel here:

....

....

Faith Focus

God gave us many kinds of emotions.

Family in Action

As a family, take time to pray together. Reflect on how you have acted on your emotions. Write a simple family prayer praising God for the wonderful array of emotions we feel daily.

....

....

....

Safer Together

Children can sometimes feel guilt or shame for their own actions and the actions of others. Review as a family the following:

- Sometimes it is difficult to talk about feelings. It is important to share our feelings.
- Doing the right thing, such as telling the truth, is always good, even though it might not always feel good.
- We are not responsible for the actions or feelings of others.

Looking Ahead

In this chapter, the Holy Spirit invites you to ▶

EXPLORE how the Cross of Jesus reminded Saint Helena to love others.

DISCOVER the events of Jesus' last days on Earth.

DECIDE ways to live as a disciple of Jesus.

CHAPTER 6

The Death and Resurrection of Jesus

What is a sacrifice? When has someone made a sacrifice for you?

Imagine that you are among the disciples with Jesus. He tells you about the work that his Father sent him to do. Jesus says,

> "We will soon be going to Jerusalem. The chief priest and scribes will hand me over to the Romans and ask that I be condemned to death. The Romans will mock me, whip me, and put me to death. Three days later I will rise from the dead."
>
> Based on Mark 10:33-34

What do you remember about the sacrifice that Jesus made for all people?

Courage

Courage, or fortitude, helps us do or say what is right even when it is hard or scary. Following Jesus means having courage as he did. Courage helps a person to be brave even when he or she is very afraid. People with courage know that God is always with them.

THE CHURCH FOLLOWS JESUS

Saint Helena of the Cross

Would you like to visit the place where Jesus lived, died, and rose from the dead? Empress Helena did. Helena was the mother of Constantine the Great, the emperor of Rome.

Empress Helena lived almost three hundred years after Jesus died and was raised from the dead. Helena made a pilgrimage from Rome to the Holy Land. A pilgrimage is a prayer journey to a holy place.

When Helena arrived in the Holy Land, she went to Mount Calvary where Jesus was crucified. According to Christian tradition, Helena dug at Calvary and found the Cross on which Jesus had died.

Empress Helena had great devotion to the Cross of Jesus. The Cross reminded her of Jesus' courage and his love for her and for all people. Looking at the Cross gave her the courage to follow Jesus and to love others as he did. Empress Helena served the poor and homeless. She had her son build the Church of the Holy Cross in Rome, the Church of the Apostles in Constantinople, and the Church of the Nativity in Palestine.

The Church has named Helena a saint and celebrates her feast day on August 18.

? What do you remember about the last days of Jesus' life on Earth?

Jesus' Last Days

Jesus and his disciples went up to the city of Jerusalem to celebrate **Passover**. This would be the last time that they would celebrate Passover with Jesus. As Jesus entered Jerusalem, a crowd welcomed him as the One whom God had promised would set them free. They cheered, "Hosanna to the Son of David" (Matthew 21:9).

Later that week, Jesus and his disciples ate the Passover meal together for the last time. Christians call this meal the **Last Supper**. At the Last Supper, Jesus gave us the gift of his Body and Blood, the Eucharist. He told his disciples to celebrate and share the Eucharist in memory of him. The Church does what Jesus did at the Last Supper at every celebration of the Mass.

After sharing the Last Supper with the Apostles, he prayed in the Garden of Gethsemane to his Father. Jesus felt the weight of his sacrifice and prayed, "My Father, if it is possible, let this cup pass from me" (see Matthew 26:39).

The suffering and Death of Jesus, or his Passion, was the greatest sacrifice of all. Jesus' Passion and Resurrection are the great signs of God's love for us.

FAITH FOCUS

What were the main events of Jesus' last days on Earth?

FAITH VOCABULARY

Passover

Passover is the Jewish feast celebrating God freeing the Israelites from suffering and slavery in Egypt and leading them to freedom in the land that he had promised them.

Last Supper

The Last Supper is the last meal that Jesus celebrated with the disciples. At this meal, he gave the Church the gift of his Body and Blood, the Eucharist.

Activity Read Matthew 26:26-28. Compare what you read here with what you see and hear at Mass.

____

____

____

____

Women Disciples of Jesus

Joanna, a follower of Jesus; Mary, the wife of Clopas; and Mary Magdalene were at the Crucifixion with Jesus' mother. Women disciples also prepared Jesus' body for burial and were the first disciples to learn about the Resurrection.

Jesus' Trial, Death, and Burial

While Jesus was praying with his disciples in the Garden of Gethsemane, Judas the Apostle led some Roman soldiers and leaders of the Jewish people to Jesus. Judas went to Jesus and kissed him. Judas used this sign of friendship to betray him.

Roman soldiers arrested Jesus and took him to Pontius Pilate, the Roman governor, and put him on trial. Pilate could not find Jesus guilty of any crime and wanted to release him. But the religious leaders who plotted against Jesus shouted, "Crucify him! Crucify him!" (Luke 23:21). So Pilate sentenced Jesus to be crucified, or put to death on a cross.

The soldiers led Jesus to Calvary, a hill outside Jerusalem where the Romans crucified criminals. They nailed Jesus to the Cross that he had carried. As he was dying on the Cross, Jesus prayed, "Father, forgive them, they know not what they do" (Luke 23:34).

Around three o'clock in the afternoon, Jesus cried out, "Father, into your hands I commend my spirit" and died (Luke 23:46). Joseph of Arimathea, a disciple of Jesus, asked Pilate's permission to bury Jesus' body. Jesus' disciples wrapped his body in a clean linen cloth and placed it in a new tomb, which was carved in the rock (see Matthew 27:57-61).

? What would you have done if you were there during Jesus' trial?

The Resurrection and Ascension

In the early morning of the third day after Jesus' Death and burial, Mary Magdalene and another disciple of Jesus, also named Mary, went to Jesus' tomb. The ground began to shake.

> An angel of the Lord descended from heaven, approached, rolled back the stone [in front of the tomb], and sat upon it. . . . Then the angel said to the women, "Do not be afraid! I know that you are seeking Jesus the crucified. He is not here, for he has been raised just as he said. Come and see the place where he lay. Then go quickly and tell his disciples."
>
> MATTHEW 28:2, 5-7

This event is called the Resurrection.

The Risen Jesus appeared to his disciples for forty days. Then he took them to a mountain in Galilee. Jesus commissioned them, or gave them work to do in his name. They were to make disciples of all people. They were to baptize people and teach them to obey all that he had commanded them. Jesus promised to always be with them and then returned to his Father. This event is called the Ascension.

Symbols

Symbols are signs that represent or point to something. The cross is a symbol of Jesus' Death and love. Christians use the cross and other symbols to remind them of the mysteries of our faith.

Activity You are the editor for the *Good News Daily Post.* Under each headline, write the first sentence for your news article.

GOOD NEWS DAILY POST

1. The Tomb of Jesus Is Empty

____

____

2. Jesus Returns to His Father

____

____

I FOLLOW JESUS

The events of the Paschal Mystery are part of your faith story. The cross is a symbol of this story. Living as a disciple of Jesus takes courage. Each time that you love others the best that you can, you are doing what Jesus did.

BY YOUR CROSS AND RESURRECTION

Decorate the cross with ways in which you can bring Jesus' life to others.

Save us, Savior of the world,
for by your Cross and Resurrection
you have set us free.

MEMORIAL ACCLAMATION, *ROMAN MISSAL*

MY FAITH CHOICE

This week, I will use the virtue of courage to be Jesus' disciple. I will

____

____

____.

"Save us, Savior of the world, for by your Cross and Resurrection you have set us free."

Chapter Review

Place these events of the last days in the life of Jesus in their proper order. Mark the first event with the number 1 and the last event with the number 7.

_____ The Resurrection

_____ The Ascension

_____ The Last Supper

_____ The Crucifixion

_____ The arrest in the garden

_____ The trial before Pontius Pilate

_____ The burial in the tomb

TO HELP YOU REMEMBER

1. Jesus celebrated the Last Supper during Passover before he was crucified.
2. Jesus suffered and died on the Cross for us.
3. Jesus was raised from the dead. Forty days later, he returned, or ascended, to his Father in Heaven.

Adoration of the Cross

Prayers of adoration are found in the Bible. Adoration is one of the five types of prayer prayed by God's people. This prayer is from the liturgy of the Church celebrated on Good Friday.

Come forward one by one. Reverence the crucifix and silently pray:

We adore you, O Christ,
and we bless you.
By your holy Cross
you have redeemed the world.

With My Family

This Week . . .

In Chapter 6, The Death and Resurrection of Jesus, your child learned:

- At the Last Supper, Jesus gave us the gift of his Body and Blood, the Eucharist.
- Jesus was betrayed, arrested, and handed over to Pilate for trial. Although not found guilty of any crime, Jesus was put to death on the Cross as a common criminal.
- On the third day after his Death and burial, Jesus rose to new life and, for forty days, appeared to the disciples on many occasions.
- After commissioning them to make disciples of all nations, Jesus ascended to his Father in Heaven.
- Courage is the virtue that allows us to do what is right even when it is hard.

For more about related teachings of the Church, see the *Catechism of the Catholic Church*, 595–667, and the *United States Catholic Catechism for Adults*, pages 91–99.

Sharing God's Word

Invite each family member to share what he or she knows about the Gospel account of Jesus' suffering and Death (Passion), Resurrection, and Ascension. Discuss the courage that Jesus showed in freely choosing to die for our sins.

We Live as Disciples

The Christian home and family is a school of discipleship. Choose one of the following activities to do as a family, or design a similar activity of your own:

- This week, take time after Mass to walk the Stations of the Cross. Imagine what it might have been like to have been with Jesus.
- Have a mealtime discussion about courage. When have family members acted with courage?
- When have you counted on God and the support of each other for the courage and strength to do what is right?

Our Spiritual Journey

In a prayer of adoration, we acknowledge that God alone is God and we are his creatures. In this chapter, your child prayed a prayer of adoration. Read and pray together the prayer on page 61. Discuss the ways in which your family keeps or can keep God first in your lives.

Faith-Filled People

Women Disciples of Jesus
Women disciples prepared Jesus' body for burial and were the first disciples to learn about the Resurrection.

For more ideas on ways your family can live as disciples of Jesus, visit **www.BeMyDisciples.com**

Reasons for Feelings

Feelings come from our bodies and minds working together. Our bodies get information through our senses. Nerves send messages to the brain. The brain responds with answers. Those answers are feelings. Some feelings are pleasant and some are unpleasant.

We have certain feelings when we are around certain people at certain times. For example, we share a sense of excitement, joy, or spiritedness with our teammates after winning a game. We feel hurt or disappointed if the team loses. Maybe we have had a bad day and we know that certain friends always cheer us up. Virtues, such as courage, can help us manage our feelings so that we act in loving and respectful ways.

Feelings can be hard to understand. Some boys and girls might feel uncomfortable around each other. That can change over time. Our bodies are always undergoing many changes. Everyone undergoes change as time passes. For example, a boy as he grows older might develop feelings for a girl that lead him to want to spend more time with her. Being close to others is important in God's plan for us. God created us to live with others. For example, in God's plan for married life, children are created through the shared love of a husband and wife.

Catholics Believe

Fortitude gives us the strength to do what is right. Courage is another name for fortitude. Fortitude helps us stand up for what is right.

Activity

Complete the sentences to help you listen to and act on your feelings. Share with your family.

You are playing outside with friends during recess. You see two older boys tease and push another child. The child begins to cry.

In this moment, I feel . . .

I choose to . . .

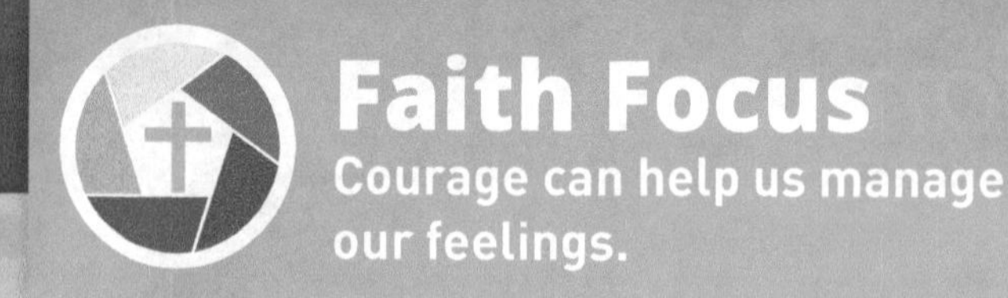

Faith Focus

Courage can help us manage our feelings.

Healthy Habits @ Home

Complete the following emotional workout as a family by inviting each family member to complete a sentence out loud.

- "I want to shout with joy when . . ."
- "I am very afraid of . . ."
- "I feel sadness when . . ."
- "I get angry when . . ."
- "I am curious about . . ."

Safer Together

Families are safer when family members trust, respect, and are loyal to each other. Review the following as a family:

- **Trust** can be earned or lost. It includes being able to depend on each other. It means believing that our parents are doing what is best for us and that God will hear our prayers.
- **Loyalty** means staying committed to the traditions and values of our faith and family. It does not mean keeping secret abusive behavior.
- **Respect** includes treating each other as unique persons created by God. It is important to respect our bodies and those of others.

Family Time

Cut out and hang at home

Have each family member respond to the following questions and encourage everyone to listen attentively.

- Is it easier for you to reveal your feelings through words or through actions?
- How have you expressed your feelings today?
- Which emotion do you find most difficult to handle? How do you normally deal with that emotion?

Family in Action

One way we show respect is by respecting each other's feelings. Another way is by listening to each other, especially during mealtime. At the end of your meal, say a prayer of thanksgiving for the respectful members of your household!

Write your prayer here:

....

....

....

....

Looking Ahead

In this chapter, the Holy Spirit invites you to ▶

EXPLORE how the Holy Spirit guided a missionary.

DISCOVER the gift of the Holy Spirit.

DECIDE how you will see the Holy Spirit at work in your life.

CHAPTER 7

Receive the Holy Spirit

How have you been helped with a task or a problem that you could not solve?

Imagine that you are with Jesus at the Last Supper. You know that he will soon be arrested and put to death. You are worried about what you will do without him. Then he says,

> "Do not be afraid. I will not leave you alone. The Father will send you the Holy Spirit in my name. He will be your helper and teacher."
>
> Based on John 14:1, 25

In which ways does the Holy Spirit help you live as a follower of Jesus?

Disciple Power

Wisdom

Wisdom is one of the seven Gifts of the Holy Spirit. This gift helps us see the world as God does. It helps us treat people with love as God treats everyone.

Family House

The Holy Spirit invites people to believe in Jesus through the lives of missionaries. Missionaries, as the Apostles did, travel to places to tell others about Jesus.

Sister Kathleen Reiley is a Maryknoll sister. She is a missionary in Japan where she helps children who have cancer. Yoshino Takashi was one of the children whom Sister Kathleen helped.

Takashi was not a Christian. A friend gave Takashi a Bible. Takashi loved reading the Bible. He underlined his favorite passages. His faith in Jesus Christ grew and grew. He soon was baptized and given the name Stephen.

Stephen heard that Sister Kathleen wanted to start a house for families of children with cancer. These families often needed a place to stay while their children were in the hospital. Without telling Sister Kathleen, Stephen told his father, "Even if I die, please help Sister build a home for these families."

Mr. Yoshino did what his son asked him. Many families are helped because of the love of young Stephen for Jesus. Now there is a Family House where families can get love and care.

Activity Find Japan on a map or globe. Now pick another country where you might like to tell others about Jesus. Write the name of that country on the line below. Underneath the line, tell what you would like to do there.

____

The Gift of the Holy Spirit

FAITH FOCUS
Why is the Holy Spirit important to the Church?

FAITH VOCABULARY
Pentecost
Pentecost is the day, fifty days after the Resurrection, that the Holy Spirit came to the disciples as Jesus had promised.

God the Father sent his Son, Jesus, into the world so that "the world might be saved through him" (based on John 3:17). For three years, during his public ministry, Jesus traveled with his disciples doing the work God the Father sent him to do.

At the Last Supper, Jesus knew his disciples were afraid. They did not want him to die. They did not want to be left alone after he died. He made this promise to them,

> "The Advocate, the holy Spirit that the Father will send in my name—he will teach you everything and remind you of all that [I] told you. . . . Do not let your hearts be troubled or afraid."
>
> JOHN 14:26-27

Jesus promised that God the Father would send them the Advocate, the Holy Spirit. An advocate is one who stands by your side and guides you. The disciples would never be alone. The Holy Spirit would always be with them to help and teach them as Jesus did.

? Why did Jesus promise to send the Holy Spirit?

Faith-Filled People

Saint Peter the Apostle

Peter and his brother Andrew were among the first disciples chosen by Jesus. Jesus chose Peter to be the leader of the Apostles and his Church. The pope is the successor of Saint Peter. The pope is the leader of the whole Church on Earth.

The Coming of the Holy Spirit

Fifty days after the Resurrection, the city of Jerusalem was crowded with Jewish pilgrims. They had come from many countries to celebrate **Pentecost**. Pentecost was a feast that the Jews of Jesus' time celebrated to thank God for the harvest.

Mary, the Mother of Jesus, and the disciples were also in Jerusalem. They were waiting for the promise Jesus made to them to come true.

> *Out of nowhere, a loud wind filled the room in which they had locked themselves. Then there appeared tongues that looked like flames of fire that came and rested on each of them. They were all filled with the Holy Spirit.*
>
> BASED ON ACTS OF THE APOSTLES 2:1-4

Jesus' promise came true. The Holy Spirit came to the disciples. Peter and the other disciples, filled with the gift of the Holy Spirit, unlocked the door and went into the marketplace. Peter boldly preached about Jesus' Death and Resurrection. Many people came to believe in Jesus Christ and asked to be baptized.

Activity Decorate the frame around the prayer. Work with a small group of your classmates. Choose gestures to use as you pray the Glory Be. Then pray giving glory and praise to God for sending the gift of the Holy Spirit.

Glory be to the Father
and to the Son
and to the Holy Spirit,
as it was in the beginning
is now, and ever shall be
world without end.
Amen.

The Work of the Holy Spirit

Peter and the other Apostles first preached the Gospel in the marketplace in Jerusalem. Then, obeying Jesus' command, they traveled by land and sea to make disciples of all nations.

Everywhere they went, the Apostles and their companions invited Jews and Gentiles, saying:

> "Repent and be baptized . . . in the name of Jesus Christ for the forgiveness of your sins; and you will receive the gift of the holy Spirit."
>
> Acts of the Apostles 2:38

God the Father, Son, and Holy Spirit always work together. The work of the Holy Spirit is the same as the work that the Father sent his Son, Jesus Christ, to do. It is the work of Salvation and Redemption. It is the work of saving us and freeing us from sin and of restoring us to the new life of God. It is the work of teaching and helping all people to live as children of God and followers of Jesus Christ.

Catholics Believe

Evangelization

Evangelization is the first work of the Church. The word *evangelization* means "the announcement of good news." Evangelization is the work of announcing the Good News to make people disciples of Jesus Christ.

Activity Design a sign or billboard that tells about the Holy Spirit's work in your parish.

I FOLLOW JESUS

Breathing or breath is an image that the Bible uses for the Holy Spirit. The Holy Spirit lives within you. The Holy Spirit gives you all of the help you need to live as a disciple, or follower, of Jesus Christ.

THE HOLY SPIRIT

Choose one of these situations and tell how you will work with the Holy Spirit to breathe new life into it.

1. A new student joins my class. Everyone is ignoring him. I can

____

____

____.

2. A good friend or a brother or sister is very sick and needs to stay in the hospital for a long time. I can

____

____

____.

MY FAITH CHOICE

This week, I will cooperate with the Holy Spirit and take part in the work of the Church, helping others come to know Jesus better. I will

____

____.

Pray, "Come, Holy Spirit, fill my heart with wisdom. Help me and teach me to live my Baptism. Amen."

Chapter Review

In the flames, write or draw three things you learned about the Holy Spirit this week.

TO HELP YOU REMEMBER

1. Jesus promised that he and the Father would send the Holy Spirit to help and teach the disciples as Jesus did.
2. The Holy Spirit came to the disciples on Pentecost.
3. The work of the Holy Spirit in the Church is the same work that the Father sent Jesus to do.

Come, Holy Spirit

Christian prayer is primarily addressed to God the Father, in the name of Jesus, through the power of the Holy Spirit. Christians also pray to Jesus and to the Holy Spirit. This prayer to the Holy Spirit is based on a prayer from the liturgy of Pentecost.

Leader: Come, Holy Spirit!

All: **Come, Holy Spirit!**

Group 1: Fill the hearts of your faithful.

Group 2: And kindle in them the fire of your love.

All: **Come, Holy Spirit!**

Group 1: Send forth your Spirit and they shall be created.

Group 2: And you will renew the face of the earth.

All: **Come, Holy Spirit!**

Leader: O God, on the first Pentecost, you taught those who believed in you by the light of the Holy Spirit. By the same Spirit, teach us what is right and share with us your wisdom and joy. Amen.

With My Family

This Week . . .

In Chapter 7, Receive the Holy Spirit, your child learned:

- The Holy Spirit, the Advocate, is God's gift to us.
- Jesus promised not to abandon his disciples. He said that he would ask the Father to send the Holy Spirit to be with them always.
- The Holy Spirit came to the disciples on Pentecost. The Holy Spirit gave the disciples the energy and courage to do the work that Jesus had commissioned them to do and to preach the Good News.
- The work of the Holy Spirit is the same work that the Father sent Jesus to do.
- The Holy Spirit dwells within us, blessing us with the gift of wisdom. This gift enables us to see life through God's eyes and make decisions accordingly.

For more about related teachings of the Church, see the *Catechism of the Catholic Church*, 683–741, and the *United States Catholic Catechism for Adults*, pages 101–110.

Sharing God's Word

Read together John 14:15-30, Jesus' promise that the Father will send the Holy Spirit to his disciples in his name. Or read the adaptation of the story on page 65. Discuss that the same Holy Spirit is with you and each member of your family, helping you take part in the work of the Church.

We Live as Disciples

The Christian home and family is a school of discipleship. Choose one of the following activities to do as a family, or design a similar activity of your own:

- Talk about how the Holy Spirit helps your family live as a Christian family.
- Make a poster of the prayer to the Holy Spirit. Hang the poster where it can serve as a reminder to everyone in your family that the Holy Spirit is always with them.

Our Spiritual Journey

The spiritual discipline of almsgiving includes sharing both our spiritual and material blessings. Practicing almsgiving energizes us to take part in the Church's work of evangelization. Read and pray together the prayer on page 69. Ask the Holy Spirit to strengthen and guide your family to live the Catholic faith.

Faith-Filled People

Saint Peter the Apostle
Feast Day: June 29
Jesus chose Saint Peter to be the first leader of the whole Church. Saint Peter was our first pope.

For more ideas on ways your family can live as disciples of Jesus, visit **BeMyDisciples.com**

All in Good Time

Growing up and becoming mature takes time. We grow physically, mentally, emotionally, and spiritually. God created us to grow over many years because things happen in their proper time. There is a proper time for things to happen for each person. This is true for our families too.

One sign of our maturing is our ability to be patient. Being patient can be very difficult. Think of patience as a way to get ready for something. Making plans, learning skills, and making friends all require time. We need time to make plans so that things will happen at the right time and in the right way. If we want to play a sport, we need time to learn the rules and plays and to develop the skills. Making friends takes time and effort too.

Being patient helps things happen in their proper time. Being patient can also mean preparing to receive something we need. Preparing includes having a pure heart. A pure heart is one that is open to receive what is needed. Keeping an open and pure heart allows us to be ready for what God will give us. Learning to be patient helps us receive the gifts God has in store for us when we are ready!

Catholics Believe

Patience and self-control help us discipline ourselves. Patience helps us to prepare for the gifts that God will provide.

Activity Think about how you have grown over the past year. Name some of the times, ways, and signs of your growth below, including spiritual growth. Share your chart with your family.

Times and Ways I Have Grown	Signs of My Growth

Family Life Connection

Healthy Habits @ Home

Patience is a good habit. Discuss these questions with your family:

- How do we show patience toward one another?
- What is one thing we can start doing to show patience toward one another?

Family Time

As a family, share stories about how family members have grown. Consider these ideas to keep the conversation on target.

- Growth can be fun and scary at the same time.
- Growth can take place both physically and spiritually.

Then ask: How can we help ourselves grow?

Faith Focus

Patience helps us to prepare for the gifts that God will provide.

Safer Together

Families are safer together when children learn about the goodness of their bodies. Review the following information to help talk to your child about the goodness of our bodies:

- God created each person in his image and likeness.
- Caring for our bodies shows that we respect God's gift of our bodies.
- Caring for our bodies shows also that we are proud of who God created us to be.
- Protecting our bodies from danger or saying "no" to inappropriate touching shows respect for our bodies.

Family in Action

The more we understand the development of an unborn child, the more we can cherish God's gift of life at all stages. As a family, discuss the development of the unborn child. Then find ways to support pro-life programs, such as:

- ☐ Contact your local pro-life, justice and peace, or mission awareness ministries.
- ☐ Provide baby clothing to agencies, become a foster family, or offer financial support to programs for pregnant teenagers.
- ☐ Collect food, clothing, or money for the homeless in your community.

Looking Ahead

In this chapter, the Holy Spirit invites you to ▶

EXPLORE who the Seven Holy Martyrs are.

DISCOVER images, or names, for the Church.

DECIDE ways to participate in the work of the Church.

CHAPTER 8

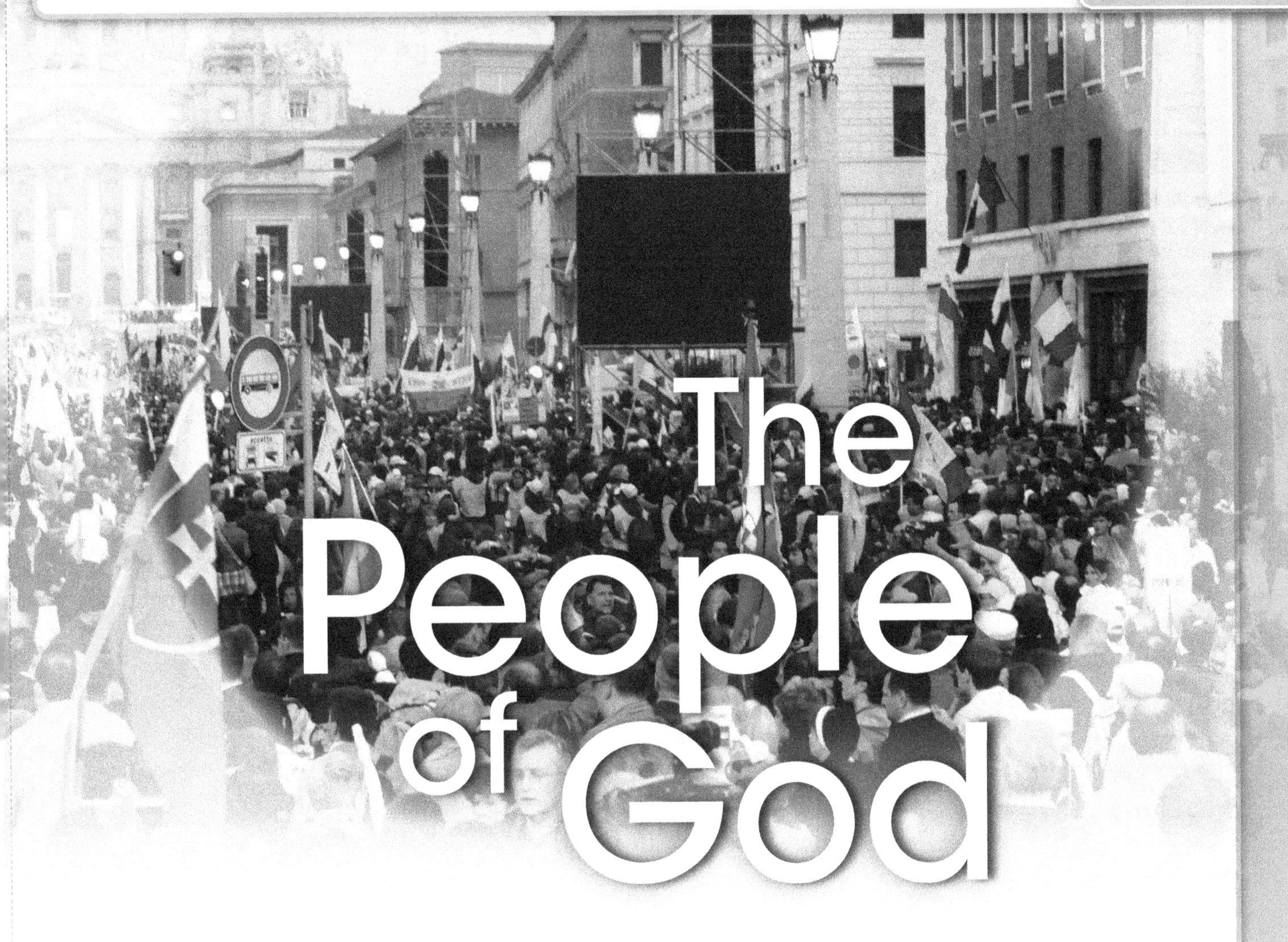

The People of God

? Which groups do you belong to? What do people who belong to one of these groups do together?

Each of us belongs to God's family. We belong to God's people. The Church is the People of God. The psalmist reminds us:

Know that the Lord is God,
He made us, his we are;
His people, the flock he tends. BASED ON PSALM 100:3

? How do you show your belief that you are part of the People of God?

Disciple Power

Understanding

Understanding is one of the seven Gifts of the Holy Spirit. Understanding helps us find the truth about God and about ourselves. It helps us discover what it means to be disciples of Jesus, the Son of God.

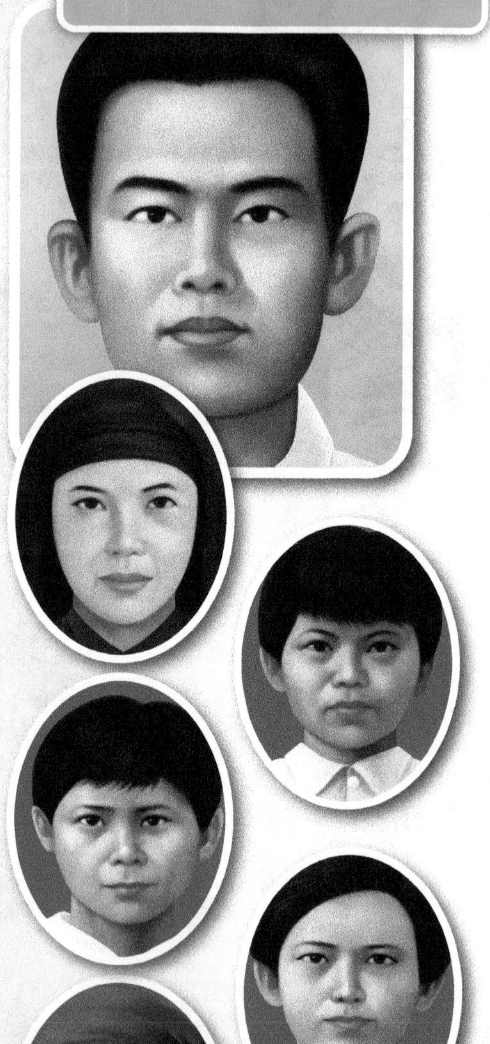

THE CHURCH FOLLOWS JESUS

The Seven Holy Martyrs of Thailand

God invites all people to be friends and disciples of Jesus. God wants to gather all people into the family of the Church.

Locate on a map the country of Thailand and the Catholic village of Songkhon on the Mekong River. In the winter of 1940, police went door to door pointing their guns at the people in the village, ordering them to abandon their faith in Christ. The village priest refused, and he was driven out of Songkhon.

Philip Siphong stepped up to help the people. He was a religion teacher in charge of the village school. He visited each home and prayed with each family. This strengthened their faith in Christ.

The police became furious with Philip. They dragged him into the forest and murdered him. Philip Siphong died for his faith in Jesus on December 16, 1940. He became the first of the Seven Holy Martyrs of Thailand. Agatha Phutta, Sister Agnes Phila, Sister Lucia Khambang, Cecilia Butsi (who was sixteen), Bibiana Khamphai (who was fifteen), and Maria Phon (who was fourteen) are the other six martyrs.

The people of Thailand celebrate the lives of these seven brave Catholics each year on December 18.

? Whom do you go to when you need help to live as a disciple of Jesus? How do they help you?

Names for the Church

The Church can be described in many ways. The Church is the People of God, the Body of Christ, and the Communion of Saints. Each of these names helps us understand the mystery of the Church.

People of God. The New Testament describes the Church as "a chosen race . . . a holy nation" (1 Peter 2:9). The Church is all of the people whom God has called together in Jesus Christ. We are called together to know, love, and serve God. God has created us to live in happiness with him forever.

Body of Christ. Baptism joins us to Jesus Christ. The Church is the Body of Christ. The Church is both human and divine. Christ is the Head of the Church, and the hierarchy, religious, and laypeople are members of the Church.

Communion of Saints. The Church is spiritual and visible. All of the faithful followers of Christ who are alive on Earth and those who have died belong to the Church. These followers include the saints in Heaven and the souls in Purgatory.

FAITH FOCUS

What does it mean to call the Church the People of God?

FAITH VOCABULARY

People of God
The People of God is a New Testament image for the Church that teaches that God has called together all people in Jesus Christ to be his people.

Body of Christ
The Body of Christ is a New Testament image for the Church that teaches that the members of the Church are made one in Christ, the Head of the Church.

Activity Describe the good works that you see members of the Church doing together in your parish.

____

____

____

____

____

____

The Apostles

The Apostles were the first shepherds of the Church. The Apostles whom Jesus chose first are named in Matthew 10:1-4. They are also called the Twelve.

The Work of the Church

The Catholic Church goes all the way back to Jesus and the Apostles. The Church continues today the work that the Apostles began. Jesus founded the Church on the Apostles. He said to Peter the Apostle, "You are Peter, and upon this rock I will build my church" (Matthew 16:18).

Jesus gave Peter and the other Apostles the authority and responsibility to baptize people, to make all people his disciples, and to teach what he had taught. Jesus Christ continues to govern, or lead, the Church today through the pope, who is the bishop of Rome, and the other bishops. The pope is the successor of Saint Peter, and the other bishops are the successors of the other Apostles.

All of the baptized are called to work with the Holy Spirit and continue the work of Christ on Earth. The words *priest*, *prophet*, and *king* describe the work of Christ. All the members of the Church share in his work. As baptized members of the Church, we do the priestly work of living holy lives. We are to tell others about God as prophets do. Our kingly work is to serve God, especially by serving people who are poor and suffering.

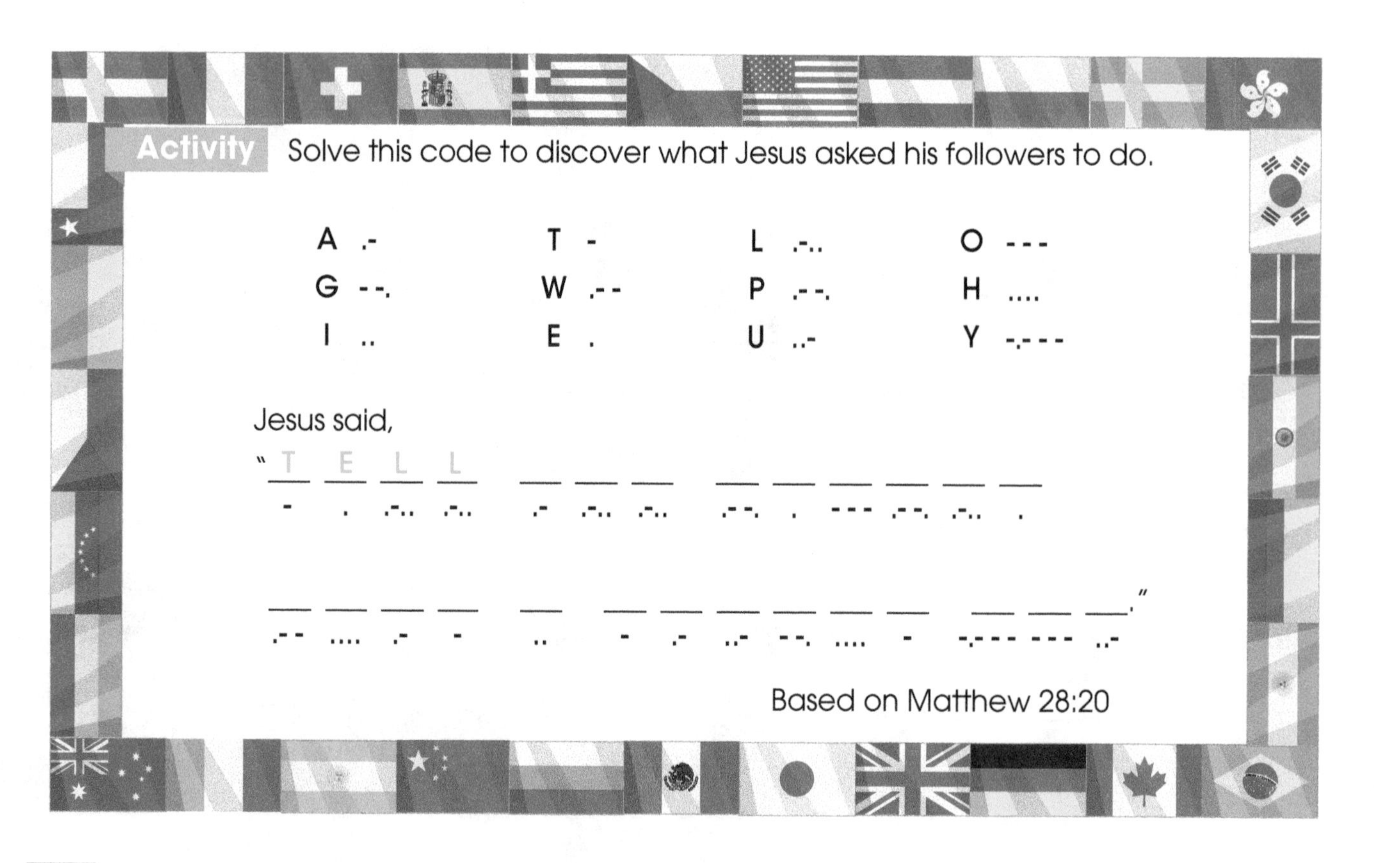

Activity Solve this code to discover what Jesus asked his followers to do.

A	.-	T	-	L	.-..	O	---
G	--.	W	.--	P	.--.	H	....
I	..	E	.	U	..-	Y	-.---

Jesus said,

"T E L L ___ ___ ___ ___ ___ ___ ___ ___ ___
- . .-.. .-.. .- .-.. .-.. .--. . --- .--. .-.. .

___ ___ ___ ___ ___ ___ ___ ___ ___ ___ ___ ___ ___ ___."
.-- .... .- - .. - .- ..- --. .... - -.--- --- ..-

Based on Matthew 28:20

The Kingdom of God

Jesus spoke of his work as building the Kingdom of God. Jesus said that the Kingdom of God, or Kingdom of Heaven, is like a treasure (read Matthew 13:44). It is something that we would be willing to sell everything we have to find and keep. It is something that we pray for every time we pray "thy kingdom come" in the Our Father.

Together with the Holy Spirit, the Church works to prepare for the coming of God's kingdom. The people of the Church around the world work to build a world of love and peace. We work together to continue the works of mercy and justice that Jesus began.

The coming of the Kingdom of God is good news for all people. It gives all people hope for the future. The Kingdom of God will finally come about when the work of Christ is finished at the end of time. Then, Christ will come again in glory. God's loving plan of Salvation and Redemption will be completed.

? How would you describe the Kingdom of God to a friend? Find a partner and share your description.

Catholics Believe

All Souls' Day

On November 2, the Church celebrates All Souls' Day. We pray for all of the souls in Purgatory. We believe that when we die, our life is changed and not ended. We support one another by our prayers.

Día de los Muertos (Day of the Dead) altar on All Souls' Day

I FOLLOW JESUS

Your parish family is made up of many people. Perhaps many languages are spoken in your parish. You help one another grow in faith and love. You pray and serve others together.

PRIEST, PROPHET, AND KING

As a baptized Christian, you are to do the work of priest, prophet, and king. Create a storyboard and show a way you fill each of these roles.

Priest	Prophet	King

MY FAITH CHOICE

You are an important member of your parish family. Your parish needs you! What will you do to work with other members of your parish? I will

____

____.

Ask the Holy Spirit for the gift of understanding so that you will come to know the truth about God and his great love for you.

Chapter Review

Use this code to decipher the message about the Church.

1 = E 2 = O 3 = S 4 = H 5 = T

T___ ___ C___ urc___ i___ ___he
4 1 4 4 3 5

Pe___ pl___ ___f G___d and
2 1 2 2

t___e B___dy ___f C___ri___t.
4 2 2 4 3

TO HELP YOU REMEMBER

1. The Church is the Body of Christ, the People of God, and the Communion of Saints.
2. Jesus founded the Church on Saint Peter the Apostle.
3. Jesus announced the coming of the Kingdom of God. His Kingdom will come about in all its fullness at the end of time.

Thy Kingdom Come!

Jesus promised that all who believe in God and live as he taught will live forever in Heaven.

Leader: Let us pray for the coming of God's kingdom.

Reader 1: We work to bring about God's kingdom

Reader 2: when we shelter the homeless,

All: **thy kingdom come.**

Reader 3: When we give food and drink to those in need,

Reader 4: when we give clothing and shelter,

All: **thy kingdom come.**

Reader 5: When we help people who are sick,

Reader 6: when we visit with those imprisoned.

All: **thy kingdom come.**

Leader: Let us all pray for the coming of God's kingdom on Earth as it is in Heaven.

All: ***(Pray the Our Father.)***

With My Family

This Week . . .

In Chapter 8, The People of God, your child learned:

- God has called us together in Christ to be the Church, the People of God, and the Communion of Saints.
- Christ is the Head of the Body of Christ, the Church. The hierarchy, religious, and laypeople are her members.
- Every member of the Church works together with the Holy Spirit to continue the work of Christ to prepare for the coming of the Kingdom of God.
- God's kingdom will finally come about in its fullness at the end of time.
- Understanding is the gift of the Holy Spirit that allows us to discover the truth about God and ourselves.

For more about related teachings of the Church, see the *Catechism of the Catholic Church*, 748–959, and the *United States Catholic Catechism for Adults*, pages 115–123.

Sharing God's Word

Read together 1 Peter 2:9-10 and Matthew 16:13-19. Emphasize and discuss what it means for your family that you are part of the Church, the People of God and the Body of Christ.

We Live as Disciples

The Christian home and family is a school of discipleship. Continue to grow in faith as a family this week. Choose one of the following activities to do as a family, or design a similar activity of your own:

- Name the ways that your family members work well together. Talk about what it means for your family to live as members of the Body of Christ.
- Talk about how peaceful people show respect and treat one another justly as members of the one family of God. Choose one thing that you will do this week to help prepare for the coming of God's kingdom of peace.

Our Spiritual Journey

Someone described the human person as *homo quaerens*, or "the searcher seeking meaning." Saint Anselm described the faithful Christian as being on a journey of "seeking the meaning of the faith." Time spent in spiritual reading and reflection is a form of prayer.

Faith-Filled People

The Apostles

the Apostles were the twelve disciples Jesus sent into the world to make disciples of all nations. The Apostles were to baptize and teach, just as Jesus had taught them.

For more ideas on ways your family can live as disciples of Jesus, visit **BeMyDisciples.com**

Being Left Out

It is time for recess. You hurry to finish your math assignment so that you can join your classmates. When you arrive on the playground, teams have been chosen for kickball. The game is just starting. You are not very good at it, but you love kickball. You want to play too. But your classmates tell you it is too late. While you watch from the sidelines, several others, the "cool" kids, are allowed to join the game. You are confused and feel hurt and disappointed.

Our feelings help us respond in different ways to the events in our lives. Virtues such as courage can help us express and manage our feelings. We can act and react to situations in loving and respectful ways. How would you feel in this situation? How would you act on your feelings?

Catholics Believe

Courage, or fortitude, helps us express our feelings and stand up for what is right.

Activity

Talk about the scenario with your family. Use this formula to express to your classmates how you feel:

I feel ____________ when you ____________.

I feel ____________ because ____________.

For example:

I feel hurt when you keep me out of the game.

I feel angry because you let the others play but not me.

Faith Focus

Jesus shows us the best ways to share our feelings with others.

Healthy Habits @ Home

Listening is one of the most important communication skills. Practice listening well to each other in your family, especially when family members are sharing how they feel.

Safer Together

Cut out and hang at home

Families are safer together when they respect and trust each other. Keep these tips in mind:

1. Keep the lines of communication open with your children.
2. Encourage your children to share their thoughts and feelings with you. Sometimes the simple act of listening can help your children sort out and express their feelings.
3. Use supportive, caring language when listening to your children and reflecting back what they say to you.
4. Communicate family rules and boundaries in a clear and concise way to your children. Have them repeat back to you what you have said to ensure that they understand.
5. Pray as a family for God's help.

Family Time

Happy and healthy families share and act on their feelings in appropriate ways. "I" messages are statements that focus on the feelings of the person speaking, rather than on the other person in an accusing way.

Talk about the examples below with family members. Add one more example. Then practice using "I" messages when expressing feelings.

Situation	Common (Accusing) Response	"I" Message
Your friends refuse to include you in their game.	You are mean to not let me play with you.	I feel left out when you exclude me from the game.
You borrowed your sister's jacket and left it outside in the rain.	You wrecked my jacket by leaving it outside!	I am upset that my jacket is damaged, because it was my favorite one. I appreciate it when you take care of things I lend you.

Unit 2 **Review**

Name ______________________________

A. Choose the Best Word

Use the words in the word bank to complete the sentences.

love	Incarnation	ministry
Last Supper	Advocate	Passover

1. The ______________ is the Son of God becoming human without giving up being God.

2. Jesus promised that God the Father would send the ______________, the Holy Spirit.

3. ______________ is the greatest of all the virtues.

4. Jesus began his public ______________ when he grew up and left home to begin the work God the Father sent him to do.

5. ______________ is the Jewish feast that celebrates God freeing the Israelites from slavery and leading them to the land promised to them.

B. Show What You Know

Match the words or phrases in Column A with the words or phrases in Column B.

Column A

1. miracle

2. pilgrimage

3. courage

4. Ascension

5. Passion

Column B

____ **a.** prayer journey to a holy place

____ **b.** the suffering and Death of Jesus

____ **c.** Jesus' return to the Father

____ **d.** wonder, something amazing and marvelous

____ **e.** fortitude, virtue that helps a person be brave

C. Connect with Scripture

Reread the Scripture passage on page 45. What connection do you see between this passage and what you learned in this unit?

____

____

____

D. Be a Disciple

1. *Review the four pages in this unit titled The Church Follows Jesus. What person or ministry of the Church shared on these pages will inspire you to be a better disciple of Jesus? Explain your answer.*

____

____

____

2. *Work with a group. Review the four Disciple Power virtues, or gifts, you have learned about in this unit. After writing your own ideas, share with the group practical ways that you will live these virtues day by day.*

____

____

____

We Worship

UNIT 3

Part One

Jesus and Lazarus

Lazarus from Bethany became sick. His sisters, Mary and Martha, asked Jesus to come at once.

Jesus arrived two days later. Lazarus had already died and had been buried. Martha said to Jesus, "Lord, if you had been here, my brother would not have died!"

Jesus told her, "I am the resurrection and the life; whoever believes in me, even if he dies, will live. Do you believe this?"

At once, Martha answered, "Yes, Lord. I have come to believe that you are the Messiah, the Son of God, the one who is coming into the world."

Jesus went to the tomb and, in a loud voice, said, "Lazarus, come out!" At that command, Lazarus came out of the tomb.

Based on John 11:1-44

What I Have Learned

WWhat is something you already know about these three faith terms?

sacraments

____

____

____

Paschal Mystery

____

____

____

vocation

____

____

____

Faith Terms to Know

Put an X next to the faith terms you know. Put a ? next to faith terms you need to learn more about.

_______ sin

_______ Exodus

_______ Gifts of the Holy Spirit

_______ sacramentals

_______ Sacraments of Christian Initiation

_______ creed

The Bible

What do you know about how the early Christians gathered to pray and celebrate?

____

____

____

The Church

What do you know about the vocation of all the people of the Church?

____

____

____

A Question I Have

What question would you like to ask about the sacraments?

____

____

____

Popular Devotions

Epiphany Blessing

A Devotion from Eastern Europe

The Solemnity of the Epiphany, or Three Kings Day, traditionally is celebrated on January 6.

The Feast of the Epiphany occurs on January 6. This is the last of the twelve days of Christmas. It is also known as Three Kings Day. It is the day the Magi arrived in Bethlehem to worship Baby Jesus. They entered the house where Jesus was and presented him with gifts of gold, frankincense, and myrrh.

This feast is celebrated in various ways. One of the most common is that of the "blessed chalk." Traditionally, the family members gather to ask the Lord to bless their home, their family, and all who visit them. They invite Jesus to be a part of their daily lives. They ask him to bless their work, study, play, and all activities that take place in the home.

They then go outside to mark the front door with chalk that has been blessed for this purpose. They write the current year and the letters C, M, and B. The four-digit year is divided in half. The century is placed first. The year is placed last. The letters in the middle mean two things. They stand for the initials of the Three Kings: Caspar, Mechior, and Balthazar. They are also an abbreviation, or short form, of the Latin prayer *Christus mansionem benedicat*. This means, "May Christ bless this house." The crosses in between each letter represent Christ.

? Why would a family ask Jesus to be part of all its daily activities?

Epiphany Blessing

On the feast of the Epiphany, families ask God to protect and bless their homes and everyone who enters them. Solve the code to see the words used in this blessing.

SECRET CODE								
A	B	C	D	E	F	G	H	I
1	2	3	4	5	6	7	8	9
J	K	L	M	N	O	P	Q	R
10	11	12	13	14	15	16	17	18
S	T	U	V	W	X	Y	Z	
19	20	21	22	23	24	25	26	

___ ___ ___
13 1 25

___ ___ ___ ___ ___ ___
3 8 18 9 19 20

___ ___ ___ ___ ___
2 12 5 19 19

___ ___ ___ ___
20 8 9 19

___ ___ ___ ___ ___ .
8 15 21 19 5

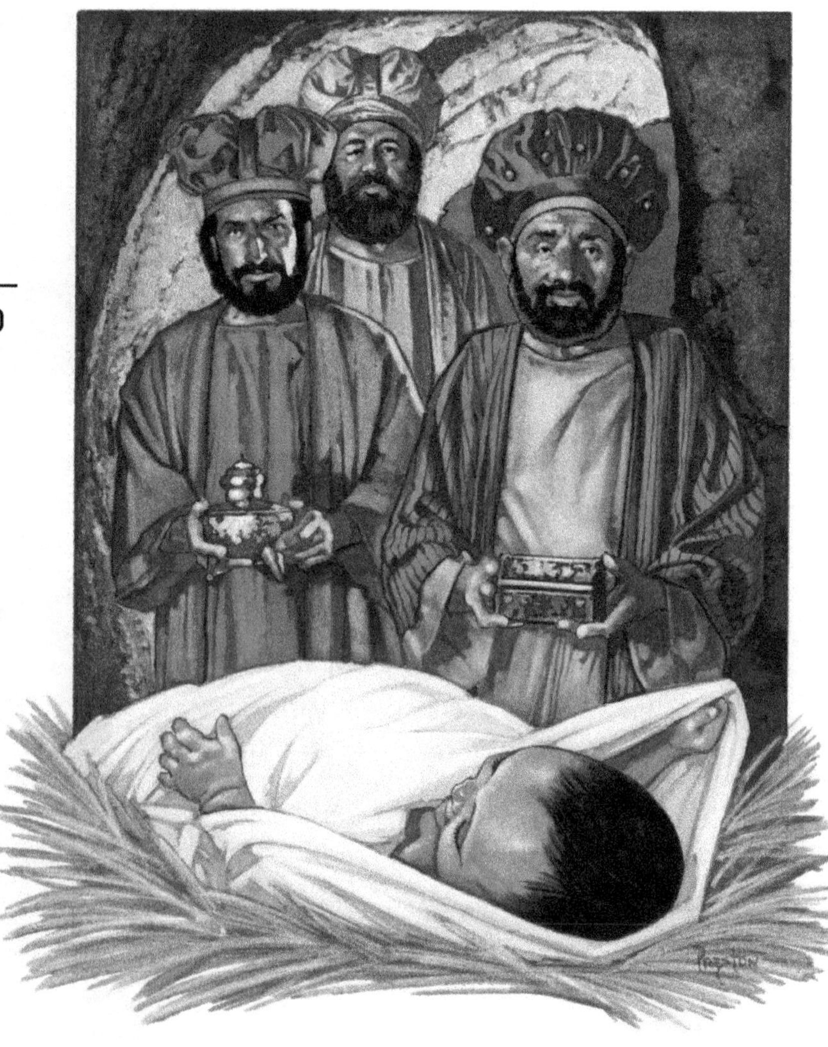

CHAPTER 9

Looking Ahead

In this chapter, the Holy Spirit invites you to ▶

EXPLORE prayer as an expression of friendship with God.

DISCOVER how the Church prays.

DECIDE how and when to pray every day.

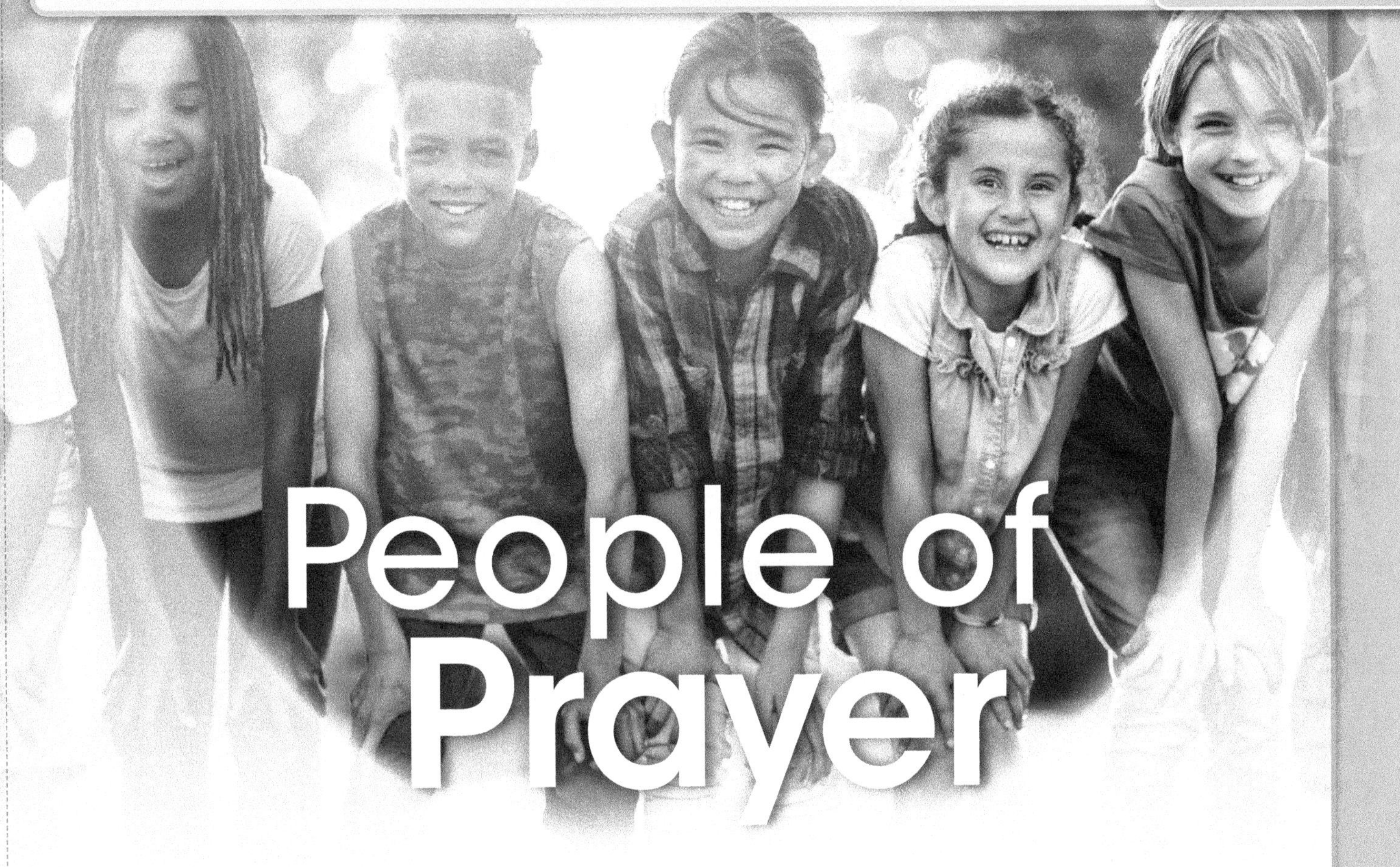

People of Prayer

? How do you like to spend time with your friends? How does this time help your friendships grow?

Spending time together and sharing thoughts and feelings with a friend helps a friendship grow. The same is true for our friendship with God. Listen to these words of Saint Paul:

> Help each other, and be patient. Look for the good in each other and in everyone. Rejoice always. Pray always. Give thanks for everything that happens to you. Let God's Spirit fill you.
>
> BASED ON 1 THESSALONIANS 5:14-19

? What does it mean to "pray always"?

Wonder and Awe

Wonder and awe, also called fear of the Lord, is a gift that sharpens our awareness of God's great love for us. It is a gift that we experience more and more as our friendship with God grows through prayer.

Dear Friend

You could hear a pin drop, and that did not happen very often in a crowded room full of teenagers! But on this special night, Mrs. Alvarez was visiting the youth group to tell them about her friendship with God.

Mrs. Alvarez was less than five feet tall, and rumor had it that she was the oldest person in the parish. The students sat around her listening carefully. Her voice was soft, almost a whisper. She talked to the teenagers about God and why she considered him a dear friend.

As they listened, the group soon came to know why Mrs. Alvarez considered God to be her dear friend. She said, "I feel like every moment of my life is a prayer. Every moment God is listening, just waiting for me to say, 'Hi!'"

Then she did something that many of the teenagers would never forget.

Quietly, she asked each of them to come forward. First, she said aloud, "Hi, God! Bless my young friends; they are your friends, too." She then gave them each a rosary. She said to each student, "Pray the Rosary, and you will learn what a friend of yours God is."

About a year later, Mrs. Alvarez died. Nearly every youth who had been there that night showed up at her funeral Mass. They came to praise and thank God for their dear friend.

? In what ways is God your "dear friend"?

God Is Always with Us

FAITH FOCUS
In what ways does the Church pray?

FAITH VOCABULARY

pray
To pray is to raise our minds and hearts to God, who is Father, Son, and Holy Spirit; it is to talk and listen to God.

Liturgy of the Hours
The daily, public, and communal prayer of the Church is called the Liturgy of the Hours.

The Holy Spirit invites us and teaches us to **pray**. When we pray, we share with God what is on our minds and in our hearts. We pray to God the Father; to Jesus, God's Son; and to the Holy Spirit. Whether we pray alone or with others, we believe that God is always with us. Whether we pray quietly in our hearts or aloud, God is always there, listening to us.

Praying strengthens our friendship with God. It celebrates our love for God. It expresses our faith and trust in God the Father, God the Son, and God the Holy Spirit. Prayer is a sign of our love for God. Praying is a sign of our trust in God.

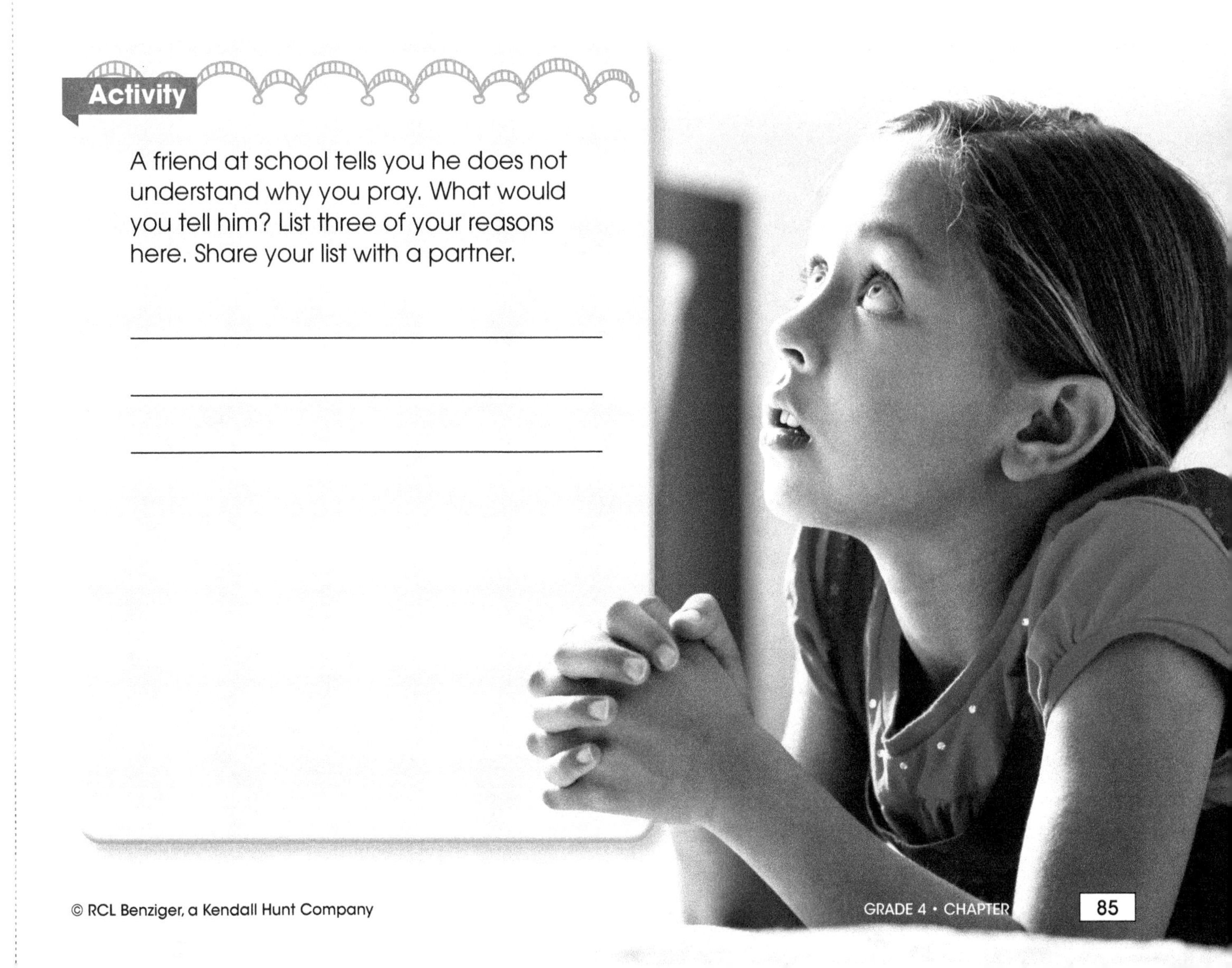

Activity

A friend at school tells you he does not understand why you pray. What would you tell him? List three of your reasons here. Share your list with a partner.

___

___

___

Faith-Filled People

Benedictines

Saint Benedict and Saint Scholastica were twins. Benedict wrote rules for people on how to live the Gospel. His rules can be summed up in the words, "pray and work." Scholastica followed the advice of her brother. Many other men and women did, too, and still do today. They are called Benedictines.

The Church Prays

The Church is a people of prayer. From the beginning of the Church, the followers of Jesus Christ have always gathered for prayer. The Church prays every day, all year long, year after year. The Church is always praying, because the Church is in every part of the world.

The liturgy is the main form of prayer for the Church. All prayer of the Church centers on the liturgy. The liturgies of the Church include the Eucharist, the other six sacraments, the **Liturgy of the Hours**, and the Benediction of the Most Blessed Sacrament.

At every part of the day, the Church is praying the Liturgy of the Hours. The Liturgy of the Hours is the daily, public, official prayer of the Church. The Church prays the Liturgy of the Hours in the morning, at midday, in the evening, and at night. We offer prayerful thanks to God for his great love for us. We ask God to help us live as his children and as followers of Christ.

? At what times of day do you pray? At which of these times do you pray with others?

Professing Our Faith in God

Praying is a sign of our faith in God. It is a sign that we believe that God is always with us and always listens. Faith is one of God's gifts to us. Faith gives us the ability to listen to God, to come to know God, and to believe in him. Faith helps us make our friendship with God the most important thing in our lives.

From her earliest days, the Church has professed her faith in God in creeds. The creeds of the Church are brief summaries of what the Church believes. We profess our faith in God the Holy Trinity and in all that God has revealed to us and done for us.

The two main creeds of the Church that we pray are the Apostles' Creed and the Nicene Creed. The Nicene Creed is the creed that we most often pray at Mass at the end of the Liturgy of the Word.

Catholics Believe

Medals and Statues

Medals and statues remind us that God is always with us. They are sacramentals. Sacramentals are sacred objects given to us by the Church that help us pray and remind us of God's love.

Activity Look up the Apostles' Creed and the Nicene Creed on page 258. Write on the lines two things that we believe about God the Father, God the Son, and God the Holy Spirit.

God the Father	God the Son	God the Holy Spirit
______________	______________	______________
______________	______________	______________
______________	______________	______________
______________	______________	______________

I FOLLOW JESUS

The Holy Spirit invites you to pray and teaches you to pray anytime and anywhere. You can pray at home, in church, on your way to school, or while you are taking a walk. God is inviting you to pray right now.

LORD, HEAR MY PRAYER

Quiet yourself for prayer. Pray Psalm 54:4. Listen. Share with God, friend to friend, what is in your heart and on your mind. Write or draw your prayer in the space. Experience wonder and awe in God's presence.

"O God, hear my prayer."

Psalm 54:4

MY FAITH CHOICE

This week, I will spend some time each day with God in prayer. I will

____

____

____.

Pray, "Our Father, who art in heaven, hallowed be thy name."

Chapter Review

Write T next to the true statements. Write F next to the false statements. Make the false statements true.

_______ **1.** We pray to God the Father, Jesus, and the Holy Spirit.

_______ **2.** Praying strengthens our friendship with God.

_______ **3.** Praying before and after meals is the main form of prayer in the Church.

_______ **4.** We pray the Nicene Creed at the end of Mass.

TO HELP YOU REMEMBER

1. The Church is a people of prayer.
2. The Liturgy of the Hours is the official prayer of the Church.
3. The creeds of the Church are short summaries of the faith of the Church.

Hail Mary

People all over the world pray the Hail Mary to honor Mary as the Mother of God and as our mother.

Leader: Lord God, Mary is our model of prayer. We honor her today as we pray.

Group 1: Hail, Mary, full of grace, the Lord is with thee.

Group 2: Blessed art thou among women and blessed is the fruit of thy womb, Jesus.

All: **Holy Mary, Mother of God, pray for us sinners, now and at the hour of our death. Amen.**

With My Family

This Week . . .

In Chapter 9, People of Prayer, your child learned:

- The Church is a people of prayer.
- Prayer is lifting our minds and hearts to God and sharing our thoughts and feelings with him.
- The Liturgy of the Hours is the daily public prayer of the Church.
- The creeds of the Church are prayers of the Church that are brief summaries of what the Church believes.
- Wonder and awe, or fear of the Lord, is one of the seven Gifts of the Holy Spirit that helps us grow in our awareness of God's greatness, power, and love for us.

For more about related teachings of the Church, see the *Catechism of the Catholic Church,* 2558–2567 and 2650–2679, and the *United States Catholic Catechism for Adults,* pages 461–495.

Sharing God's Word

Read Psalm 54:4 together. Talk about how prayer is both talking and listening to God. Prayer is conversation and communication with God. It is living our friendship with God.

We Live as Disciples

The Christian home and family is a school of discipleship. Your family grows in faith together. Choose one of the following activities to do as a family, or design a similar activity of your own:

- Use your family's prayer before meals as a time to thank God for his presence in your household.
- Sacramentals, such as medals or statues, remind us of God's love for us and help us pray. Find all of the sacramentals in your home. If they are not displayed, choose a few to display around your home.

Our Spiritual Journey

Mary is the Mother of God and the Mother of the Church. She is a woman of prayer. She is our constant companion on our spiritual journey. Praying the Hail Mary acknowledges and reminds us of this reality. Pause during your busy day to pray the Hail Mary. Invite Mary to accompany you on your spiritual journey.

Faith-Filled People

Benedictines

Saint Benedict and Saint Scholastica founded monasteries based on the ideas of "pray and work." The followers of this form of monastic life are called Benedictines.

For more ideas on ways your family can live as disciples of Jesus, visit **BeMyDisciples.com**

Developing Discipline

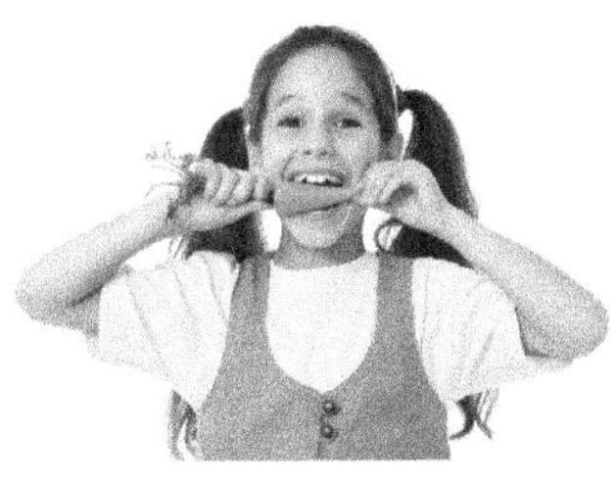

If we discipline ourselves, we can be as healthy and holy as God wants us to be. God wants us to love and take care of ourselves. Many healthy habits can help us do this. We can eat healthy foods, exercise, and get enough sleep. We show discipline and self-control when we take care of our bodies and develop healthy habits.

Our bodies need proper nutrition, or fuel. We can practice the good habit of eating a balanced diet. The good habit of exercising every day—such as playing ball, riding a bike, dancing, hiking, and other fun activities—will help our bodies and our spirits. A person is never too young or too old to develop the habit of being physically and spiritually active every day.

At the end of the day, our bodies do need a break. Without enough sleep, we are more likely to get sick and more likely to be tired, cranky, and unable to think clearly. By practicing the good habit of temperance, we take care of our bodies, minds, and spirits. God created us in such a way that our actions affect our health, both physically and spiritually. Taking care of ourselves is a way of showing that we are grateful for God's gift of life.

Catholics Believe

Temperance is the virtue of self-control and discipline. Temperance helps you know how much is too much, whether it be food, play, or even work!

Activity Complete the chart with your family. Discuss ways that family members can help each other keep fit.

Family Member	Hours of Sleep	Minutes of Activity

Faith Focus

Temperance is the virtue of self-control and discipline. It gives balance in the way we act and speak.

Cut out and hang at home

Decide which nutritious foods your family wants to eat this week. Discuss their nutritional value and why you chose the foods you did.

Nutritious foods this week:

....

....

....

....

....

Healthy Habits @ Home

In our families we can support each other in developing healthy habits. With family members, identify healthy habits you want to develop and ways to support each other.

Habits to develop:

- ☐ ....
- ☐ ....
- ☐ ....

Ways to support:

- ☐ ....
- ☐ ....
- ☐ ....

Family in Action

Some families struggle to put nutritious food on the table. As a family, investigate ways you can help other families eat more nutritiously. Then make a commitment to help.

We will help by

Safer Together

Review the following key elements to help your child recognize the unique dignity that God has created in all of us:

- **Self-awareness**—Who am I? How do I feel? What have I done?
- **Honesty**—Am I honest with myself?
- **Trust**—Do I trust others and myself?
- **Self-reflection**—Do I reflect on my own life and learn from others?
- **Freedom**—Am I making good choices?
- **Perspective**—Do I step back and assess my actions?

Looking Ahead

In this chapter, the Holy Spirit invites you to ▶

EXPLORE why Catholics in Mexico celebrate Las Posadas.

DISCOVER the liturgy of the Church and the liturgical year.

DECIDE to show reverence and thanks to God.

CHAPTER 10

Celebrating God's Love

❓ What are some special times when your family gathers to celebrate?

Listen to how Saint Luke describes why the members of the early Church gathered. Imagine you and your family are there. Luke writes:

> The members of the early Church devoted themselves to listening and learning the teachings of the Apostles. They came together to help each other, for the breaking of the bread, and for the prayer. Every day they praised God.
>
> BASED ON ACTS OF THE APOSTLES 1:42, 46-47

❓ When do you gather with your parish to pray?

Piety

Piety, also called reverence, is one of the seven Gifts of the Holy Spirit. Piety is a deep respect for God and for the Church. A person who practices piety gives reverence and honor to God.

THE CHURCH FOLLOWS JESUS

Las Posadas

Today, people in countries all over the world gather as the Church. We grow and celebrate our faith in Jesus. We celebrate our faith using cultural traditions unique to our country. The Church in the United States of America is blessed with people from many cultural families. The Hispanic and Latino people are examples of those families. A traditional Latino celebration is Las Posadas.

People in Mexico celebrate Las Posadas each year during Advent. The celebration takes place during the eight days before Christmas. Celebrating Las Posadas helps the people get ready to celebrate Christmas. The celebration of Las Posadas is an expression of piety honoring God. It is a celebration of faith in Jesus Christ.

During Las Posadas, the people of a town act out Mary and Joseph's search for a place to stay in Bethlehem. The word *posada* means "inn." The people carry candles and walk in procession through the streets behind two people who represent Mary and Joseph. Mary and Joseph stop at homes along the way and ask for a place to stay. They are turned away until, finally, a family welcomes them into their home.

Las Posadas reminds us that we always need to be ready to open our hearts to God's love. It is a wonderful, joyful celebration that shares with everyone the good news of God's love.

? How does your parish celebrate Advent? What are your favorite family Advent traditions? What is special to you about these traditions?

The Liturgy of the Church

When the Church gathers to celebrate the **liturgy**, the People of God are doing an important work. The word *liturgy* means "a public work," or "work of the people." The liturgy is the work of the whole Church, the Body of Christ. It is the work of the faithful joining with Christ, the Head of the Church, in his work of giving praise and glory to his Father. As we gather, we sing out with the writer of Psalm 66:

How wonderful are you, Lord God. Everyone on earth worships you and sings praises to you.

Based on Psalm 66:3, 4

The liturgy is also the work of God, the Holy Trinity. God the Father blesses us with the gift of the Son, Jesus. The Son of God blesses us with his Body and Blood. God the Holy Spirit blesses us with the gift of God's own life and love.

The priest leads the assembly of the faithful gathered to worship God. The priest acts together with and in the name and Person of Christ. The faithful gather with Jesus Christ. They ask for God's blessings and give thanks to the Father through the power of the Holy Spirit.

FAITH FOCUS

Why does the Church gather to celebrate the liturgy?

FAITH VOCABULARY

liturgy
The liturgy is the work of the Church, the Body of Christ, as we worship God.

Paschal Mystery
The Paschal Mystery is Jesus' passing over from suffering and Death to new and glorious life; Christ's work of Salvation accomplished by his Passion (his suffering and Death), Resurrection, and Ascension.

Activity Think about a special blessing or gift that your family has received from God, and write it here. Then write some words of prayer and thanks to God.

____

____

____

Faith-Filled People

Saint John the Apostle

John was the youngest of the Apostles. He is also the writer of the fourth Gospel and the Book of Revelation. In the Book of Revelation, John writes about the liturgy in Heaven, where all of the angels and saints constantly give glory and praise to God.

Celebrating God's Saving Work

The liturgy of the Church centers on the Eucharist and the six other sacraments. In the liturgy, we do not simply remember what Jesus did in the past. Through the celebration of the liturgy, we are made sharers in the **Paschal Mystery** and in the life of God. We celebrate and are made sharers in God's work among us today.

The Paschal Mystery is the work of God saving all people in Jesus. It is Christ's work of Salvation and Redemption accomplished by his suffering, Death, Resurrection, and Ascension. During the liturgy, we proclaim the saving work of Christ until he comes again in glory at the end of time.

Activity Complete the word web with ways in which you have shown by your good actions that you believe in the Paschal Mystery.

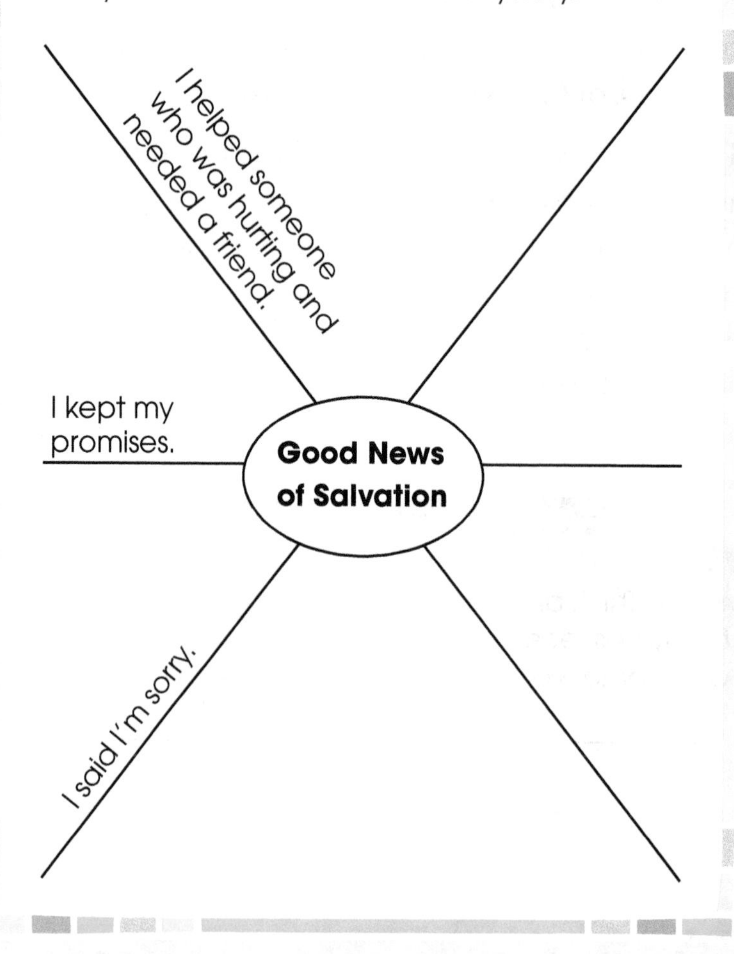

The Liturgical Year

The Church celebrates the liturgy every day of the year. This is called the liturgical year. The liturgical year is made up of feasts and seasons that celebrate God's great plan of saving love in Christ. These are the seasons and times of the liturgical year.

Advent. We wait and prepare for the coming of Jesus. We prepare for our celebration of Christ's birth, his first coming among us. We also celebrate his presence with us now and prepare for his Second Coming in glory at the end of time.

Christmas. We celebrate the birth of Jesus Christ, the Savior of all people.

Lent. We prepare for Easter. Lent is a time to prepare to welcome new members into the Church and to renew our own baptismal promises.

Triduum. The word *triduum* means "three days." The Triduum is the center of the liturgical year. It is our three-day celebration of the Paschal Mystery on Holy Thursday, Good Friday, and the Easter Vigil/Easter Sunday.

Easter. For fifty days, from Easter Sunday to Pentecost, we celebrate that Christ is risen, is always with us, and will come again in glory at the end of time.

Ordinary Time The remaining weeks of the liturgical year are called Ordinary Time. We listen and respond to God's Word. We grow in love for God and others.

What is your favorite time of the liturgical year? Tell why it is your favorite time.

Catholics Believe

Frequent Communion

The Church encourages the faithful to receive Holy Communion frequently. Receiving Holy Communion deepens our union with Christ and the Church. It strengthens us to work with people in need.

I FOLLOW JESUS

We want nothing to keep us away from God. During the season of Advent, we remember and respond to the message of John the Baptist:

Prepare the way of the Lord. MARK 1:3

We prepare ourselves to welcome Jesus, the Savior of the world.

ON YOUR WAY

You can help "prepare the way of the Lord" all year long. Place a check mark in the box (✔) next to the things that show how you are responding to John the Baptist's words. In the space, draw another action you take to prepare the way of the Lord.

- ☐ I help at home after school.
- ☐ I say a short prayer of thanks to God in the morning when I wake up.
- ☐ I tell others about the low grade my friend got on the test.
- ☐ I play with my friends and am late for dinner.

MY FAITH CHOICE

I will do my best to prepare the way of the Lord. I will

____

____.

Take a quiet moment to thank and bless God for his love.

Chapter Review

Fill in the blanks with the word or phrase from the box that correctly completes the paragraph.

Triduum	liturgy	Holy Trinity
God	Paschal Mystery	Lent

The ______________ is the Church's work of worshiping ______________. The liturgy is the work of the Church and the ______________. The liturgy celebrates the ______________. The ______________ is the center of the liturgical year. ______________ is a time to prepare to welcome new members into the Church.

TO HELP YOU REMEMBER

1. The liturgy of the Church is her work of worshiping God.
2. In the liturgy, we are made sharers in the Paschal Mystery of Jesus Christ.
3. The Church celebrates and shares in God's plan of Salvation all year long.

Holy, Holy, Holy Lord

God is the source of all our blessings. At Mass, we begin our prayer of thanks, the Eucharistic Prayer, by praying an acclamation from the writings of Isaiah the Prophet. An acclamation is a prayer that honors God.

Leader: Let us join together with all the angels and saints and give honor and glory to God, the Holy One.

All: **Holy, Holy, Holy Lord God of hosts.**
Heaven and earth are full of your glory.
Hosanna in the highest.
Blessed is he who comes in the name of the Lord.
Hosanna in the highest.

From Preface, *Roman Missal*

With My Family

This Week . . .

In Chapter 10, Celebrating God's Love, your child learned:

- The liturgy is the Church's work of worshiping God.
- In the liturgy, the members of the Church gather with Christ, the Head of the Church, to give praise and glory to the Father. We remember and are made sharers in the Paschal Mystery of Christ.
- The Paschal Mystery is the saving Passion (suffering and Death), Resurrection, and Ascension of the Lord Jesus.
- The liturgical year is the cycle of seasons and feasts that make up the Church's year of worship.
- Piety, or reverence, is one of the seven Gifts of the Holy Spirit that helps us honor and respect God and the Church.

For more about related teachings of the Church, see the *Catechism of the Catholic Church*, 1076–1109, 1136–1186, and 1200–1206, and the *United States Catholic Catechism for Adults*, pages 165–179.

Sharing God's Word

Read together Psalm 66:1-4. Talk about how the words of the psalm reflect the attitude of your family as you join with the Church in worshiping God.

We Live as Disciples

The Christian home and family is a school of discipleship. Your family grows in faith together! Choose one of the following activities to do as a family, or design a similar activity of your own:

- On the way home from Mass, recall all of the people who assisted the priest, such as the deacon, the readers, the choir, the altar servers, and the extraordinary ministers of Holy Communion. Talk about the many ways that your family and the rest of the assembly took part in the celebration of Mass.
- The word *eucharist* means "thanksgiving." The next time your family shares a meal, talk about the things your family is doing that show you are thankful to God for his blessings.
- Invite each family member to share which of the liturgical seasons is his or her favorite. Ask each person to share his or her reasons.

Our Spiritual Journey

When Jesus entered Jerusalem, he was greeted with the acclamation "Hosanna!" Your words and deeds can be acclamations of your discipleship. The way that you greet others, what you say to them, or what you do for them can be signposts that reveal the direction of your life as well as invitations for others to follow the Lord.

Faith-Filled People

Saint John the Apostle
Feast Day: December 27
John was the brother of James and the youngest of Jesus' disciples. John taught that God is love.

For more ideas on ways your family can live as disciples of Jesus, visit **BeMyDisciples.com**

In Little Ways

More than one hundred years ago, a fifteen-year-old French girl was sure about how she wanted to show her love for God. She wanted to honor God with great love. She begged the pope to let her become a nun, even though she was only fifteen. The pope agreed. Soon, Thérèse Martin entered the Carmelite convent in Lisieux and became a Carmelite nun.

Thérèse was an ordinary girl from a small town in France. Her life was not easy. She suffered from bad headaches and fevers, and she had difficulty sleeping. Thérèse did not let these things stop her from doing God's work. She realized that she did not have to do great things to serve God, the nuns in her community, and other people. Doing little, ordinary things was Thérèse's way of doing God's work.

Thérèse knew in her heart that God was calling her to love him by helping others. This was her vocation, or call from God. Every day she found little ways to love God. Sometimes this meant being patient with and kind to others who were hard to get along with. When Thérèse was sick or tired, she would pray the Lord's Prayer and the Hail Mary very slowly. She prayed in her own little way.

Activity Write down some of the little ways you can show your love for God. Then share them with your family.

Catholics Believe

God calls us to witness and proclaim the Gospel in loving ways. Like Saint Thérèse, we can love even in the littlest of ways.

Faith Focus

God calls us to love, even in the littlest ways.

Healthy Habits @ Home

As a family, reflect on the gifts God has given each member of your family. How do you use the gifts God has given you?

Gifts	How We Use God's Gifts

Safer Together

You can help your child stay safe by reviewing these tips:

- Remind your child that God never asks anything of him or her that would cause harm.
- If your child is ever asked to do something harmful or secret "because God wills it," he or she should say "no," get away, and tell you or another trusted adult.

Family Time

Cut out and hang at home

God speaks to us through the Church, as in the example of saints and other good people. As a family, identify ways that God has been speaking to each of you this week.

Ways God speaks in our family:

....

....

....

Family in Action

As a family, summarize what you have learned from the example of Saint Thérèse. Then make a banner as a reminder of what you have learned. Perhaps it could read: "Little things can mean a lot." Hang the banner in your home as a reminder.

What will your family banner read?

....

....

....

Looking Ahead

In this chapter, the Holy Spirit invites you to ▶

EXPLORE how workers continue the work of Christ in the world.

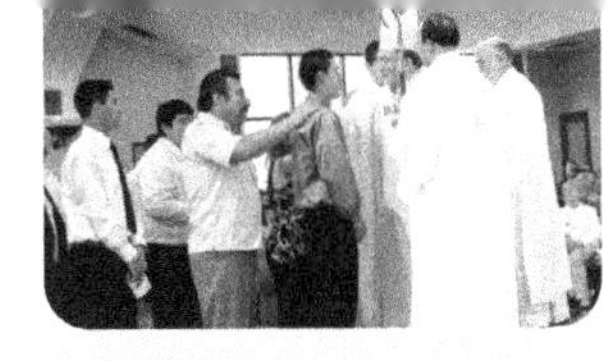

DISCOVER the three Sacraments of Christian Initiation.

DECIDE ways to use a gift of the Holy Spirit.

Sharing in Christ's Life and Work

? What are some signs and symbols used by the Catholic Church?

Jesus used signs and symbols. Imagine yourself back in the time of Jesus. You have come to the village well to draw water for drinking. You hear Jesus say to a Samaritan woman,

> Whoever drinks the water I shall give will never thirst.
>
> BASED ON JOHN 4:14

? What does the water that Jesus speaks of symbolize? Where in your parish church do you see the Church use this symbol?

Knowledge

Knowledge is one of the seven Gifts of the Holy Spirit. It helps us see the truth of everything that God has made known to us. A person who uses this gift tries to learn more about God and what it means to be a child of God.

Bread for the World

Bread is not only a food that we eat; it is also a symbol for all that is life-giving, a spiritual food. Jesus used bread as a symbol. In John's Gospel, Jesus said that he is the Bread of Life.

The Holy Spirit helps the Church bring true bread to the world. The Holy Spirit teaches the Church what that bread is. The Holy Spirit helps the Church, or gives the Church the grace, to bring that bread to the world.

Over fifty years ago, a group of Catholics and other Christians were serving food in church halls to people who lived on the streets. This small group of Christians wanted to do more. They wanted to do things to stop hunger before it began. They learned about the harm that hunger was doing to so many people all over the world. They prayed for knowledge about how they could help make a difference. In 1972, they began Bread for the World.

Today there are over 44,000 Bread for the World workers. They work with government leaders and Church leaders to set up programs that fight the things that cause hunger. The work of Bread for the World is also a symbol. It points to the loving care of God for all people, especially people in need.

? How can you help people who need food? Talk with a partner about your ideas.

God Among Us

The liturgy of the Church centers on the Eucharist and the other six sacraments. The Seven Sacraments are Baptism, Confirmation, Eucharist, Penance and Reconciliation, Anointing of the Sick, Holy Orders, and Matrimony.

The **sacraments** are celebrations of our faith. Given to us by Jesus, the sacraments make us, through the power of the Holy Spirit, sharers in the saving work of Christ and in the life of the Holy Trinity. That is why the Church teaches that, for believers in Jesus Christ, the sacraments are necessary for Salvation.

FAITH FOCUS
What do we celebrate in the three Sacraments of Christian Initiation?

FAITH VOCABULARY

sacraments
The sacraments are the seven main liturgical signs of the Church, given to us by Jesus Christ. They make us sharers in the saving work of Christ and in the life of the Holy Trinity through the power of the Holy Spirit.

Sacraments of Christian Initiation
Baptism, Confirmation, and Eucharist, which are the foundation of the Christian life, are called the Sacraments of Christian Initiation.

Activity Name the sacraments that you have received or have seen other people receive. Describe what you saw and heard.

____

____

____

____

____

____

____

____

____

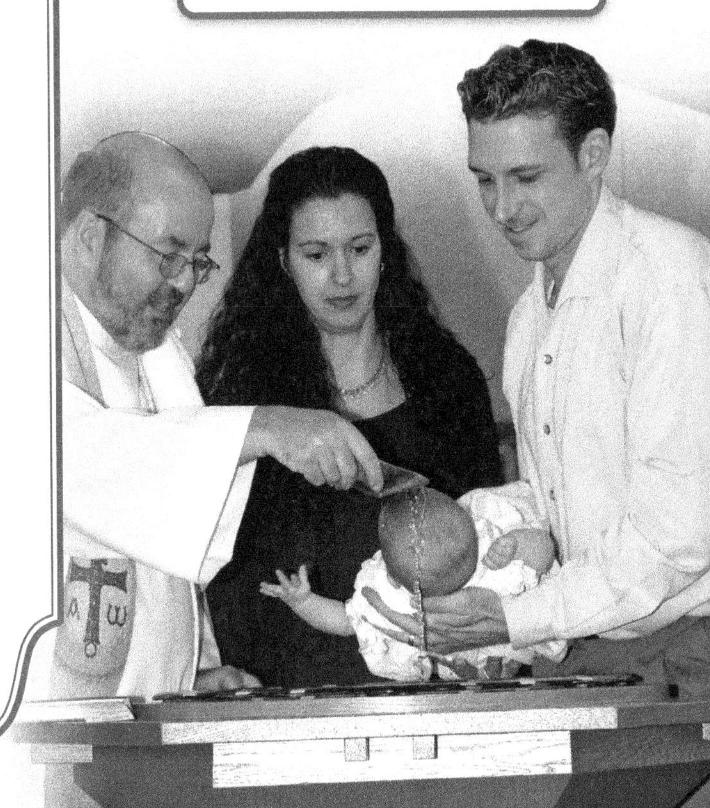

Faith-Filled People

Saint Kateri Tekakwitha

Kateri Tekakwitha was a member of the Mohawk people. At age 11, she heard Catholic missionaries preaching about Jesus. Kateri tried to live as a follower of Jesus even before she was baptized, which was when she was 20 years old. Her life of prayer and service to the sick and elderly drew many Native Americans to ask to be baptized. Saint Kateri Tekakwitha is the patron of Native American Catholics.

Baptism and Confirmation

Baptism, Confirmation, and Eucharist are the **Sacraments of Christian Initiation**. These three Sacraments are the foundation of the Christian life. Through the celebration of these three sacraments, a person is joined to Christ and becomes a full member of the Church.

Baptism is the first sacrament that we receive. It is called the doorway to the Christian life. Through Baptism, we are joined to Christ and become members of the Body of Christ, the Church. Saint Paul teaches that we have all been baptized into the one body of Christ:

> "We are all part of Christ's body."
>
> Based on 1 Corinthians 12:27

At Baptism, we first receive the gift of the Holy Spirit. We are reborn as God's adopted daughters and sons and begin our new lives in Christ. Original Sin and all personal sins are forgiven. Since Baptism marks us forever as belonging to Christ, we can receive it only once.

Confirmation strengthens the graces of Baptism. In Confirmation, we are strengthened to share with others the Good News of all that God has done in Jesus Christ. In Confirmation, as in Baptism, we receive a lasting character, or indelible mark, on our souls that marks us as belonging to Christ forever.

? What does it mean that you are marked as belonging to Christ forever?

Eucharist

Eucharist is the third Sacrament of Christian Initiation. In every celebration of the Eucharist, the whole Church on Earth and in Heaven joins with Christ, the Head of the Church. We give praise and thanksgiving to God the Father through the power of the Holy Spirit.

Jesus Christ is present and leads us in every celebration of the Eucharist. By the power of the Holy Spirit, Christ is present

- in the people gathered for worship;
- in the priest who leads the celebration;
- in the Word of God proclaimed in Sacred Scripture;
- and, most especially, under the appearances of bread and wine, which have become his Body and Blood. We call this the Real Presence of Christ in the Eucharist.

Through our participation in the celebration of the Eucharist, we become sharers in God's life and the saving work of Christ's Paschal Mystery. We receive the Body and Blood of Christ in Holy Communion and are united more closely with Christ and one another.

Catholics Believe

Sacramentals

Sacramentals are objects and actions given to us by the Church that help us remember God's presence and the mysteries of our Catholic faith. Holy water, the crucifix, and blessed ashes are objects that are sacramentals. The blessing of a person, of a meal, of an object, or of a place are common sacramental actions.

Activity With a partner, prepare a scenario in which a young person is showing, by his or her action, that Christ is present in the world.

I FOLLOW JESUS

When you were baptized, you received the gift of the Holy Spirit. The Holy Spirit helps you to live as a follower of Jesus and to continue his work in the world. The Holy Spirit gives you the gift of knowledge so that you can learn more about the Church and how to follow Jesus.

THE GIFT OF KNOWLEDGE

Think about two things that Jesus taught that you want to learn more about. Then tell how you will learn.

I want to learn more about . . .

____

____

____

____.

I will learn by . . .

____

____

____.

MY FAITH CHOICE

This week, I will do my best to learn more about what it means to live as a member of the Body of Christ, the Church. I will

____

____.

Pray to the Holy Spirit. Ask the Holy Spirit to help put your decision into practice.

Chapter Review

Draw a line to connect the sacrament in the left column with the description in the right column that best describes it.

Confirmation	This sacrament is at the center of the Church's celebration of the liturgy and completes our initiation into the Body of Christ, the Church.
Eucharist	Through the celebration of this sacrament, we are first joined to Christ and become members of his Body, the Church.
Baptism	This sacrament strengthens the graces of Baptism.

TO HELP YOU REMEMBER

1. The Seven Sacraments have been given to the Church by Christ. They make us sharers in the life of God through the power of the Holy Spirit.
2. Baptism, Confirmation, and the Eucharist are the three Sacraments of Christian Initiation.
3. By receiving the Sacraments of Christian Initiation, we are fully joined to Christ and become full members of the Church.

Anointing

Anointing with Chrism is a sacramental. It is a sacred and ancient ritual of the Church. When we are anointed in Baptism, the priest or deacon rubs Sacred Chrism on the top of our heads, making the sign of the cross.

Leader: Come forward one at a time. Let us remember that we belong to Christ.

All: *[Come forward and touch the oil with your right hand. Then rub your hands together and return to your seat.]*

Leader: Let us remember that the Holy Spirit helps us to live as children of God and disciples of Jesus.

All: **In the name of the Father, and of the Son, and of the Holy Spirit. Amen.**

With My Family

This Week . . .

In Chapter 11, Sharing in Christ's Life and Work, your child learned:

- The sacraments are the seven major celebrations of the liturgy given to us by Christ. Taking part in the celebration of the sacraments makes us sharers in the life of the Holy Trinity.
- Baptism, Confirmation, and the Eucharist are the Sacraments of Christian Initiation. These three sacraments are the foundation of the Christian life.
- By receiving these three sacraments, we become fully united with Christ and with one another, and we become full members of the Church, the Body of Christ.
- Knowledge is one of the seven Gifts of the Holy Spirit. This gift helps us learn the truth about what God has made known to us.

For more about related teachings of the Church, see the *Catechism of the Catholic Church*, 1113–1130, 1210–1274, 1285–1314, and 1322–1405, and the *United States Catholic Catechism for Adults*, pages 181–199, 201–211, 213–232, 527.

Sharing God's Word

Read together Romans 6:3-4. Talk about what it means to say that taking part in the celebration of the sacraments makes us sharers in the saving work of Jesus Christ.

We Live as Disciples

The Christian home and family form a school of discipleship. Choose one of the following activities to do as a family, or design a similar activity of your own:

- Keep a bowl of holy water near the entrance to your home. Encourage each other to use the holy water to bless yourselves when you go out and to remind yourselves that you are disciples of Jesus.
- Talk about your family's sacrament stories. Share memories of your family members' Baptism, Confirmation, and First Eucharist celebrations.
- Find out about hunger where you live and about how it is affecting people. Decide what your family can do to help.

Our Spiritual Journey

At Baptism, we are made sharers in the work of Jesus the Priest, Prophet, and King. We take part in the priest's work of sacrifice; the prophet's work of calling people to live the Word of God faithfully; and the king's work of caring for people, especially those in need and those who are being treated unjustly. Use the prayer on page 105 to remind your family of their baptismal responsibilities.

Faith-Filled People

Saint Kateri Tekakwitha
Feast Day: July 14
Saint Kateri was a Native American. Her life of prayer and service drew many Native Americans to Christ.

For more ideas on ways your family can live as disciples of Jesus, visit **BeMyDisciples.com**

Family Life Connection

Belonging to Community

Jesus never excluded anyone. He invites everyone to be his disciples and to belong to the Church. Jesus welcomed many different kinds of people. He especially welcomed those whom others excluded from their groups. Jesus made friends with people who were less fortunate than others.

By welcoming others with respect, you act the same way Jesus did. When we welcome others, we can become a community. When people form a community, they often have things in common. We welcome those who have things in common with us as well as those who are different from us.

Each of us belongs to a community. A family is a community. A group of friends is a community. Classmates are a community. Neighbors are a community. Loving our neighbors, classmates, friends, and families is a way we can show our love for God.

Catholics Believe

Every community, with the aid of God's grace, is to support each person within that community by living the virtues. Love of neighbor and love of God are inseparable.

Activity Complete the chart. Then share with your family.

Ways that I am similar to other people...	Ways that I am different from other people...

Family Life Connection

Healthy Habits @ Home

Discuss the times when you have welcomed others who are different from you. As a family, identify ways that your family can welcome people.

We welcome others by

....

....

....

Cut out and hang at home

Family Time

As a family, brainstorm a list of all the communities each family member belongs to. Share stories about each.

Communities we belong to:

....

....

....

Faith Focus

Love of neighbor and love of God are inseparable.

Safer Together

Share these strategies with your child about how to deal with tension within a community.

- Invite everyone to take a deep breath to calm down.
- Do not focus on the problem that caused the tension but on listening to the different perspectives of the community members.
- Ask God for the strength to heal, forgive, listen, and love.
- Recall what unites the members as a community—what everyone shares in common.
- Celebrate the diversity of the members of the community as gifts from God.

Family in Action

During family prayer, invite each family member to offer intentions. Suggest that the intentions be for others, such as friends, classmates, or neighbors. Write the intentions here:

....

....

....

....

Looking Ahead

In this chapter, the Holy Spirit invites you to ▶

EXPLORE how two priests listened and responded to God's call.

DISCOVER that Baptism calls us to serve God and others.

DECIDE ways to listen and respond to God's call.

CHAPTER 12

Responding to God's Call

? When is it especially important to listen to others?

In the Bible, we read about a young Jewish boy named Samuel. His mother, Hannah, brought him to the shrine at Shiloh to serve God by helping the priests.

> One night Samuel thought he heard Eli calling him. Eli understood that it was God calling Samuel. He told Samuel if he heard the voice again to say, "Speak, Lord, for your servant is listening." Samuel heard his name called out again. This time he answered, "Speak, Lord. Your servant is listening."
>
> Based on 1 Samuel 3:8-10

? Where and when do you listen to God?

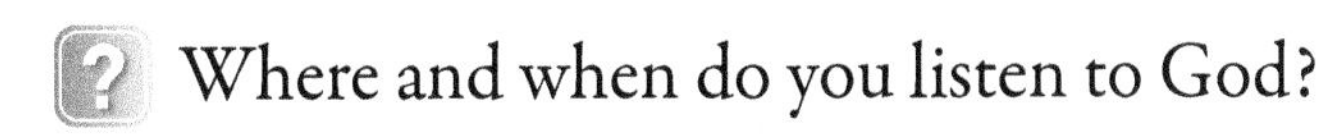

Disciple Power

Joy

Joy is one of the Fruits of the Holy Spirit. It is a sign that we are living our Baptism. Joy comes from knowing that we are deeply loved by God. The gift of joy helps us be aware that life is a gift from God.

THE CHURCH FOLLOWS JESUS

Hearing God's Call

Father Joe was in charge of the altar servers at Most Precious Blood Parish. He taught the altar servers the meaning of the Mass responses and how to help at Mass.

Glenn was one of the altar servers. He listened carefully to everything Father Joe said. He watched how Father Joe treated everyone with respect.

One day, Glenn said to his mom, "Do you think I could be like Father Joe some day?" Glenn's mom said, "I think that you could. Talk it over with Father Joe."

Fourteen years later, Glenn was ordained a priest. He presided over his first Mass at Most Precious Blood Parish. Like Samuel, Father Joe and Father Glenn heard God and said, "Speak, Lord, your servant is listening."

Activity Write the names of the people who have helped you listen to God's call to help others. Circle one name, and tell a partner how that person helped you.

____

____

____

____

Called to Serve

FAITH FOCUS
How does Baptism call us to serve?

FAITH VOCABULARY
vocation
A vocation is the work that we do as members of the Church. We are called to use our talents to carry on Christ's mission in the world.

During his public ministry, Jesus called his disciples to continue the work that his Father had sent him to do. At the Last Supper, Jesus said,

"This is how all will know that you are my disciples, if you have love for one another." JOHN 13:35

Just before the Risen Jesus returned to his Father in Heaven, he said,

"Go, therefore, and make disciples of all nations." MATTHEW 28:19

After the Ascension, Mary, Jesus' mother, the Apostles, and other disciples were gathered in an upper room in Jerusalem. As they waited and prayed, the sound of a strong wind filled the room. Small flames danced over their heads. They were filled with the Holy Spirit. They were now ready to begin the work Jesus gave them.

Later, Peter left the place they were staying and boldly proclaimed to all:

Jesus from Nazareth is the Messiah. He is the one everyone has been looking for. He is risen. We have seen, and we believe. BASED ON ACTS 2:1-4, 36

Today the Holy Spirit helps and guides the Church, under the leadership of the pope and bishops, to carry out the work of Jesus Christ. The pope is the bishop of Rome and the successor of Saint Peter. The other bishops are the successors of the other Apostles.

? Where and how do you see the people in your parish doing what Jesus said?

Faith-Filled People

Saint John Bosco

John Bosco juggled and did other tricks. This really attracted people's attention, and they listened to him. Homeless boys were among the people who gathered around John Bosco to watch and listen to him. John Bosco said, "God has given me these gifts. I use them to teach my boys about the love of God." Saint John Bosco's feast day is January 31.

The Call to Serve

At your Baptism, the Church welcomed you into the Body of Christ. You were joined to Christ. You became an adopted son or daughter of God. You received the gift of the Holy Spirit and the grace to live as a sign of God's love for the world. Your parents and godparents promised to help you know, love, and serve God.

God created you in his image and likeness. There is no one else quite like you. God has a special work, or vocation, in mind for you and for every person. God has given you the gifts and talents you need to do this special work as a member of the Church.

God gives people their gifts and talents to use to help others come to know, love, and serve him, and share his love with the world. As you discover these gifts and talents, you can grow in your understanding of the vocation that God is calling and inviting you to accept. This is the great adventure of being a disciple of Jesus Christ!

? What are your gifts and talents? How might you use one of these gifts right now to share God's love with the world? How might you use this gift or talent when you grow up?

Our Vocation

The work that God calls us to do to serve God and others is called a **vocation**. The word *vocation* means "a call." All vocations are important. Each of us has different talents, but we share in the work of Christ. We each bring the light of Christ to the world.

Every person who is baptized receives the vocation to serve God and other people as a member of the Church. God gives some members of the Church the vocation to lead and serve the Church as bishops, priests, or deacons. This is called the ordained ministry.

Other members of the Church carry on Christ's mission as members of a religious community approved by the Church. They receive the vocation to live the consecrated life. Most of the baptized serve the Church as the lay faithful. Some laypeople marry; some remain single and do not marry.

You can come to know your vocation in many ways. Like Samuel, you need to pray and talk things over with God. Like Father Glenn, you talk things over with your parents and other adults.

Catholics Believe

Vocation

The Church helps you know how God is calling you to use your gifts, talents, and interests to continue to build the Kingdom of God announced by Jesus.

Activity Read the headline about one way that people do Christ's work in parishes. Think about all the people who serve others through your parish. Write your own headlines about persons or groups of people in your parish who serve others.

Teens Run Homework Help Center

____

____

____

I FOLLOW JESUS

You are part of the Body of Christ. God has given you gifts and talents to use in serving others. As you grow and develop your talents, you will discover how you can best use them to share in Christ's work. This will be your vocation, and it will bring you joy.

SPEAK LORD, I AM LISTENING

Write a gift or talent you have in each balloon. At the base of the balloon bouquet, write how you are using some of your gifts for others. Which gift needs to grow stronger? Circle that gift and tell how you could strengthen it.

____

____

____

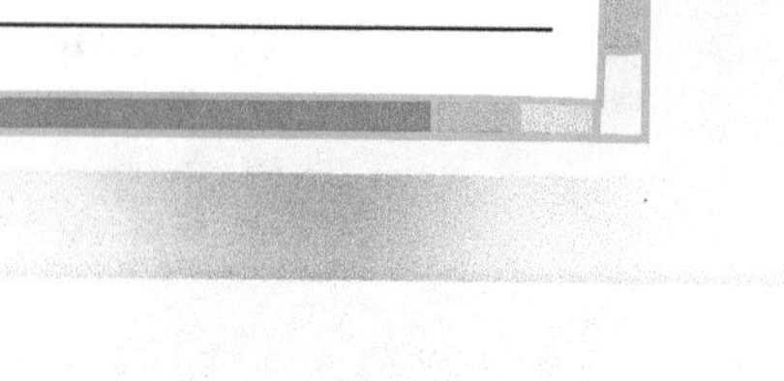

MY FAITH CHOICE

I need to develop the gift or talent of ______________________________ more fully. This week, I will

______________________________.

Pray, "Jesus, you have made me part of your Body. Help me to live my life with joy as I use my gifts in your service. Amen."

Chapter Review

Use three of the words or phrases below in a short paragraph that tells how we listen and respond to God's call to take part in the work of the Church.

ministry	gifts and talents	vocation
Holy Spirit	baptismal call	disciple

____

____

____

____

____

TO HELP YOU REMEMBER

1. Samuel listened to God to learn what God wanted him to do.
2. God calls all of the baptized to do the work of the Church.
3. Every person who is baptized has a vocation to know, love, and serve God.

Speak, Lord, I Am Listening

Spending quiet time with God and listening to him is called a prayer of meditation. In a prayer of meditation, we try to understand God's Word and how we will live it. Use these steps and pray a prayer of meditation:

1. Sit quietly. Close your eyes. Breathe slowly.
2. Picture yourself someplace where you can talk and listen to God.
3. Think about the Bible story of Samuel.
4. Take time to talk and listen to God. Say, "Speak, Lord, I am listening."
5. Reflect for a moment, then ask, "What is God saying to me?"
6. Write key words or phrases that you remember.

With My Family

This Week . . .

In Chapter 12, Responding to God's Call, your child learned:

- ▶ It is important to listen and respond to the Word of God.
- ▶ Samuel was called by God, and he listened attentively and learned from Eli how to respond to God's call.
- ▶ All of the baptized receive the vocation to take part in the work of the Church. The Holy Spirit helps and teaches us how to live that vocation.
- ▶ When we listen to and respond to God's call, we are filled with joy. Joy is a Fruit of the Holy Spirit.

For more about related teachings of the Church, see the *Catechism of the Catholic Church*, 54–61, 121–130, 157–165, and 1373–1381, and the *United States Catholic Catechism for Adults*, pages 37–45.

Sharing God's Word

Read together 1 Samuel 3:3-5, 8-10, or read the adaptation of the story on page 107. Emphasize that Samuel asked for Eli's help, and then listened and responded to God.

We Live as Disciples

The Christian home and family form a school of discipleship. Choose one of the following activities to do as a family, or design a similar activity of your own:

- ▶ Use your family mealtimes for conversations about gifts and talents of family members. Talk about how the gifts and talents of each of your family members help your family to take part in the work of the Church.
- ▶ As part of a bedtime ritual, look back on the day and recall the moments of joy in your day. Say a prayer of thanks to God for these moments.

Our Spiritual Journey

A prayer of meditation can help a person come to know God. Spending time with God this way reminds us that we belong to Christ. The spiritual practice of meditating on God's presence is a source of great joy. In this chapter, your child learned to pray a meditation. Read and follow together this prayer on page 113.

Faith-Filled People

Saint John Bosco
Feast Day: January 31
Saint John Bosco cared about children and showed them how much God loved them through games and play.

For more ideas on ways your family can live as disciples of Jesus, visit **BeMyDisciples.com**

Family Life Connection

A Dinnertime Dilemma

One evening your mother has cooked your family's favorite meal. You are all going to sit down to eat together. This is something you have not been able to do in a while. The meal is served. Everyone starts to eat. "Haven't we forgotten something?" your mother asks. "What about saying grace?"

After grace, phones begin to ring and buzz. Soon, your brother is responding to a text message. Your sister is watching a video. Everyone's eyes are glued to their screens. No one is talking to each other. Your mother watches you all in disbelief. Her hope for a joyful family dinner has vanished. "Well," she says, getting everyone's attention. "It's obvious to me that we have at least two unhealthy habits to break!"

Joyful people practice habits and virtues that show they are grateful for God's many gifts. Practicing good habits is one way we love and take care of ourselves and our family members. But sometimes we fall into bad habits. What two habits do you think need to change in the scenario?

Catholics Believe

We practice the Christian virtues in our families.

Activity

Decide on two habits that are important to your family.

Tell how they help you to love and support God and each other.

1 Our family habit of ________________ helps us love and support God and each other by ________________.

2 Our family habit of ________________ helps us love and support God and each other by ________________.

Faith Focus

We love and take care of ourselves and others when we practice good habits.

Healthy Habits @ Home

We can bear witness to and proclaim the Gospel in the littlest things we do for each other. In our families, we can develop the habit of offering small, simple actions to show our love for each other. Talk about what these actions might be (for example, offering a kind word, a helpful gesture, or a simple blessing).

Safer Together

Use these tips to help your children change habits that may be harmful to their physical or spiritual health.

1. **Awareness.** Help your children become aware of the habit, such as biting their nails, forgetting to brush their teeth, or using improper language. Help them identify what triggers the bad habit.
2. **Support.** Offer gentle reminders when you observe your children engaging in the habit. Help them find a substitute for it.
3. **Mutuality.** Tell your children about an unhealthy habit you want to change. Join forces with them and hold each other accountable to the changes.
4. **Persistence.** Remind your children that they will slip up every now and then. Changing a habit takes time, patience, and persistence.

Family Time

Cut out and hang at home

Discuss how the family can incorporate the following virtues and habits into daily life at home.

VIRTUE	HABIT
Gratitude	Say "thank you."
Forgiveness	Say "I forgive you." "I am sorry."
Respect	Say "please."

Unit 3 **Review**

Name ______________________________

A. Choose the Best Word

Fill in the blanks, using the words from the word bank.

Blessed Sacrament	Advent	Baptism	Lent
Confirmation	Christmas	Mass	Easter

1. ______________, ______________, ______________, and ______________ are liturgical seasons.

2. The Sacrament of ______________ seals, or completes, our Baptism.

3. The ______________ is the central gathering of the Church.

4. ______________ welcomes new members into the Church. It is the "doorway to the Christian life."

5. The consecrated bread, which is the Body of Christ, is called the ______________.

B. Show What You Know

Match the items in Column A with those in Column B.

Column A	**Column B**
1. knowledge	____ **a.** when Jesus gave us the Eucharist, the gift of his Body and Blood
2. sanctifying	____ **b.** helps us know that God is more important than anything else in life
3. liturgical year	____ **c.** grace received at Baptism
4. Sacraments of Christian Initiation	____ **d.** the yearly cycle of the Church's celebration of the liturgy
5. Last Supper	____ **e.** Baptism, Confirmation, and Eucharist

C. Connect with Scripture

Reread the Scripture passage on page 81. What connection do you see between this passage and what you learned in this unit?

____

____

____

D. Be a Disciple

1. *Review the four pages in this unit titled The Church Follows Jesus. What person or ministry of the Church on these pages will inspire you to be a better disciple of Jesus? Explain your answer.*

____

____

____

2. *Work with a group. Review the four Disciple Power virtues, or gifts, you have learned about in this unit. After writing your own ideas, share with the group practical ways that you will live these virtues day by day.*

____

____

____

We Worship

UNIT 4

Part Two

Feed My Sheep

Peter and the other disciples had been fishing all night. When they were returning to shore, they saw Jesus who had started a charcoal fire. "Come, have breakfast," Jesus said.

When they had finished breakfast, Jesus asked Simon Peter at three different times, "Simon, son of John, do you love me?" Each time Peter answered, "Yes, Lord, you know that I love you." After the first time Peter answered, Jesus said, "Feed my lambs."

After the second time Peter answered, Jesus said, "Tend my sheep." After the third time, Peter was upset and said, "Lord, you know everything; you know that I love you." And Jesus said, "Feed my sheep."

Based on John 21:3-17

What I Have Learned

What is something you already know about these three faith terms?

Bread of Life

____

____

____

Sacraments at the Service of Communion

____

____

____

Sacraments of Healing

____

____

____

Faith Terms to Know

Put an X next to the faith terms you know. Put a ? next to faith terms you need to learn more about.

_______ sin

_______ manna

_______ contrition

_______ absolution

_______ suffering

_______ domestic church

_______ deacons

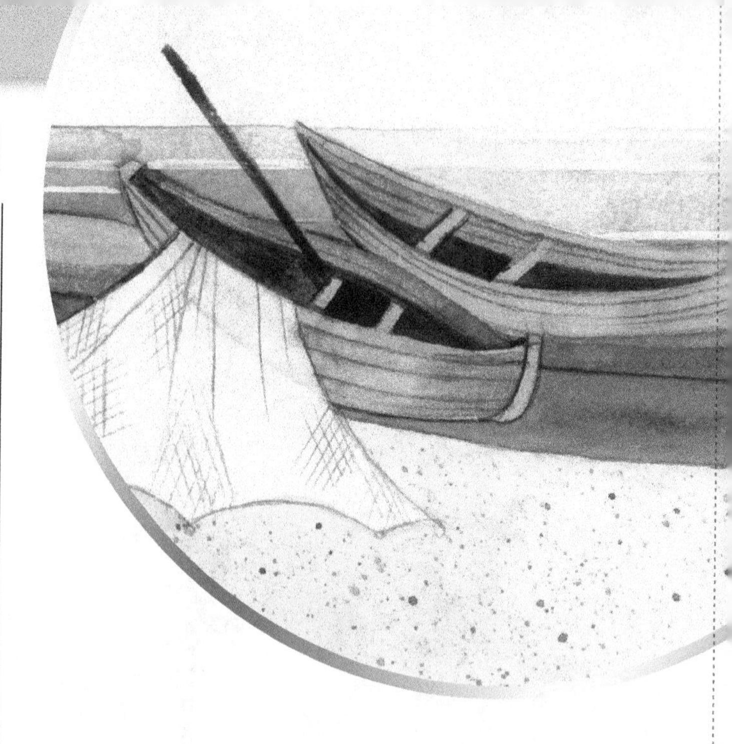

The Bible

What do you know about the Jewish feast of Passover?

____

____

____

The Church

What do you know about how the Church celebrates the Sacraments of Healing?

____

____

____

A Question I Have

What question would you like to ask about the Sacrament of Holy Orders?

____

____

____

Popular Devotions

Alfombras

A Devotion from Guatemala

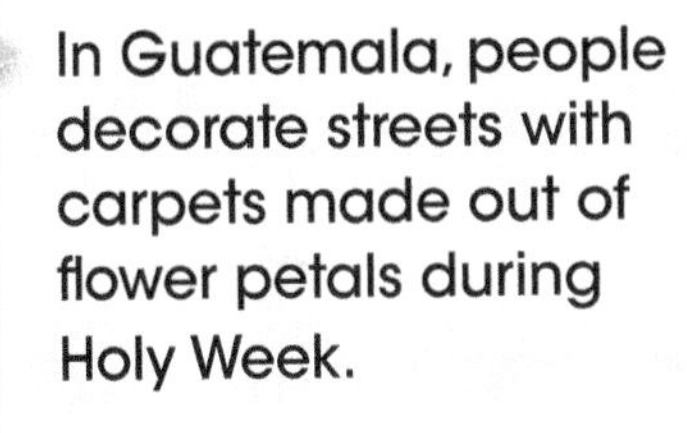

In Guatemala, people decorate streets with carpets made out of flower petals during Holy Week.

Holy Week celebrations all over the world honor the Passion and Death of Jesus. Guatemala has some of the most elaborate Holy Week celebrations. One of the best known is in Antigua, the original capital of Guatemala.

During Holy Week, faithful Christians decorate the streets with *alfombras. Alfombras* are elaborate carpets. They are made out of flower petals, fruits, vegetables, and sawdust. Families, religious groups, and even businesses spend months making the carpets for the celebrations.

During Holy Week, the carpets are spread on the streets. In the processions that take place over the carpets, religious floats carry people in costumes. The people act out the Stations of the Cross. People walk behind the floats to express sorrow for their sins. The carpets are ruined by the processions. The *alfombras* are seen as sacrifices, or acts of giving, to God in thanksgiving for the gift of Jesus the Savior.

? Why do you think the people make the beautiful *alfombras* if they are going to be ruined?

Popular Devotions

Alfombras

The people of Guatemala spend weeks making *alfombras*. These beautiful carpets are then ruined by the Holy Week processions. Find the words below. Then use them to explain the way Holy Week is celebrated in Guatemala.

WORD BANK

- HOLY WEEK
- SACRIFICE
- CARPETS
- FLOWERS
- PROCESSION
- SORROW
- JESUS
- GUATEMALA
- ALFOMBRAS

N	W	U	P	O	L	N	T	K	S	V	J	A
C	C	J	A	L	A	M	E	T	A	U	G	U
W	E	J	E	S	U	S	O	L	C	O	Y	O
L	P	P	Q	S	I	K	D	M	R	Y	R	C
R	W	L	R	P	O	T	M	R	I	M	S	W
D	K	L	S	O	V	Q	A	D	F	M	O	P
P	F	O	T	D	C	N	D	O	I	J	R	C
O	H	O	L	Y	W	E	E	K	C	X	R	B
I	T	V	A	B	Q	U	S	M	E	J	O	N
A	L	F	O	M	B	R	A	S	L	B	W	L
P	A	S	E	I	N	I	P	R	I	N	V	A
U	E	S	R	E	W	O	L	F	W	O	Y	G
M	Y	Q	U	I	L	E	O	A	T	A	N	Z
K	L	I	E	N	S	C	A	R	P	E	T	S

Looking Ahead

In this chapter, the Holy Spirit invites you to

EXPLORE how God provided for a Franciscan community.

DISCOVER how three Bible stories tell of God's loving care for us.

DECIDE how you can be a sign of God's loving care.

CHAPTER 13

Jesus Feeds Us

Tell about a time when you were tired and hungry. Who cared for you? How?

In the Old Testament, we read about a time when God's people began to lose trust in God. They grumbled about how miserable their lives were. God heard their complaining. Listen to what God told their leader, Moses:

> "I will now rain down bread from heaven for you. Have the people go out every day to gather enough bread to eat so that they are no longer hungry."
>
> Based on Exodus 16:4

What other Bible stories do you know about bread? What do they tell about how God cares for you?

Disciple Power

Kindness

A kind person is loving and caring toward others. A kind person always treats people with respect. We live the virtue of kindness by treating others as we want to be treated.

THE CHURCH FOLLOWS JESUS

Give Us Our Daily Bread

"Pssst! Father Solanus!" A Franciscan Capuchin brother tried to catch the eye of Father Solanus Casey. "We have no more bread, and hundreds of men are waiting for something to eat," the worried brother said.

The white-bearded Father Solanus nodded his head. He understood, but he stayed calm. Pouring hot coffee, he made his way down the rows between tables.

Father Solanus and others had opened a soup kitchen to help the many hungry, troubled people they met. Every day, people came from all over Detroit for a free meal—their only meal of the day. They experienced the kindness of others.

But the Capuchins also depended on others to provide the food. Dinner was whatever was available. If a farmer gave bushels of potatoes, then they ate potato soup. When a crate of clucking chickens was left near the back door, a kettle of chicken soup was soon simmering on the stove.

Word quickly spread through the room, "The kitchen is out of food." When the room grew quiet with fear, the soft-spoken Father Solanus asked for prayer. "Why shouldn't we ask God for our daily bread?"

Five minutes later, cheering erupted in the waiting line. Men slapped each other on the back. A bakery truck, loaded with food, had just arrived.

"See?" grinned Father Solanus, "God provides." Father Solanus was not at all surprised by the sudden blessing at the back door.

? How does your parish reach out to share God's loving care with others?

Signs of God's Love

There are many stories about bread in the Bible. On the first page of this lesson, you listened to the beginning of an important bread story in the Old Testament. It is part of the **Exodus** story.

The Exodus is the journey of the Israelites from slavery in Egypt to freedom in the land God promised them. Here is what happened next:

In the morning there was a layer of dew all about the camp, and when the layer of dew evaporated, fine flakes were on the surface of the wilderness, fine flakes like hoarfrost on the ground. On seeing it, the Israelites asked one another, "What is this?" for they did not know what it was. But Moses told them, "It is the bread which the LORD has given you to eat." EXODUS 16:13-15

Each day the Israelites gathered enough **manna** for the day. They baked it and ate it until they were satisfied. For Moses and the Israelites, the manna was a sign of God's loving care for them. This is an example of Divine Providence, God's loving care for us.

FAITH FOCUS
What is God saying to us through the Bible story of Jesus feeding people with bread?

FAITH VOCABULARY

Exodus
The Exodus is the journey of the Israelites, under the leadership of Moses, from slavery in Egypt to freedom in the land promised them by God.

manna
The bread-like food the Israelites ate in the desert during the Exodus is called manna.

Activity What are some signs of God's loving care for you? Write one next to each place listed.

Home______________________________

School ______________________________

Community______________________________

Parish ______________________________

Blessed Solanus Casey

Solanus Casey was born in Wisconsin in 1870. He was baptized Bernard Francis. On a small farm and in a big family, the future Father Solanus first learned to trust God. Working as a doorkeeper, this Capuchin priest helped thousands with sound spiritual advice and encouragement. Father Solanus also had a gift of healing. He was named Blessed in 2017.

Jesus Feeds Five Thousand People

Here is another bread story. It is another story of God's loving care love for us. This story is from the Gospel according to Luke in the New Testament:

> *A crowd of people followed Jesus to a deserted place. The people were hungry and tired. Jesus said to the disciples, "Give the people some food." The disciples replied, "We only have five loaves and two fish." Jesus took the five loaves and the two fish. Looking up to heaven, he said the blessing over them, broke the bread, and gave the food to the disciples to give to the crowd. They all ate and were no longer hungry.*
>
> Based on Luke 9:11-13, 16-17

Jesus performed a miracle to feed five thousand people with only five loaves of bread and two fish. There were even twelve baskets of food left over. Jesus performed many miracles. A miracle is something that only God can do. Jesus performed many miracles to show people how much God loves them and cares for them.

? Pretend you are in the crowd that followed Jesus. What would you tell your family and friends about Jesus?

The Bread of Life

The miracle of the manna in the desert points to the Eucharist. In the Gospel, Jesus fed the people with bread.

This early Christian story reminds us that Jesus, the Bread of Life, gave us the Eucharist:

> [At the Last Supper, Jesus] took the bread, said the blessing, broke it, and gave it to them, saying, "This is my body, which will be given for you; do this in memory of me."
>
> LUKE 22:19

The Eucharist is the spiritual food which gives us strength to live as disciples of Jesus. Jesus said,

> "Whoever eats my flesh and drinks my blood remains in me, and I in him. . . . This is the bread that came down from heaven. Unlike your ancestors who ate and still died, whoever eats this bread will live forever."
>
> JOHN 6:56, 58

At Mass, by the power of the Holy Spirit, the bread and wine become the Body and Blood of Christ in the Sacrament of the Eucharist. Christ is fully present in a true and real way in the bread and wine.

Catholics Believe

Almsgiving

Almsgiving is sharing our blessings with others, especially with people in need. The word *alms* comes from a Latin word meaning "an act of mercy or kindness." God is merciful and kind to us. Christians treat others in the same way.

Activity What can you do to help people come to know God's love for them? In the blank hearts, use words or pictures to show how you can share the good news of God's love with others.

Give food to people who are hungry.

Smile.

Listen to someone who has a problem.

I FOLLOW JESUS

You can be kind to people in many ways. When you are, you are a sign to others of God's loving care for them. Your kind words and actions help people see how much God loves them and cares for them. Ask for God's forgiveness when you sin.

KINDNESS

Write a poem, song, or story that describes you and your friends being kind to others.

____
Title

____
____
____
____
____
____
____
____
____

MY FAITH CHOICE

This week, I will look for people who are hungry not only for food but also for other important things like friendship and kindness. I will

____
______________________________.

Sit for a moment in the stillness. Remember God's kindness and care towards you and your family. Say a prayer of thanks.

Chapter Review

Compare and contrast the story of Moses and the manna in the desert with the story of Jesus feeding the crowd. How are the two stories alike and how are they different?

Moses
(Exodus 16:13-15)

____

____

____

Jesus
(Luke 9:11-13, 16-17)

____

____

____

TO HELP YOU REMEMBER

1. God fed his people, the Israelites, with manna during the Exodus.
2. Jesus fed five thousand people with five loaves of bread and two fish.
3. The Bible invites us to believe and trust in God's loving care for us.

Jesus, the Bread of Life

A litany is a series of petitions that each has a response. This litany is based on part of a poem that is read at Mass on the Solemnity of the Body and Blood of Christ.

Leader: Jesus, Good Shepherd and true Bread,

All: **be merciful and kind to us.**

Leader: Jesus, source of our happiness,

All: **be merciful and kind to us.**

Leader: Jesus, you know and can do all things,

All: **be merciful and kind to us.**

Leader: Jesus, make us your guests in Heaven,

All: **be merciful and kind to us. Amen.**

With My Family

This Week . . .

In Chapter 13, Jesus Feeds Us, your child learned that:

- God fed the Israelites with manna in the desert during the Exodus.
- Jesus fed five thousand people by multiplying five loaves of bread and two fish.
- In both stories, God reveals his ever-present loving care for people.
- The Gospel story of Jesus feeding the people also reminds Christians of the Eucharist, the spiritual food of the Body and Blood of Jesus.
- We live the virtue of kindness by treating others as we want to be treated.

For more about related teachings of the Church, see the *Catechism of the Catholic Church*, 302–314, 1094, 1334, 1363, and 1391–1405, and the *United States Catholic Catechism for Adults*, pages 220–229.

Faith-Filled People

Blessed Solanus Casey
Feast Day: November 3
Solanus helped many people with his spiritual advice and encouragement. He was known for his great kindness.

Sharing God's Word

Read together Luke 9:10-17, the account of Jesus feeding the crowd. Or read the adaptation of the story on page 122. Emphasize that Jesus feeding the people is a sign of God's loving care.

We Live as Disciples

The Christian home and family is a school of discipleship. Choose one of the following activities to do as a family, or design a similar activity of your own:

- We all know that good nutrition and exercise help keep our bodies healthy. Next time your family gathers to share a meal, talk about how participating in Mass helps our spiritual health.
- Jesus fed the crowd to help people understand God's love for them. How do the members of your family help each other know God's love for them?
- The Bible story about Jesus feeding the crowd is in all four Gospels. Read and compare all four stories: Matthew 14:13-21, Mark 6:30-44, Luke 9:10-17, and John 6:1-15.

Our Spiritual Journey

God in his infinite kindness and generosity invites us to live in communion with him. "Prayer is a living relationship of the children of God with their Father who is good beyond measure, with his Son Jesus Christ, and with the Holy Spirit" (CCC 2565). God gave us the gift of the Eucharist to nourish that communion. Frequent Communion is vital to the Christian life.

For more ideas on ways your family can live as disciples of Jesus, visit **BeMyDisciples.com**

Family Life Connection

A Call For All

A vocation is a call from God to live a certain way. We might define the word "vocation" as the way we are going to love our way through life. Our lives are adventures of discovering how we will love God and love others. Everyone has a vocation to be generous. God calls us to give and share out of love.

Members of the Church have various callings to love generously. For example, some people join religious communities. God calls certain men to the priesthood. God calls certain people to the married life. A husband and wife show their love for God by loving and serving one another and raising a family together. God calls some people to the single life. God calls all of us to serve one another out of love.

God calls each person to a vocation and gives each person the gifts to live out that vocation. As we grow older, we discover the best ways to use our gifts. We might find little ways. We might find big ways. The world has many needs. The world needs many different kinds of people doing many different things. Only we can choose to follow the vocations God invites us to live.

Catholics Believe

Generosity is the virtue of giving and sharing out of love for God. Generous people use their gifts and talents to help make the world a place where God's love is present.

Activity

Imagine what God might be calling you to do in service to others. In the space provided, draw yourself using your gifts in service to others out of love for God. Share your drawing with your family.

Faith Focus

Generosity is the virtue of giving and sharing out of love for God.

Family Time

Cut out and hang at home

Decide on a family activity that responds to a need in your community while using your gifts and talents.

Need in the Community:

....

....

Our Gifts and Talents:

....

....

Healthy Habits @ Home

The family is a wonderful place to practice the virtue of generosity—of sharing our gifts. Choose two ways to practice generosity in your home this week.

We will practice generosity by:

1. ....
2. ....

Safer Together

Your family can be safer together if they learn and practice the 3 R's of Safety: **Recognize**, **Respond**, and **Report**. Review the following together:

1. **Recognize** the situation when you are with a group of friends. Be aware of your physical environment as well as the interaction of the group.
2. **Respond** appropriately if you begin to feel uneasy or if someone is in danger. Be prudent and ask for help or find a safe place to go.
3. **Report** the situation to a trusted adult. Be strong and tell the truth to an adult whom you trust.

Family in Action

As a family, write a message to encourage other families to be generous with their time, talents, and treasures.

Looking Ahead

In this chapter, the Holy Spirit invites you to ▶

EXPLORE the story of Blessed Zepherin Namuncurá.

DISCOVER how the Church continues Jesus' work of healing.

DECIDE to continue the forgiving work of Jesus.

CHAPTER 14

Jesus Forgives

? When has someone forgiven you for something wrong that you did? Describe how you felt when you were forgiven. What do you remember about how Jesus forgave people?

Imagine you are walking from village to village with Jesus and his disciples. Listen in as Peter asks Jesus,

> "Lord, if my brother sins against me, how often must I forgive him? Do I have to forgive him seven times?"
>
> Jesus answers Peter, "You need to forgive him not just seven times, but seventy-seven times! You must forgive over and over again. You must never stop forgiving!"
>
> Based on Matthew 18:21-22

? Why do you think Jesus teaches that we need to forgive over and over again?

Forgiveness

Forgiveness is an act of kindness or mercy. It is an action of the Beatitude, "Blessed are the merciful." People who generously practice forgiveness are peacemakers. They do not hold grudges.

THE CHURCH FOLLOWS JESUS

Blessed Zepherin

When Zepherin Namuncurá was a boy, he was challenged to forgive boys who teased him because he was an Araucano Indian. Because he forgave them, they became friends, and he taught them a valuable lesson.

"Can I shoot first when the bows are done?" begged Juan. He fell to his knees to beg his friends Ricardo, Felipe, and Zeph as they laughed. Juan was always the comedian.

A few minutes later, the four boys were shrieking with laughter. Juan, Ricardo, and Felipe tried to hit a target on a tree. Their arrows flew this way and that. "Not even close," they all laughed together.

Then Zeph, whom they called the "Little Chief," fit an arrow to his bow. Breathing in deeply, Zeph pulled back the arrow and bowstring. Squinting at the target, he let his arrow fly. Then, as his friends shouted praise, he shot others. "Zzzzzip. Zzzzip." A bull's-eye every time!

"Shooting a bow means something different to me now that I am a Christian," said Zeph. Then, he quietly explained this to his friends. "My life is like my arrow," the "Little Chief" said as he pulled lightly on his bowstring. "I can go in many directions. I could even hurt someone if I go the wrong way. But I want to fly toward God. He is my target, my true target." Zeph died of tuberculosis in 1905 when he was nineteen. He was beatified, or declared "blessed," by the Church in 2007.

? What do you do to keep your "arrow" pointed toward the right target?

Jesus Forgives

People sometimes choose to move in a direction that is away from God's love. God sent his Son, Jesus, to help us when we do.

Jesus, the Son of God, is the Savior and Redeemer. He brought the gift of God's forgiveness and healing to the world. The writers of the Gospels describe many times that Jesus healed people:

> The friends of a man who could not walk carried him on a stretcher to Jesus. There were so many people that they lowered him down through a hole in the roof to get to Jesus.
>
> Jesus saw the people's faith and said, "Courage, child, your sins are forgiven."
>
> He then said to the person who was paralyzed, "Rise! Pick up your stretcher. Go home." The man got up and went home. When the crowds saw this, they were struck with awe. They glorified God for what they had just seen.
>
> Based on Matthew 9:1-8

The Church continues Jesus' work of forgiveness and healing. If we sin after we are baptized, the Church makes this present among us in a special way through the two **Sacraments of Healing**—the Sacrament of Penance and Reconciliation and the Sacrament of the Anointing of the Sick.

FAITH FOCUS

How does Jesus' work and mission of forgiveness continue in the world today?

FAITH VOCABULARY

Sacraments of Healing
The Sacrament of Penance and Reconciliation and the Sacrament of the Anointing of the Sick are the two Sacraments of Healing.

sin
Sin is freely choosing to turn away from God's love and weakening or breaking one's friendship with God and the Church.

Activity Choose one of these Gospel passages to read. Then tell a partner what you learned about Jesus' work of forgiveness.

Matthew 18:35 Mark 11:25 Luke 6:37

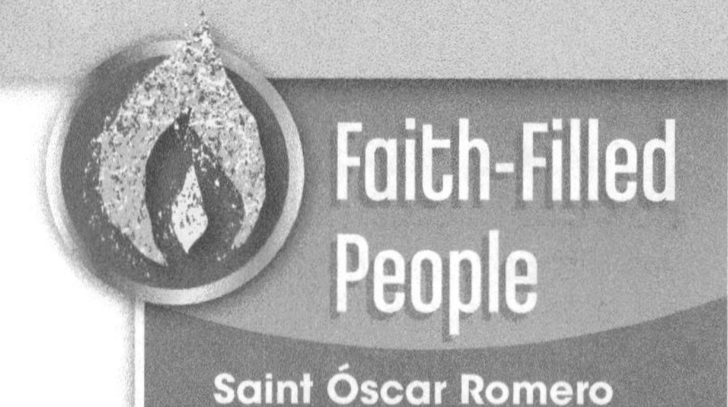

Saint Óscar Romero

Óscar Romero was the archbishop of San Salvador in the country of El Salvador. In his homilies and weekly radio program, Archbishop Romero often spoke for justice and against violence. As Jesus did, he called both rich and poor to lives of justice and forgiveness. Because of his work, Archbishop Romero was assassinated as he celebrated Mass on March 24, 1980.

Sin and Forgiveness

Jesus taught that forgiveness is an important kind of healing. God forgives our sins through the work of Jesus Christ. If we **sin**, we turn away from God's love. We weaken or break our friendship with God and the Church.

When people sin, they walk in a direction that leads them away from God's love. Sometimes a person may freely choose to turn his or her back completely away from God's love. When a person does this, he or she commits a mortal sin.

When we sin, the Holy Spirit invites us to ask for forgiveness and to heal the harm our sin has caused. We do this in the Sacrament of Penance and Reconciliation for any sins we have committed after Baptism. This sacrament is sometimes called Confession, Penance, or Reconciliation. In this sacrament, we are reconciled with God and the Church.

The Celebration of the Sacrament

To prepare to celebrate the Sacrament of Penance and Reconciliation, you first examine your conscience. You look closely at your life. You name and take responsibility for the times when you have freely chosen to turn away from God's love and to hurt others and yourself.

The celebration of Penance and Reconciliation always includes

Confession. We tell our sins in private to a priest. We must tell the priest our serious, or mortal, sins.

Contrition, or repentance. We are truly sorry for our sins and promise to try not to sin again.

Penance, or satisfaction for our sins. We accept the prayer or action the priest gives us as a way to heal the damage caused by our sin.

Absolution. God forgives us through the words and actions of a bishop or a priest.

? What are some of the ways you can show that you forgive others?

Sharing in God's Forgiveness

We receive God's healing love in the Sacrament of Penance and Reconciliation. God's gift of forgiveness gives us the grace to turn our lives toward him. We receive the grace to move our lives in the right direction. God's grace heals and strengthens our relationship with God and with the Church.

For people who have confessed mortal sins, this sacrament restores the relationship with sanctifying grace. They live in friendship with God now, and they live in hope that they will live forever with God and all the saints in Heaven.

In this sacrament we also receive the grace to say no to the things that hurt ourselves and others. We receive the grace to avoid temptation and to say no to sin in the future. Temptation is everything that tries to get us to walk away from God and his love.

Penance and Reconciliation also gives us the gift of peace. This peace comes from knowing that our lives are heading in the right direction. We are back on the right path toward God. Things are right once again among God, the Church, other people, and us.

Catholics Believe

Examination of Conscience

God gives every person the gift of a conscience. Your conscience is the ability to judge when an action is right or wrong. An examination of conscience is thinking about your words and deeds in the light of the Gospel to see how you may have sinned. It is a way to prepare for the Sacrament of Penance and Reconciliation.

Activity Follow this advice to avoid temptations and to make good choices. Then use the first letter in each line to fill in the blanks and discover a message about the Sacrament of Penance and Reconciliation.

Figure out your choices.
Rest your brain awhile, then pray.
Ease off—do not decide in a hurry.
Stop and think about the consequences.
Hold off until you are pretty sure.

Set your conscience in action.
Take it slow and easy.
Ask what Jesus would do.
Review all the facts and advice.
Then make a right choice.

The Sacrament of Penance and Reconciliation gives you a

___ ___ ___ ___ ___   ___ ___ ___ ___ ___.

I FOLLOW JESUS

You are sometimes faced with situations in which someone deliberately chooses to hurt you. When this happens you must decide whether to forgive or not to forgive that person. There are consequences to both of these decisions.

IN YOUR HANDS

Think of a time when someone has chosen to hurt you. On one handprint, write or draw what would happen if you refused to forgive the person. On the other handprint, write what would happen if you did forgive. Which is the better way? Why?

On one hand . . .

On the other hand . . .

MY FAITH CHOICE

I will remember that Jesus asked me to forgive over and over again. This week, I will do my best to continue the forgiving work of Jesus. I will

____

____.

Pray, "Jesus, give me the strength and courage to forgive those who hurt me. Amen."

Chapter Review

For each of the letters in the word "Forgive" write something about the Sacrament of Penance and Reconciliation.

F
C O N T R I T I O N
R
G
I
V
E

TO HELP YOU REMEMBER

1. Jesus continues his work of healing and forgiveness through the Church in the Sacraments of Healing.
2. In the Sacrament of Penance and Reconciliation, we receive forgiveness for sins committed after we are baptized.
3. The Sacrament of Penance and Reconciliation gives us the grace to say no to sin in the future.

Act of Contrition

In an act of contrition, we accept responsibility for our sins. We promise that we will do our best not to sin anymore, and to make up for our sins. Pray it at bedtime each day.

My God,
I am sorry for my sins with all my heart.
In choosing to do wrong
and failing to do good,
I have sinned against you
whom I should love above all things.
I firmly intend, with your help,
to do penance,
to sin no more,
and to avoid whatever leads me to sin.
Our Savior Jesus Christ
suffered and died for us.
In his name, my God, have mercy.
Amen.

With My Family

This Week . . .

In Chapter 14, Jesus Forgives, your child learned that:

- The two Sacraments of Healing are the Sacrament of Penance and Reconciliation and the Sacrament of the Anointing of the Sick.
- In the Sacrament of Penance and Reconciliation, we ask for and receive God's forgiveness for the sins we have committed after we have been baptized.
- The graces we receive in the Sacrament of Penance and Reconciliation strengthen our relationship with God and the Church and help us to say no to sin in the future.
- Forgiveness is a virtue that helps us show mercy to others.

For more about related teachings of the Church, see the *Catechism of the Catholic Church,* 1420–1484 and 1499–1525, and the *United States Catholic Catechism for Adults,* pages 168, 233–247.

Sharing God's Word

Read together Matthew 18:21-22, the account of Peter's questioning Jesus about forgiveness. Emphasize that Jesus continues his work of forgiveness through the Church.

We Live as Disciples

The Christian home and family is a school of discipleship. Choose one of the following activities to do as a family, or design a similar activity of your own:

- As a family, name several ways that you celebrate forgiveness when a family member says "I am sorry." Continue to put them into practice as a family.
- Include a simple prayer of petition in your grace before meals, both asking God's forgiveness for the times family members have hurt each other and for the grace to accept the forgiveness of each other.

Our Spiritual Journey

An examination of conscience is an ancient and proven spiritual discipline that helps us to discern where and when we have loved God and others through word and action, as well as where and when we have fallen short of loving God and others. Encourage your child to examine his or her conscience at bedtime and to pray an act of contrition.

Faith-Filled People

Saint Óscar Romero
Feast Day: March 24
In his homilies and weekly radio programs, Saint Óscar Romero spoke for justice and against violence.

For more ideas on ways your family can live as disciples of Jesus, visit **BeMyDisciples.com**

Acting on Feelings

Feelings themselves are neither good nor bad, right nor wrong. How we act on our emotions is important. Our actions can be good or bad, right or wrong. Sometimes doing what is wrong makes us feel good, but this does not make the action right.

Showing and receiving feelings of affection are very important actions. God blesses people with many ways to show true affection. One way to show affection is with words. We might say, "I like you," to a friend. Another way is through actions. We might give our parents a hug. We use the gift of our consciences to help us make good choices in expressing our feelings.

Married people show affection in special, private ways. This is a part of God's plan for families and for the creation of new life. As we grow older, our feelings of affection change, and the words and actions we use to express those feelings will also change. Our words and actions should always be right for our age and proper between people.

Catholics Believe

We use the gift of our consciences to guide us in making good choices. Our consciences work best for us when we train them to choose good and then follow them.

Activity

Collect and share with your family images of people showing affection as God intended and explain why you chose them. Then complete this sentence:

People show affection as God intended by

....

....

....

....

....

....

....

....

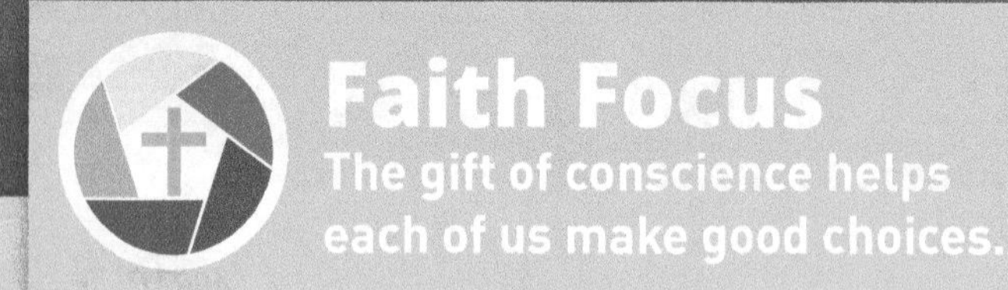

Faith Focus

The gift of conscience helps each of us make good choices.

Healthy Habits @ Home

As a family, consider these questions when striving to make good decisions:

- Is the act itself good?
- Is the intention good?
- Is the situation good?

Safer Together

As a family, talk about dealing with emotions appropriately. Here are some tips to review:

1. Recognize when you feel strong emotions.
2. Name what you are feeling.
3. Express what you feel in an appropriate way.
4. Identify what caused your strong emotion.
5. Take responsibility for how you act on your feelings.

Family Time

Cut out and hang at home

Review these steps for making good decisions.

1. Identify what you want to do.
2. Decide whether the action is right or wrong.
3. Act only on a good decision.

Family in Action

Focus on how family members show respect for God, themselves, and others by making a Family Examination of Conscience.

We show respect for God by:

....

We show respect for ourselves by:

....

We show respect for others by:

....

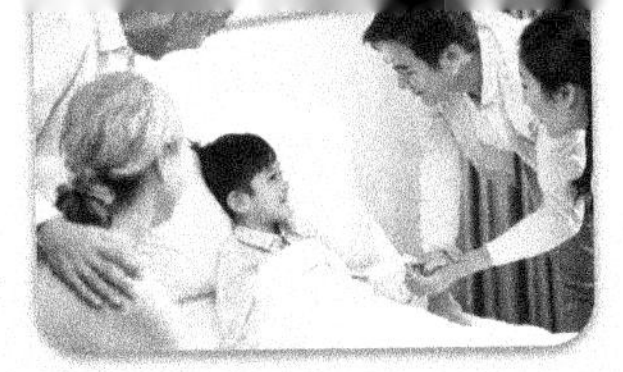
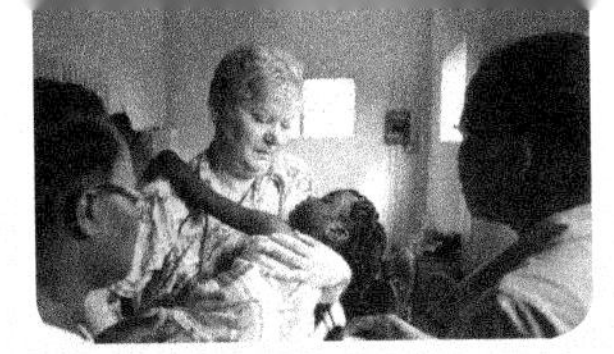

Looking Ahead

In this chapter, the Holy Spirit invites you to ▶

EXPLORE how Jesus continues to serve the sick and suffering.

DISCOVER how Jesus' ministry to the sick continues today.

DECIDE how to be a sign of God's love to someone who is sick.

CHAPTER 15

Jesus Heals the Sick

? When has someone comforted and cared for you when you were sick?

The Bible has many stories about people who were sick and suffering. Imagine you are with Jesus and Peter and the other disciples:

> Peter's mother-in-law was very sick. She had a high fever. Her family was very worried about her. They asked Jesus to help her. They had faith that he could comfort her. Jesus came and stood over her. He ordered the fever to leave her, and it did. She got up out of bed and immediately began to care for her family and guests.
>
> Based on Luke 4:38-39

? What does this story tell you about Jesus' concern for people who are suffering?

Compassion

A person who has compassion feels the suffering someone else is having and reaches out to help that person. The parable of the Good Samaritan (Luke 10:29-37) is a good example of what Jesus teaches us about a person who has compassion.

THE CHURCH FOLLOWS JESUS

Comfort Those Who Suffer

The Church has reached out with compassion to people who were sick from her very beginning. In fact, there is evidence that hospitals were set up by early Christians. Here is one story that tells one way the Church continues to care for the sick today.

Michael was in the hospital preparing for his surgery. The doctors were to remove a small tumor on his lung, and they would not know how serious it was until they operated. It was a scary time for Michael and his family—and his friends.

The night before his surgery, Michael's family and three of his classmates were visiting with him. There was a knock on the door. Turning, they saw a woman who asked, "May I come in? I have come to pray with Michael and bring him Holy Communion," she said. "Will that be okay?" she asked. Michael's family immediately recognized her to be Mrs. Barna whom they had often seen at church on Sunday.

Michael felt a little embarrassed, but welcomed her. After Mrs. Barna and his family and friends prayed with him, Michael felt peaceful.

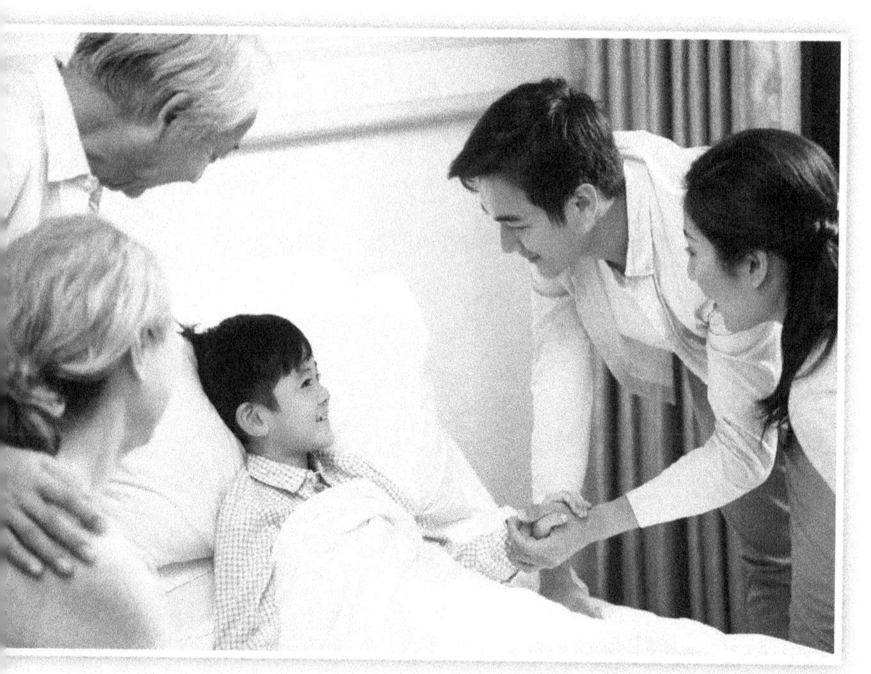

Mrs. Barna was one of many members of their parish who visit the sick. They remind parishioners from their parish who are sick and their families that Jesus is present with them. They are signs to the sick that the whole Church is with them.

Just as Jesus reached out with compassion to the mother of Saint Peter's wife, Mrs. Barna reached out to Michael and his family.

? How are the members of your parish who visit the sick signs of God's love?

God's Healing Love

The Bible story of creation tells us that God created everyone "very good." God created us to be happy here on Earth and forever in Heaven. God's plan of creation did not include sickness and **suffering**. Illness and death and other forms of suffering came into the world as a result of Original Sin, our first parents' sin.

Some people wrongfully blame God for the suffering in the world. They sometimes turn away from God. Other people trust in God's great love for them even when they suffer. They reach out to God in prayer as the writer of this psalm verse did.

> Give ear to my words, O LORD;
> understand my sighing.
>
> PSALM 5:2

People who truly believe in God know that he is always present with them. He is present with them when they are healthy and when they are sick.

FAITH FOCUS

How does Jesus' work of healing continue in the world today?

FAITH VOCABULARY

suffering
Suffering is a consequence of Original Sin, the sin of our first parents. In the Sacrament of the Anointing of the Sick, our suffering is united with the saving work of Jesus.

synagogue
The synagogue is where Jewish people gather to pray, read, and study the Scriptures and the Law of God and other teachings of the Jewish religion

Activity Look up Psalm 4 in the Bible. Choose a verse to comfort someone who is sick or suffering in some other way. Write the verse in the space. Learn it by heart. Pray it alone. Pray it with others.

____

____

____

____

Saint John of God

John of God served his country as a soldier, worked as a shepherd, and, at times, sold books. In 1538, after listening to a sermon, John decided to dedicate his life to caring for people who were sick. Today more than 40,000 followers of Saint John of God care for people who are sick and suffering all over the world. Saint John of God is the patron saint of hospitals, of people who are sick, and of nurses. His feast day is celebrated on March 8.

Jesus Heals a Young Girl

Jesus revealed God's healing love to people over and over again. People turned to Jesus in times of suffering. The Gospel tells us that Jairus, an official of the **synagogue** whose daughter was very sick, came to Jesus. Read and discover what happened:

One day when Jesus and his disciples were entering a town, Jairus came to Jesus. He fell on his knees and begged Jesus to come to his house because his twelve-year-old daughter was dying.

Jesus went with him and as they came toward Jairus' home, someone from his house came and said to Jairus, "Your daughter is dead; do not trouble the teacher any longer."

On hearing this, Jesus said, "Do not be afraid; just have faith and your daughter will be saved."

Jesus went over to Jairus' daughter, took her by the hand, and called to her, "Child, arise!"

The girl immediately arose.

BASED ON LUKE 8:40-42, 49-50, 53-55

We, too, believe and trust in Jesus. We turn to him when we or other people are sick or suffering in another way. We know that he is always true to his promise:

"I am with you always." MATTHEW 28:20

? What did Jairus ask Jesus? What might you ask Jesus when you or a member of your family is sick?

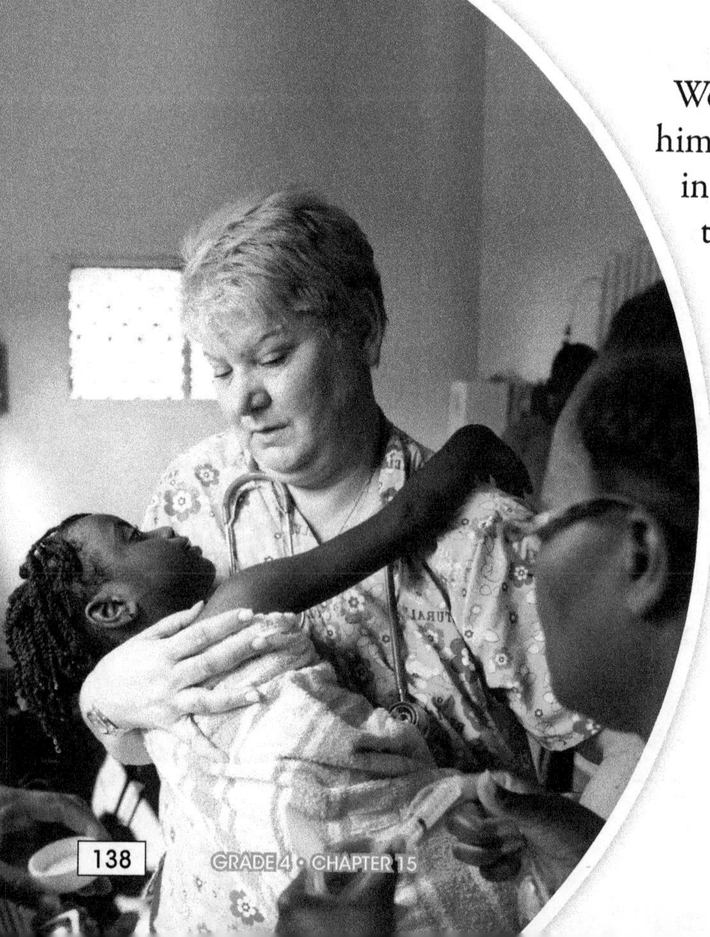

Anointing of the Sick

Jesus continues his ministry of healing among the sick through the Church today. The Sacrament of the Anointing of the Sick invites people to have faith and trust in God.

The Church has done this from her earliest days. James the Apostle wrote:

> If there is anyone among you who is sick, he should call the priests of the Church. And they will pray over him or her and anoint him or her with oil in the name of Jesus. And the prayer of faith will save the sick person.
>
> BASED ON JAMES 5:14-15

The Church celebrates this sacrament with us when we are seriously ill, weak from old age, or in danger of death. A priest anoints our hands and forehead with the Oil of the Sick.

The Graces of the Sacrament

We receive special graces when we celebrate this sacrament. These are the graces we receive:

We are united more closely to Christ and his suffering.

We receive the strength, peace, and courage to deal with our suffering.

We receive forgiveness for our sins if we are not able to confess our sins in the Sacrament of Penance and Reconciliation.

Our health may be restored if that would help us grow in holiness.

We are prepared for death and our journey to God in Heaven.

Activity On art paper, create a get-well note. Include a faith message to the person who is sick.

Catholics Believe

Oil of the Sick

Oil helps to heal us. The Church uses the Oil of the Sick in the celebration of Anointing of the Sick. All the holy oils are kept in a special place in the church called an ambry.

I FOLLOW JESUS

When have you helped a member of your family who was sick? When have you visited a friend who was sick or sent your friend a get-well card? When you did, the Holy Spirit helped you be a sign of God's caring and healing love for that person. You were doing the same work that Jesus did.

CARING FOR OTHERS

List some of the things you and other young people can do to help people who are sick or are suffering in some way.

___

___

___

___

___

___

___

___

___

___

___

MY FAITH CHOICE

This week, when I hear or read about some people who are suffering, I will be a sign of God's love. I will reach out with compassion. I will

___

___.

Quiet yourself for a moment to say a prayer for someone you know who is sick. Pray, "Dear God, bless and keep ______ in your loving care. Amen."

Chapter Review

Use the words in the word bank to complete each sentence.

synagogue	Jairus	John
graces	Church	healing

1. Anointing of the Sick is a Sacrament of ____________________.
2. A ____________________ is the place Jewish people gather to pray.
3. Those who receive the Sacrament of the Anointing of the Sick receive special ____________________.
4. ____________________ asked Jesus to heal his daughter.

TO HELP YOU REMEMBER

1. The Bible has many stories that describe how people deal with their sickness and suffering.
2. Jairus believed and trusted that Jesus would heal his daughter.
3. We are to reach out to Jesus in faith and trust when we are sick or suffering in any way.

Lord, Hear Our Prayer

In a prayer of intercession, we pray for other people. Pray this prayer of intercession for people who are sick or suffering in any way.

Leader: God of love, you are always present with us.

All: **Comfort *(name)* with your love.**
(Each child repeats the sentence with the name of a friend or family member.)

Leader: Send your Holy Spirit to comfort all the sick and suffering with the gift of your love and presence. We ask this through Christ, our Lord.

All: **Amen.**

With My Family

This Week . . .

In chapter 15, Jesus Heals the Sick, your child learned:

- The Holy Spirit gives us comfort and courage in times of sickness and suffering.
- The Holy Spirit strengthens our faith and trust in God so we can deal with our sufferings.
- We receive the comfort and the courage to join our sufferings to those of Christ and witness God's ever-present love in our lives.
- Compassion is feeling the pain and suffering of a person and reaching out to and caring for a person who is hurting.

For more about related teachings of the Church, see the *Catechism of the Catholic Church,* 309–314 and 1500–1510, and the *United States Catholic Catechism for Adults,* pages 69–70, 168, 249–259.

Sharing God's Word

Read Together Luke 8:40-55, the account of Jesus healing the daughter of Jairus. Or read the adaptation of the story on page 138. Emphasize that Jesus desires and invites us to turn to him when we or other people are suffering. Recall the meaning of Jesus' promise "I am with you always" (Matthew 28:20).

We Live as Disciples

The Christian home and family is a school of discipleship. Choose one of the following activities to do as a family, or design a similar activity of your own:

- Find out if your parish has a group that prays every day for people in the parish who are sick. If your parish does, have your family become part of that group.
- Name some ways that your family can reach out to others who are suffering. Choose one thing that you will do as a family this week.

Our Spiritual Journey

The Spiritual Works of Mercy provide us with a series of disciplines to share our spiritual blessings with others. These works include "Comfort those who suffer." How well is the practice of this discipline and the virtue of compassion integrated into your life? Also encourage your child to pray for the sick and to let the sick person know about the prayer.

Faith-Filled People

Saint John of God
Feast Day: March 8
Saint John of God dedicated his life to caring for the sick. He is the patron saint of hospitals and nurses.

For more ideas on ways your family can live as disciples of Jesus, visit **BeMyDisciples.com**

Our Amazing Bodies

God created us according to a magnificent plan. He created each of us with a body and a soul. God wants us to be healthy and holy. God created our bodies with many systems. All of these body systems have an order, a particular way to help keep us healthy. In science class we can learn more about the body systems. When we are healthy, our bodies are working as God intended.

All of our body systems depend on each other to work properly. This is part of God's plan for our bodies. For example, our bodies cannot work without a digestive system, which includes a mouth, stomach, and intestines. When we eat healthful foods, the digestive system works best. And when the digestive system is working best, the rest of the body and its systems can work better too. The correct working order of the whole body is vital to our health.

We can cooperate with God's plan for our bodies by choosing healthy habits. We can take the right steps for staying healthy, but sometimes we become sick through no fault of our own. There are times when the body cannot be healed easily. This can be difficult, especially when the body's systems are seriously damaged.

Catholics Believe

When we are healthy, our bodies are working as God intended. The Cardinal Virtues help us to respect ourselves and properly maintain healthy bodies and live holy lives.

Activity

Draw an image of your face. Identify the major parts, and label each one with its body system name. Share your drawing with your family.

Faith Focus

When we are healthy, our bodies are working as God intended.

Healthy Habits @ Home

Create a family health plan with a checklist of good habits to do on any given day.

Our Health Plan

- ☐ ....
- ☐ ....
- ☐ ....
- ☐ ....
- ☐ ....
- ☐ ....

Safer Together

Children, as they mature, may feel uncomfortable with how they look. They can be susceptible to inappropriate comments from others. Reinforce these points as a family:

1. God made everyone beautiful with different body shapes and sizes.
2. Our physical differences reflect the amazing diversity of God's creation.
3. Respecting our own bodies and the bodies of others is mature behavior and necessary for living healthy and holy lives.

Family Time

Cut out and hang at home

As a family, discuss the amazing workings of the human body. To keep the conversation on topic, consider these ideas:

- The framework of bones and joints holds the body together and gives us our shapes.
- The muscular system makes movement possible.
- The brain is the control center.
- Humans share in God's creation through the reproductive system.

Family in Action

We can learn a great deal about the sacredness of human life. Ask family members to respond to the following questions:

- What excitement and fears did you have or do you still have about growing up?
- How does our culture show or fail to show respect for the human body?
- How do we, as a family, show respect for the human body?
- What more can we do, as a family, to show respect for the human body?

Looking Ahead

In this chapter, the Holy Spirit invites you to ▶

EXPLORE the work of Blessed Maria Romero Meneses.

DISCOVER how Holy Orders and Matrimony call some to serve.

DECIDE how you can live a holy life.

CHAPTER 16

Signs of God's Love

? What do people in your town or city do to help the community?

Close your eyes and listen. One day Jesus is teaching his disciples. He wants them to know that, as his disciples, they are to share his love with the world. Jesus says:

> "I am the vine, you are the branches. If you remain in me, and I in you, you will bear much fruit. Be my disciples. As the Father loves me, so I also love you. Remain in my love. This is what I ask you to do: Love one another, as I love you." BASED ON JOHN 15:5, 6, 8, 12

? How do members of the Church work together to show their love for one another?

Holiness

Holiness is living in communion with God. People who are holy are living signs of God's love in the world. Every person has the vocation to grow in holiness.

THE CHURCH FOLLOWS JESUS

Blessed Maria Romero Meneses

Christ is the vine. The members of the Church are the branches. Here's a story of how the love we show others comes from our connection to Jesus.

Blessed Maria Romero Meneses was born in Nicaragua in 1902 to a wealthy family. When she was twelve, she became very sick. She was paralyzed for six months. During her illness, she discovered her vocation to be a religious sister.

When she felt better, Maria joined the Salesian religious community. As a Salesian sister, she first went to Costa Rica. She shared Christ's love with girls living in wealthy families and with those from families living in poverty.

Sister Maria taught music, drawing, and typing to the girls from wealthy families. She taught trades to people who were poor so that they could make a living.

Sister Maria inspired many of her students to join her in her work. She showed wealthy people how they could share God's love with people who were poor by sharing their blessings with them. She set up recreational centers, food pantries, a school for girls who were poor, and a health clinic. Together they were wonderful signs of God's love.

Today the Church honors Sister Maria as Blessed Maria Romero Meneses. Blessed Maria is an example of how we can share the love of Christ the Vine with others.

? How do men and women serve the Church as members of a religious community?

At the Service of Communion

God created everyone holy. He calls each of us to live a life of holiness. Our words and actions are to show that we are children of God.

Most members of the Church are called to live lives of holiness as laypeople. Some marry, and others remain single. Some members are called to live lives of holiness in a religious community, as Blessed Maria did. Some baptized men are called to lives of holiness in the vocation of bishop, priest, or deacon.

Members of the Church who are called to the vocation of marriage or Holy Orders are chosen to help us live our Baptism and our call to holiness. They are consecrated, or set aside, and given God's grace for this work in the **Sacraments at the Service of Communion**. These sacraments are Holy Orders and Matrimony.

FAITH FOCUS
What do the Sacrament of Holy Orders and the Sacrament of Matrimony celebrate?

FAITH VOCABULARY

Sacraments at the Service of Communion
Holy Orders and Matrimony are called the Sacraments at the Service of Communion.

domestic church
The domestic church is the church of the home.

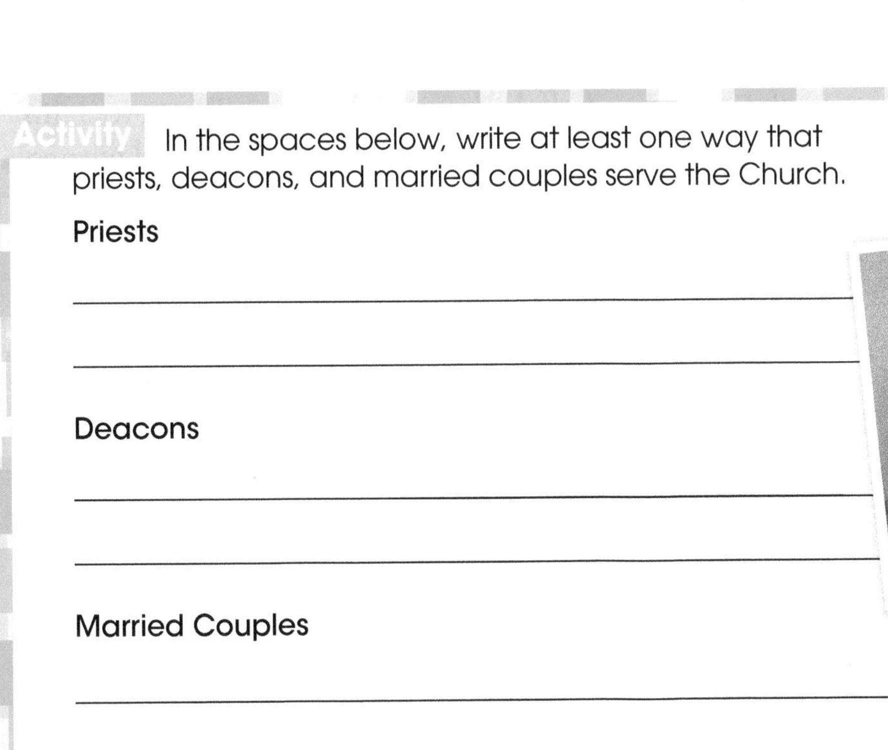

Activity In the spaces below, write at least one way that priests, deacons, and married couples serve the Church.

Priests

____

____

Deacons

____

____

Married Couples

____

____

Faith-Filled People

The Pope

The pope is the successor of Saint Peter the Apostle and the bishop of Rome. He is the shepherd of the whole Church. He is also called the Holy Father and has supreme authority over the Universal Church. By his life and teachings, he guides all the people of the Church to live holy lives.

Sacrament of Holy Orders

Since the beginning of the Church, bishops, priests, and deacons have served the whole Church. Without bishops, priests, and deacons, one cannot speak of the Church. The ordained ministry is part of the Church founded by Jesus Christ.

Bishops, priests, and deacons are ordained for this service in the Sacrament of Holy Orders. They serve the Church by teaching what Jesus taught, by leading the Church in divine worship, and by governing the Church.

Bishops. Jesus chose the Apostles to serve the Church in his name (read Mark 3:13-14). Bishops are the successors of the Apostles. Under the authority of the pope, the bishop of Rome, and together with him, the bishops are the chief teachers in the Church.

Priests. Priests are co-workers with the bishops. They preach the Gospel and lead us in the celebration of the sacraments. Priests guide us in understanding Sacred Scripture and the teachings of the Church.

Deacons. Deacons, who are sometimes married, are also ordained. They help bishops and priests. They proclaim God's Word, baptize, and witness the marriage of people. They care for the sick and those in need.

? Look at the photos on this page. How do ordained ministers help you live your call to holiness?

Matrimony

Matrimony is the other Sacrament at the Service of Communion. In this sacrament, a baptized man and a baptized woman freely promise to enter into a lifelong marriage with each other. They receive God's grace to love and serve each other and the family of our Church. Their love and service become a sign of Jesus' love for the Church.

In the Sacrament of Matrimony, the couple promises to answer God's call to have a family. The Christian family is called the **domestic church**. The word *domestic* comes from the Latin word *domus*, which means "home" or "household."

The members of our families are the first people to tell us about Jesus. From them we first learn about God and his love for us. Our families helps us learn the ways that we can live lives of holiness, loving God and others as Jesus taught.

Catholics Believe

Vows and Promises

The members of religious communities make sacred promises or vows to God and to the Church. This helps them live their call to holiness. They promise not to marry, to live simple and poor lives, and to obey the leaders of their community and the Church.

Activity Look at each photo. Then write how the family in the photo is being the domestic church.

____

____

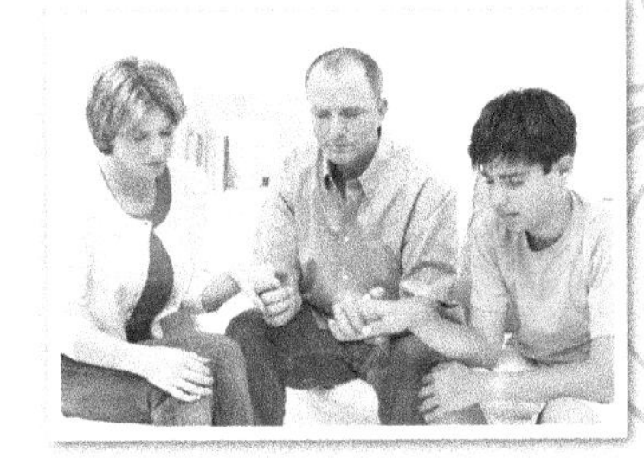

____

____

____

____

____

____

I FOLLOW JESUS

You are a member of both your family and your parish. Together members of your family and your parish help one another live their call to holiness.

SERVING OTHERS

Create a poster that will encourage you and your friends to help one another live holy lives. Write or draw your ideas in the space provided.

MY FAITH CHOICE

This week, I can try to work with my family or members of my parish to live a holy life. I will

____

____.

Jesus tells us, "Remain in my love" (John 15:9). Close your eyes and reflect on the meaning of Jesus' words for you.

Chapter Review

These three statements are false. On the lines, write the word or words that would make them true.

1. The two Sacraments at the Service of Communion are Holy Orders and Reconciliation.

   ____

2. In Holy Orders, a baptized man and a baptized woman promise to be faithful to each other.

   ____

3. Bishops, priests, and married couples are called in a special way through the Sacrament of Holy Orders.

   ____

TO HELP YOU REMEMBER

1. The Sacraments at the Service of Communion set aside members of the Church to help all the members of the Church live holy lives.
2. Bishops, priests, and deacons are ordained in the Sacrament of Holy Orders to serve the whole Church.
3. In Matrimony, a baptized man and a baptized woman receive the grace to love and serve one another and the Church.

Prayer for Vocations

God calls each of us to live a holy life. He calls us to do this in different ways. We call this our vocation. Pray this prayer for vocations now as a group, and pray it alone each day.

Lord God,
help me understand
how you want me to live.
I will give all my heart to the work
of being a sign of your love
for all to know.
Amen.

With My Family

This Week . . .

In Chapter 16, Signs of God's Love, your child learned:

- All people are called to lives of holiness.
- The Sacraments at the Service of Communion—Holy Orders and Matrimony—set aside some members of the Church to serve the whole Church.
- In the Sacrament of Holy Orders, a baptized man is ordained to serve the whole Church as a bishop, priest, or deacon.
- In the Sacrament of Matrimony, a baptized man and a baptized woman are united in a lifelong bond of faithful love as a sign of Christ's love for his Church.
- Holiness is living in communion with God; we are all called to holiness.

For more about related teachings of the Church, see the *Catechism of the Catholic Church*, 1533–1589 and 1601–1658, and the *United States Catholic Catechism for Adults*, pages 262–292.

Sharing God's Word

Read together Luke 10:1-2, the account of Jesus sending his disciples on a mission. Emphasize that while all of the baptized are called to serve one another as Jesus commanded, members of the clergy, married people, and single people are all called to serve the whole Church.

We Live as Disciples

The Christian home and family is a school of discipleship. Choose one of the following activities to do as a family, or design a similar activity of your own:

- Talk about how your parish priests and deacons live out their vocations to serve the Church. Name ways that they help you and other members of the parish live out your Baptism. Discuss how your family can help them.
- Families are holy. Talk about all the ways your family helps each other grow in holiness. Promise to continue doing these things.

Our Spiritual Journey

The grace of discernment enables us to come to know and to live lives of holiness. Discernment is the discipline of prayerfully coming to a deeper knowledge and understanding of one's vocation and of the means of living it. Asking the advice of a spiritual director or a confessor enables us to grow in the wise practice of this spiritual discipline.

Faith-Filled People

The Pope

The pope is the successor of Saint Peter the Apostle (the first pope) and the Bishop of Rome. He is also called the Holy Father. By his life and teachings, he guides all the people of the Church to live holy lives.

For more ideas on ways your family can live as disciples of Jesus, visit **BeMyDisciples.com**

A Sign of God's Love

Catholics Believe

Through our words and actions, we are living signs of God's love in the world.

Your family has just learned that the pastor of your parish will be leaving. He has been assigned as the pastor of another parish. He has been a generous, loving, and compassionate presence in your faith community and for your family. While sad that he is leaving, your family is grateful for the many things he has taught you.

Each of us is called to be living signs of God's love in the world. Everyone has a vocation to holiness. This means we continue Jesus' work in the world through our loving actions. In what way has your pastor been a sign of God's love in the world?

Activity

Think about two ways your pastor has helped your family grow in holiness. Write the ways here:

....

....

....

....

....

....

....

....

....

....

Faith Focus

Things we do and say that show our love for God are holy.

Healthy Habits @ Home

Help your children identify and practice healthy and holy habits. Healthy habits show respect for our bodies. Holy habits help us grow closer to God and share his love through our words and actions.

Safer Together

Help your children stay safe with these guidelines. Make sure your children:

1. know your address and telephone number.
2. check with a parent or the person in charge before they go anywhere or get into a car, even with someone they know.
3. check with a parent or trusted adult before they accept anything from anyone, even from someone they know.
4. know to say "no" if someone tries to touch them or treat them in a way that makes them feel uncomfortable, scared, or confused.
5. know they are strong, smart, and have the right to be safe.

Family Time

Cut out and hang at home

Discuss how family members are loving signs of God's presence in the world. Talk about times when you have done each of the following:

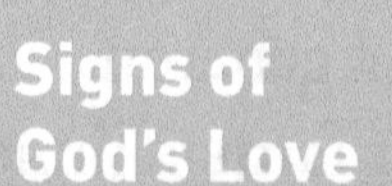

Signs of God's Love	What We Did
Shared an act of kindness	
Forgave someone	
Cared for someone who was hurting	
Spent time in prayer	
Made a good choice	

Unit 4 **Review**

Name ______________________________

A. Choose the Best Word

Use the words in the word bank to complete the sentences.

healing	Service	Exodus
holiness	domestic church	pope

1. Holy Orders and Matrimony are the Sacraments at the ________________ of Communion.

2. ________________ is living in communion with God. Every person has the vocation to grow in this.

3. The ____________________ is the church of the home.

4. The ________________ was the journey of the Israelites from slavery in Egypt to freedom in the land God promised them.

5. The ________________ is the successor of Saint Peter the Apostle and the bishop of Rome.

B. Show What You Know

Place a T in front of the sentence if it is true. Place an F if it is false. Tell your class how to make the false statements true.

_____ **1.** Penance and Reconciliation and Anointing of the Sick are Sacraments of Service.

_____ **2.** The Church uses oil in the Sacrament of Penance and Reconciliation.

_____ **3.** The domestic church is the church of the home.

_____ **4.** Sin is freely choosing to turn away from God.

_____ **5.** We receive absolution when we confess our sins in the Sacrament of Penance and Reconciliation.

C. Connect with Scripture

Reread the Scripture passage on page 117. What connection do you see between this passage and what you learned in this unit?

____

____

____

D. Be a Disciple

1. *Review the four pages in this unit titled The Church Follows Jesus. What person or ministry of the Church on these pages will inspire you to be a better disciple of Jesus? Explain your answer.*

____

____

____

2. *Work with a group. Review the four Disciple Power virtues, or gifts, you have learned about in this unit. After writing your own ideas, share with the group practical ways that you will live these virtues day by day.*

____

____

____

We Live UNIT 5

Part One

Well Done!

A man called his servants together. He gave to one servant five coins, to another two coins, and to a third servant, one coin. Then the master went away.

The servant who received five coins went and traded them and earned five more. The one who received two earned two more. But the man who received one coin dug a hole in the ground and buried it.

When the master returned, the man who buried the coin said, "I was afraid of losing your money, so I buried it. Here it is back."

The master took the coin and gave it to the servant who had already made five coins. He said to this servant, "Well done, my good and faithful servant. Come, share your master's joy."

Based on Matthew 25:14-26

What I Have Learned

What is something you already know about these faith concepts?

holiness

____

____

____

happiness

____

____

____

Cardinal Virtues

____

____

____

Faith Terms to Know

Put an X next to the faith terms you know. Put a ? next to faith terms you need to learn more about.

_______ soul

_______ free will

_______ conscience

_______ prudence

_______ Beatitudes

_______ sanctifying grace

_______ emotions

_______ Gifts of the Holy Spirit

The Bible

What do you know about God giving Moses the Ten Commandments?

____

____

____

The Church

Which saint or organization of the Church would you like to learn more about?

____

____

____

A Question I Have

What question would you like to ask about being a moral person?

____

____

____

Popular Devotions

The Black Christ of Esquipulas

A Devotion from Guatemala

The Black Christ of Esquipulas is celebrated on January 15, March 9, and Ascension Thursday.

The people of Guatemala have a devotion to the Crucified Christ. The devotion seems to have begun in the city of Esquipulas. An image of Christ is kept in the basilica there. It has been honored for four centuries.

The image is called the Black Christ because it was carved from dark-colored wood. One legend says the wood was light and miraculously turned dark overnight. The truth may be that the wood turned dark over time because of candle smoke and people touching it.

The Black Christ of Esquipulas is celebrated on January 15, March 9, and Ascension Thursday. Visitors come from across Central America to honor the image. They come to ask for forgiveness and peace.

People in the streets buy colorful craft items during the celebrations. When the visitors arrive in the church, they light candles or leave gifts. The gifts are small wax figures in the shape of body parts or other objects. They represent healings, favors, or miracles the people have received from the Lord.

? Why do you think the image of the Crucified Christ is so important to the people of Guatemala?

Popular Devotions

The Black Christ of Esquipulas

The people of Guatemala have a devotion to the Black Christ of Esquipulas. Solve the crossword puzzle to discover words that remind us of their practices.

Down

1. The people of Guatemala have a _____ to the Black Christ.
2. The image of the Crucified Christ is located in the _____ in Esquipulas.
4. Guatemala is located In ____ America.

Across

3. Visitors leave gifts that represent _____ they have received from God.
5. People come to Esquipulas to ask for _______.
6. People visit the basilica to light candles and _____.

Looking Ahead

In this chapter, the Holy Spirit invites you to ▶

EXPLORE how Saint Augustine chose to follow Jesus.

DISCOVER how we use intellect and free will to make good choices.

DECIDE to make good choices.

CHAPTER 17

Created in God's Image

What is one way that you are different from other people? What is one way that you are the same? What is special about how God created people?

There are many places in the Bible where God tells us that there is something very special about every person. Think about what is so special about people. Now listen to what God says to us in these words from Psalm 119:

> *[Lord God,] your hands made me and fashioned me.*
> *Help me learn your commands*
> *and help me choose to follow them.*
>
> Based on Psalm 119:73

What does it mean that God's hands made you and fashioned you?

Prudence

One of the four Cardinal Virtues, prudence is a virtue that helps us know what is truly good for us. It also helps us know how to choose what is right and good.

THE CHURCH FOLLOWS JESUS

Augustine's Choices

Augustine spent many years trying to learn God's commands and to follow them. He made many bad choices when he was young. However, he became a model decision maker. Augustine's choice to follow Jesus has become famous. It has helped many people make good choices.

When Augustine was a young man, he made many bad choices that he thought would bring him happiness. His mother, Saint Monica, prayed over and over again for her son. She prayed that Augustine would learn to stop making choices that were hurting him and others.

When he was twenty-nine years old, Augustine heard Bishop Ambrose preach. Ambrose made Augustine think about his life and the choices he had been making. Augustine started to put the virtue of prudence into action. He soon made the decision to change his ways and live as Jesus had taught.

Augustine wrote a book about his life. The book is called *Confessions*. People all over the world still read this book today. Reading it continues to help people make good choices and live holy lives.

? Who helps you learn to make good decisions?

In God's Image

In the creation story, God tells us the most important thing that we can ever know about ourselves and other people:

God created mankind in his image;
in the image of God he created them;
male and female he created them.

GENESIS 1:27

God creates every person in his image and likeness. He creates every person with a soul. The soul is the spiritual part of every person that makes us like God and that lives forever.

Our souls also gives us two wonderful powers—**intellect** and **free will**. With the power of intellect, we can come to know God, ourselves, other people, and the wonders and mysteries of creation. With the power of free will, we can choose to love and serve God and others, or we can choose not to.

Jesus reminds us that

"You shall love the Lord your God with all your heart, with all your soul, with all your mind, and with all your strength. . . . You shall love your neighbor as yourself."

MARK 12:30-31

FAITH FOCUS

Which powers has God given us to make choices to live holy lives?

FAITH VOCABULARY

intellect
Intellect is the part of every person that gives him or her the ability to know God, oneself, and other people, and know how God wants us to live.

free will
Free will is the part of every person that gives him or her the ability to choose to love and serve God and others as he has created us to do, or to choose not to love and serve God and others.

Activity Work with a partner. Create a skit in which a person is using his or her free will correctly. Describe the situation in this space.

____

____

____

Faith-Filled People

Saint Paul the Apostle

Paul traveled by land and sea to preach the Gospel. He preached about what it means to be a disciple of Jesus and about the choices we make every day to live holy lives. People did not always welcome him. He was arrested, put in prison, and finally put to death because of his faith in Jesus. The Church celebrates the feast of the Conversion of Saint Paul on January 25, and the feast of Peter and Paul, Apostles, on June 29.

Choices! Choices! Choices!

Every day we use intellect to learn more and free will to make choices. The choices that we understand and make freely are called *deliberate actions*. We have the responsibility to use intellect and free will to make good deliberate actions.

We use intellect and free will responsibly when we choose to say or do what we know is good. When we choose something that we know is against God's Laws, we are not using our intellect and free will responsibly. We are always responsible for our deliberate actions.

It is not always easy to know what is good and to choose it. When we are not sure about what to do, we need to ask for help. We need to learn what the Church teaches about good and bad choices. We need to pray to the Holy Spirit. The Holy Spirit gives us the help to know, do, and say what is good and to avoid what is against God's Laws.

All of our choices, even the simple choices that we make each day, have consequences. Consequences are the good or bad effects of our choices. We are morally responsible for the consequences of our actions.

? What gets in the way of making good choices? Tell a partner about it.

Our Feelings

Just as you have a free will and an intellect, you also have feelings or emotions. These are God's gifts to us, and they have the power to influence the choices that we make.

Emotions are feelings inside us. They are part of what makes us human. They can help us choose to do or say what is good. They can also influence us to choose to do or say what is evil. Emotions are neither good nor bad; it is how we use them that is important.

Anger and sadness are two emotions or feelings. They are not bad, and sometimes they can help us do good. Through each and every emotion, God calls us to live good and holy lives.

We might feel angry when we see someone being treated unfairly. We can use the feeling of anger to work for justice and kindness.

We might feel sad when we see a friend who is sick. We can use the feeling of sadness to help people when they are sick or in trouble.

Catholics Believe

Papal letters

One way that the Church teaches is through letters. For example, Pope Saint John Paul II wrote several official letters that teach us about the faith of the Church. One of these letters, "The Gospel of Life," teaches that every person is created in the image of God.

Activity Read Luke 22:54-62 and answer these questions.

Feelings and Choices

What feelings do you think Peter had that influenced the choices he made?

____

____

Name a feeling that helped you choose to say or do something good. Describe what happened.

____

____

I FOLLOW JESUS

You are created in the image and likeness of God. You show that by the many choices you make each day to live a holy life. The good choices that you make have consequences that help you and others live as children of God.

MAKING DIFFICULT DECISIONS

Read the situation below. Think about how you can practice the virtue of prudence. Fill in two consequences for a good choice that you could make and two consequences for a bad choice.

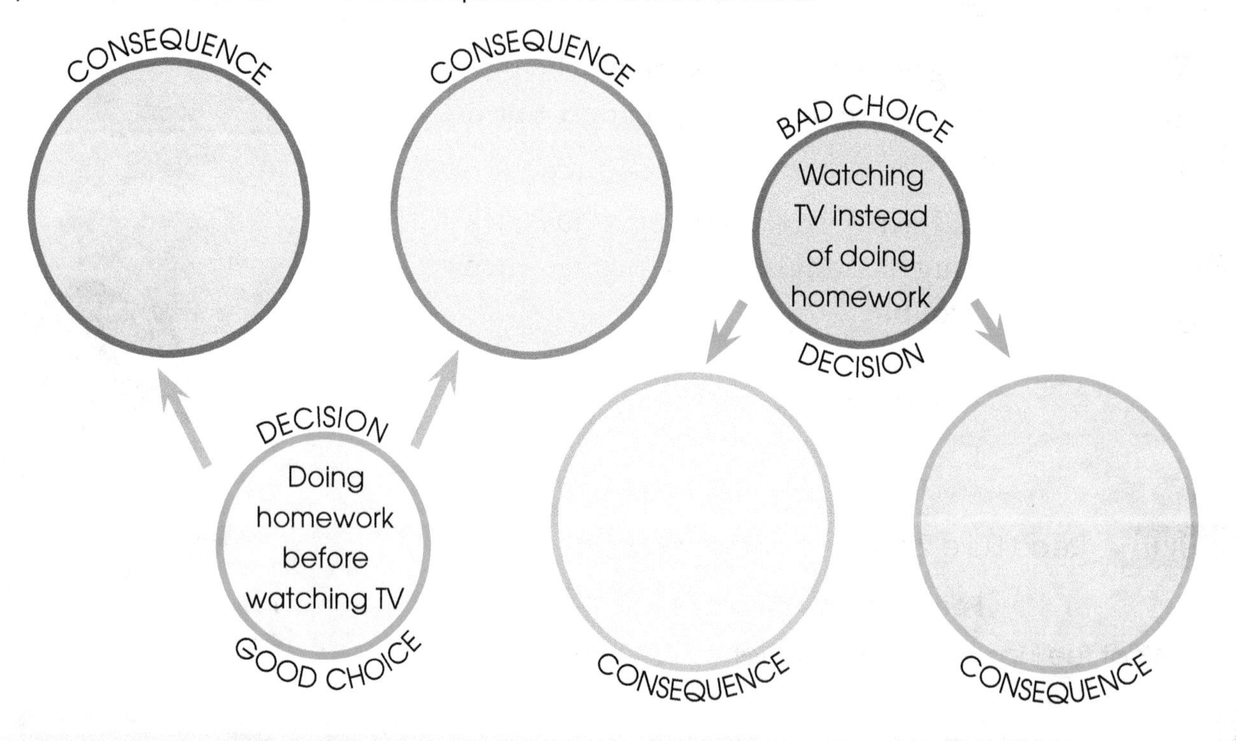

MY FAITH CHOICE

This week, I will think carefully about the consequences of my decisions before I make them. As a reminder to do this, I will

____

____.

Take a moment and ask God for the gift of prudence in making good choices.

Chapter Review

Unscramble the letters of the faith words. Match the words to the descriptions.

1. G E M A I ____________________

2. E R E F L W L I ____________________

3. O N M O T I S E ____________________

4. T E L L C T E N I ____________________

Descriptions

_____ **a.** Term used in the Bible that reveals that we are created in God's likeness

_____ **b.** Feelings that we experience that influence our choices

_____ **c.** The power to know God, others, and ourselves, and to learn new things

_____ **d.** The power to choose between good and evil

TO HELP YOU REMEMBER

1. We are each created with a soul that makes us like God and that lives forever.
2. We are each created with the gifts of intellect and free will to help us make good decisions.
3. We are each created with emotions, or feelings, that influence our decisions to live holy lives.

Prayer of Saint Augustine

Many prayers are written by the saints. Pray this prayer of Saint Augustine. Ask the Holy Spirit to help you live a holy life.

All: **Guard me, then, O Holy Spirit,**
That I always may be holy.

Group 1: Breathe in me, O Holy Spirit,
That my thoughts may all be holy;

Group 2: Act in me, O Holy Spirit,
That my work, too, may be holy;

All: **Guard me, then, O Holy Spirit,**
That I always may be holy.

Group 1: Draw my heart, O Holy Spirit,
That I love but what is holy;

Group 2: Strengthen me, O Holy Spirit,
That I defend all that is holy;

All: **Guard me, then, O Holy Spirit,**
That I always may be holy. Amen.

With My Family

This Week . . .

In Chapter 17, Created in God's Image, your child learned:

- Every person is created in the image and likeness of God. God creates every person with a soul.
- God gives each of us intellect and free will. These wonderful gifts help us to know, love, and serve God and others.
- God has also blessed us with emotions, or feelings. These gifts, which are neither good nor bad in themselves, influence the way in which we make choices.
- All of our choices have consequences. We are responsible for our choices and their consequences.
- The Cardinal Virtue of prudence helps us to know what is good for us and helps us to choose what is good.

For more about related teachings of the Church, see the *Catechism of the Catholic Church*, 33–35 and 1699–1742, and the *United States Catholic Catechism* for Adults, pages 56-57, 67–68, 310, 319.

Sharing God's Word

Read together Genesis 1:27, the story of God creating people, or read the adaptation of the story on page 157. Emphasize that God created all people in his own image.

We Live as Disciples

The Christian family is a school of discipleship. Choose one of the following activities to do as a family, or design a similar activity of your own:

- Name and discuss the many ways that your family members help each other make good decisions.
- Make a list of the steps that your family can use to make good decisions. Post it where all the family members can see it and be reminded to follow the steps.

Our Spiritual Journey

Many people have come before us to show us how to live holy lives. The saints of the Church model what it means to be disciples of Jesus Christ and how to make life-giving choices. The prayers that they have written can be a rich source for your family's prayer life. In this chapter, your child prayed the Prayer of Saint Augustine. Read and pray together the prayer on page 161.

Faith-Filled People

Saint Paul the Apostle
Feast Day: June 29
Paul traveled by land and by sea to teach people about Jesus. He invited them to believe in Jesus.

For more ideas on ways your family can live as disciples of Jesus, visit **BeMyDisciples.com**

Both Body and Soul

Catholics Believe

God created each of us with a unique body and a unique soul. The body is mortal. The soul is immortal. The body lives because of the soul.

God desires us to be healthy and holy. We take care of our bodies so that they work as God intended. The good news is that we are more than just our bodies. As amazing as our bodies are, we are much more! God created each of us with both a body and a soul. Our bodies are the physical parts of who we are. Our souls are the spiritual parts of us that never die. Our souls are the innermost aspect of who we are. The soul is created immediately by God and is immortal. God gave us souls at the first moments of our lives.

We are especially created in God's image because of our souls. Even if our bodies are sick or damaged, we are still persons. For example, just because someone needs eyeglasses to see does not make him or her less of a person.

Our bodies and souls work together. When we think, feel, and choose, our souls are active in us. We use our bodies to help us put these thoughts, feelings, and choices into action. Growing as followers of Jesus means growing as persons with both bodies and souls.

Activity

Share with family members your responses to the following situations.

1. When I see someone who is sad, I will

....

....

....

....

2. When I see or hear about someone in need, I will

....

....

....

3. When I see someone hurting another person, I will

....

....

....

Faith Focus

God created each of us with a unique body and a unique soul.

Healthy Habits @ Home

As a family, identify ways to practice the Cardinal Virtues that show respect for both your bodies and your souls

Respect for our bodies:

....

Respect for our souls:

....

Safer Together

Review these tips for talking with your child about his or her changing body:

- Emphasize that God uniquely created his or her body.
- Some areas of a person's body are considered private.
- No one has a right to touch the private area of another person's body inappropriately.
- Emphasize the importance of respecting one's own body and the bodies of others.

Family Time

Cut out and hang at home

Evaluate your family's weekly activities. Discuss how these activities address both physical and spiritual health.

Ways we address our physical health:

....

Ways we address our spiritual health:

....

Family in Action

We can honor the way God created each of us—with a unique body and unique soul. As a family, identify two ways family members can care for both body and soul this week.

We can care for our bodies:

1. ....
2. ....

We can care for our souls:

1. ....
2. ....

Looking Ahead

In this chapter, the Holy Spirit invites you to ▶

EXPLORE the story of Saint Mother Teresa of Calcutta.

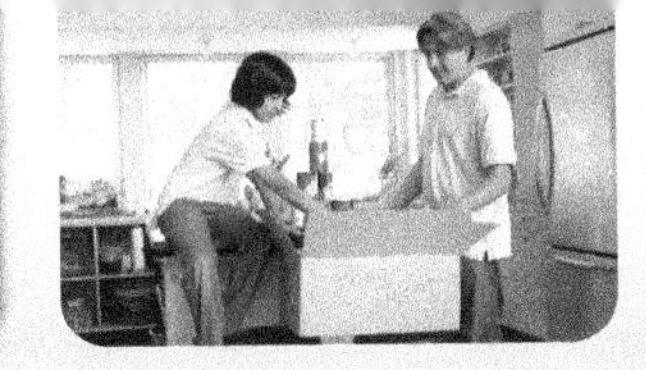

DISCOVER what the Beatitudes teach us about being a discipline.

DECIDE to live the Beatitudes.

CHAPTER 18

The Beatitudes

? What makes you happy? What did Jesus teach about what really will make people happy?

Everybody wants to be happy. Listen carefully to what God tells us about being happy, and then think about what God says to you in this Scripture passage from the Book of Proverbs:

Happy is the person who is kind and generous to people who are poor. — Based on Proverbs 14:21

? How does being kind and generous to people who are poor make a person happy?

Disciple Power

Generosity

Generous people freely share what they have. They share because of their love for God and for people. Generous people truly believe that we are all members of the family of God.

THE CHURCH FOLLOWS JESUS

Something Beautiful for God

The story of our Church is filled with giving people who were really happy. These people were happy because they knew they were true friends of God. They had generous spirits. They looked for ways to love God by loving others. Saint Teresa of Calcutta is one of these people.

As a young nun, Teresa traveled to Calcutta, India, to teach at a school for girls. During that time, she was deeply moved by the number of sick and dying people on the streets.

One day, she heard God calling her. She felt called to share God's generous love with people she saw. She did just that. She took care of the sick and dying. She washed them and cleaned their sores. She fed them and gave them fresh water. She found a place that she could bring them to and give them a home.

Eventually, other women joined Teresa. Some of these women were her former students. Soon she started an order of religious women called the Missionaries of Charity. Over time, the Missionaries of Charity built homes throughout the world to care for the poor.

In 1979, Mother Teresa received the Nobel Peace Prize. Millions of people admire her life of holiness and love. She is an example of humble and generous service. In 2016, she was canonized, or named Saint Teresa of Calcutta, by Pope Francis.

? Mother Teresa's simple message was, "We are put on Earth to do something beautiful for God." How can being generous help a person do this?

The Way to Happiness

Many people and things here on Earth bring us happiness. The happiness that we experience here is only a glimpse of the happiness that God wants us to have.

Real happiness is the happiness that God created us to have. Jesus taught his disciples that real happiness is being with God. It is being a friend of God now on Earth and forever in Heaven. We come to know and discover this real happiness when we live as Jesus taught us.

One day, a lawyer who knew all about God's Law came to Jesus. He asked Jesus how he could find real happiness:

> The man told Jesus, "I have kept all of God's Laws." Jesus then told the man, "Go sell everything you have and give it to the poor. Come, follow me."
>
> BASED ON MATTHEW 16:19-21

Jesus was telling the man to be as generous to others as God is to him.

FAITH FOCUS
What do the Beatitudes teach us about making good choices that bring us true happiness?

FAITH VOCABULARY
Beatitudes
The Beatitudes are the sayings or teachings of Jesus that describe real happiness, the happiness that God created people to have.

Activity Use the code to discover a message about real happiness.

A	B	C	D	E	F	G	H	I	J	M	L	M
1	2	3	4	5	6	7	8	9	10	11	12	13
N	O	P	Q	R	S	T	U	V	W	X	Y	Z
14	15	16	17	18	19	20	21	22	23	24	25	26

___ ___ ___ ___ ___   ___ ___   ___ ___ ___
8 1 16 16 25   9 19   20 8 5

___ ___ ___ ___ ___ ___   ___ ___ ___   ___ ___ ___ ___ ___ ___
16 5 18 19 15 14   23 8 15   20 18 21 19 20 19

___ ___   ___ ___ ___   ___ ___ ___ ___.
9 14   20 8 5   12 15 18 4

BASED ON PROVERBS 16:20

Faith-Filled People

Saint Louise de Marillac

Louise de Marillac grew up never knowing her mother. As an adult, she founded the Daughters of Charity with Saint Vincent de Paul. The Daughters of Charity work with poor and sick people and with children whose parents had left them when they were born. Saint Louise de Marillac is the patron saint of social workers. The Church celebrates her feast day on March 15.

The Beatitudes

The **Beatitudes** are sayings and teachings of Jesus that describe real happiness. In each of the Beatitudes, Jesus describes one thing that people can do that leads to the happiness that God wants us to have. It is the happiness of people who give their hearts to God.

Read the Beatitudes to discover what Jesus teaches about the happiness that comes from being blessed by God:

"Blessed are the poor in spirit,
for theirs is the kingdom of heaven." MATTHEW 5:3

The poor in spirit have faith in God and trust in his love for them.

"Blessed are they who mourn,
for they will be comforted." MATTHEW 5:4

Those who mourn are sad because people suffer. They show compassion by doing what they can to help.

"Blessed are the meek,
for they will inherit the land." MATTHEW 5:5

The meek are kind and treat others with respect.

"Blessed are they who hunger and thirst
for righteousness,
for they will be satisfied." MATTHEW 5:6

People who hunger for righteousness treat others fairly and work for justice.

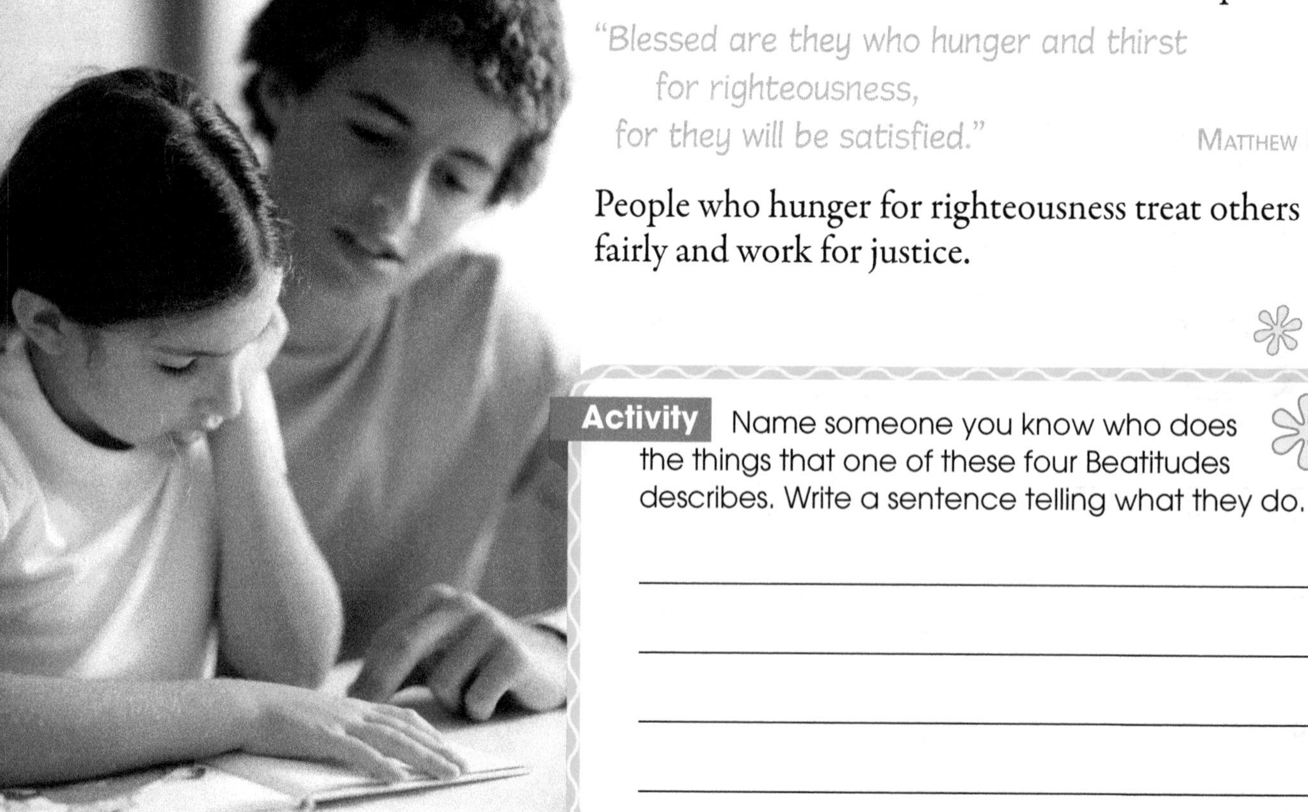

Activity Name someone you know who does the things that one of these four Beatitudes describes. Write a sentence telling what they do.

____

____

____

____

More Beatitudes

The Beatitudes are like signposts on the road of life. They point us in the right direction. They guide us to make choices that lead to the happiness that God wants every person to enjoy. Here are four more Beatitudes that Jesus taught.

"Blessed are the merciful,
for they will be shown mercy." MATTHEW 5:7

People who are merciful forgive others just as God forgives them.

"Blessed are the clean of heart,
for they will see God." MATTHEW 5:8

The clean of heart keep God first in their lives.

"Blessed are the peacemakers,
for they will be called children of God." MATTHEW 5:9

Peacemakers solve problems without hurting anyone.

"Blessed are they who are persecuted for
the sake of righteousness,
for theirs is the kingdom of heaven."
MATTHEW 5:10

Those who are persecuted for the sake of righteousness do what God wants even when others laugh at them or threaten to harm them.

? What Beatitudes are the people in the pictures living?

Catholics Believe

Beatitude and Vocation

The teachings in the Beatitudes reflect God's promises made to the Chosen People since Abraham. They describe the vocation of all of the People of God.

I FOLLOW JESUS

Like everyone else, you want to be happy. When you think of it, the choices you make each day are ways of looking for happiness. Living the Beatitudes is the path to true happiness.

THE WAY TO TRUE HAPPINESS

Write or draw how you can live one of the Beatitudes. Describe the consequences of living that Beatitude.

Beatitude

Consequence

MY FAITH CHOICE

This week, I will try my best to live the Beatitude that I described in the activity. I will

____

____.

Spend a moment quietly praying one of the Beatitudes. Ask for God's grace to understand it better and to live it!

Chapter Review

Write the Beatitude that would help you respond best to this situation.

No one ever seems to choose Sam to be on his or her team. One day at recess, you are chosen to be one of the two captains who will choose players for the kickball teams.

____

____

____

____

____

TO HELP YOU REMEMBER

1. God wants everyone to be blessed and truly happy.
2. The Beatitudes guide us in making choices that lead to the happiness that comes from being blessed by God.
3. Living the Beatitudes leads to the happiness God wants us to have.

Praying the Beatitudes

Praying the Scriptures helps us discover the path to the happiness that God has created us to have. Together, join in praying this ancient form of prayer.

Leader: Dear God, we know that you created us to be happy. We remember that your Son, Jesus, said, "It is your Father's pleasure to give you the kingdom" (based on Luke 12:32).

All: **You show us the path of life. In your presence there is fullness of joy. In your right hand, happiness forever.**

Leader: *(Read Matthew 5:3-10 prayerfully from the Bible. Pause after each Beatitude.)*

All: ***(Respond after each Beatitude.)***
You show us the path of life.

Leader: Holy God, bless us always. Show us the path of life.

All: **Amen.**

With My Family

This Week . . .

In Chapter 18, The Beatitudes, your child learned:

- The Beatitudes are the teachings from the Sermon on the Mount that describe the qualities and actions of the people blessed by God.
- Many things can bring us happiness, but some things do not give true and lasting happiness.
- Living the Beatitudes helps us discover the happiness that God wants us to have.
- People who practice generosity are giving and sharing people. Generous people are happy people.

For more about related teachings of the Church, see the *Catechism of the Catholic Church*, 1716–1724, and the *United States Catholic Catechism for Adults*, page 308.

Sharing God's Word

Read together the Bible verses known as the Beatitudes. You can find these verses on pages 166-167 or in Matthew 5:3-10. Emphasize that in each Beatitude, Jesus describes one thing people do that leads to the happiness God wants us to have.

We Live as Disciples

The Christian family is a school of discipleship. Choose one of the following activities to do as a family, or design a similar activity of your own:

- Play a game of charades using the Beatitudes as the statements to be acted out.
- At your next family meal, discuss the virtue of generosity. How is your family a generous family? Choose a way together to be even more generous with your time, talent, or treasure.

Our Spiritual Journey

Jesus gave his disciples a comprehensive description of what it takes to be a disciple. The Beatitudes describe the kind of life that each of us, as Jesus' followers, are called to live. In this chapter, your child prayed the Beatitudes. Read and pray together the prayer on page 169.

Faith-Filled People

Saint Louise de Marillac
Feast Day: May 9
Saint Louise de Marillac founded the Daughters of Charity, who work with the poor, the ill, and the orphaned.

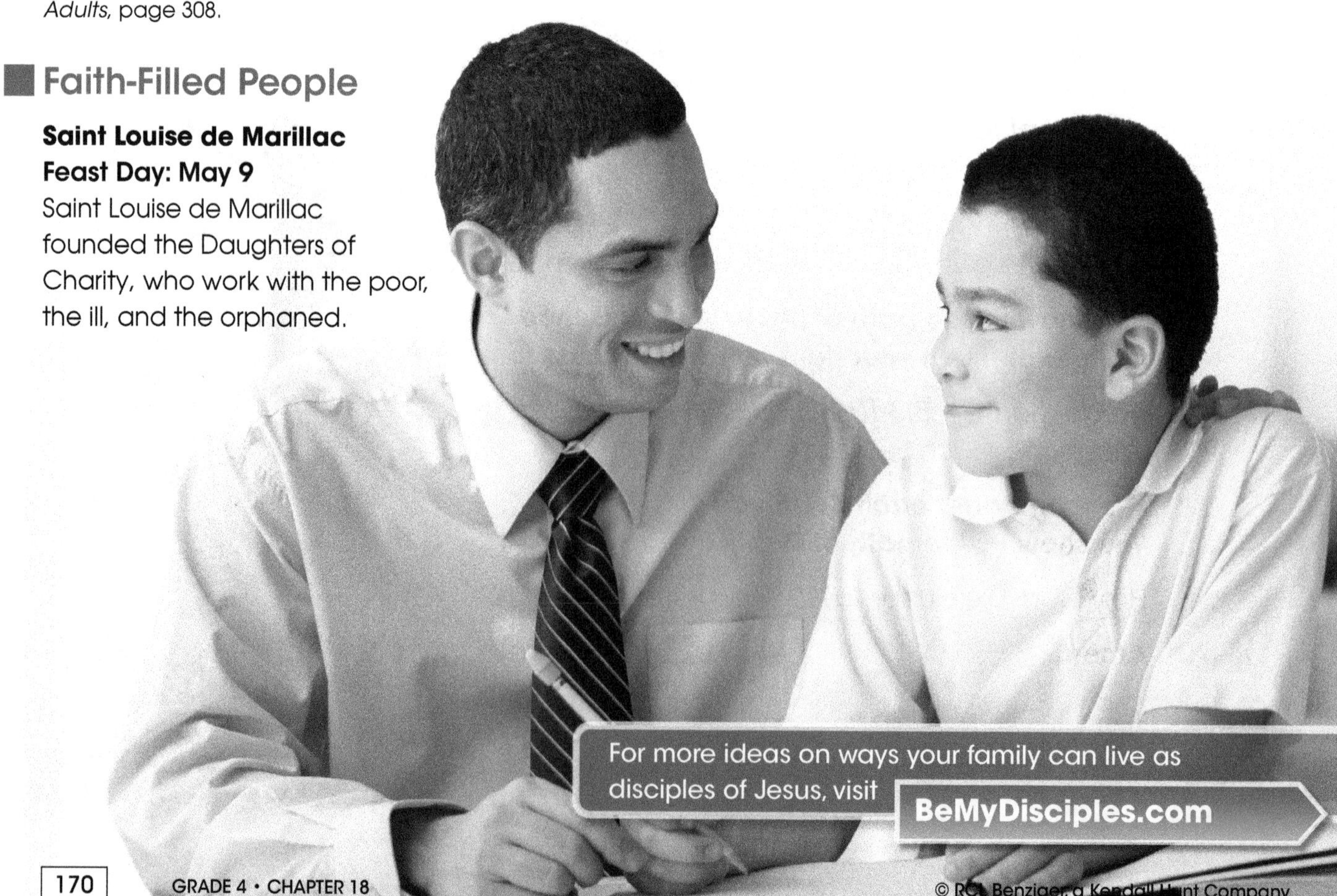

For more ideas on ways your family can live as disciples of Jesus, visit **BeMyDisciples.com**

Putting Others First

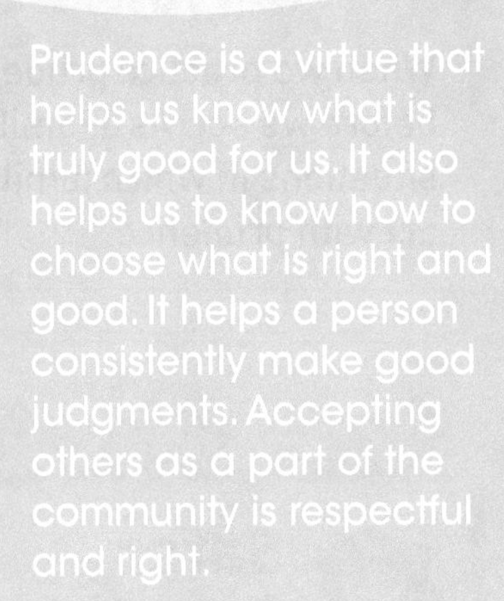

Prudence is a virtue that helps us know what is truly good for us. It also helps us to know how to choose what is right and good. It helps a person consistently make good judgments. Accepting others as a part of the community is respectful and right.

We sometimes feel like treating others in a way that we know is not caring. When this happens, we are being tempted not to live as Jesus taught us to live. Jesus teaches that we are to love God and our neighbors, even those we do not like or understand. We are not to be mean or selfish. This way of loving is called the Greatest Commandment. It says: "You shall love the Lord, your God, with all your heart, with all your soul, and with all your mind. . . . You shall love your neighbor as yourself" (Matthew 22:37, 39).

Jesus also taught an important rule called the Golden Rule. He said, "Do to others whatever you would have them do to you" (Matthew 7:12). We show love by caring for others through our thoughtfulness. A thoughtful person considers the needs of other people. We can practice the Golden Rule by putting ourselves in another's place and thinking about how we would like to be treated.

One person who lived what Jesus taught was Saint Teresa of Calcutta. She formed her own religious community, the Missionaries of Charity, to serve the poor, particularly in India. Mother Teresa believed that with a pure heart you could see God in every person. She once said, "Love does not measure; it just gives."

Activity

List people who are not always treated with respect. Then decide on actions that you will take to show them you care. Share with your family.

PEOPLE WHO ARE NOT TREATED WITH RESPECT:

HOW I WILL SHOW THAT I CARE:

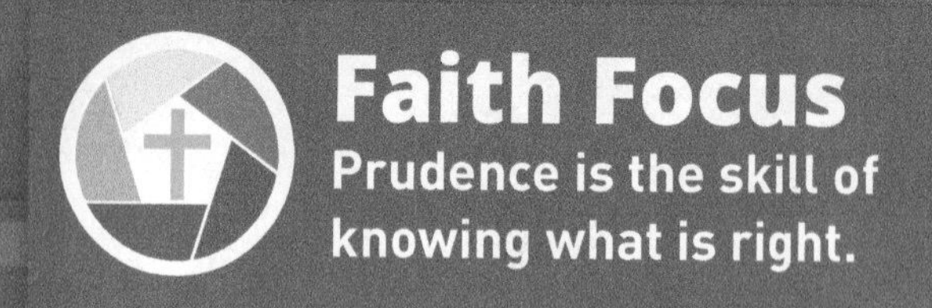

Faith Focus

Prudence is the skill of knowing what is right.

Healthy Habits @ Home

When we practice prudence, we think before we act. As a family, identify two situations in which family members can act with prudence.

1. ....

2. ....

Safer Together

Family members are safer when they know what to do and how to identify and respond to abusive situations. Review the following with your child:

- Teasing can be a form of abuse.
- Intentionally hurting the feelings of another can be a form of abuse.
- You should get away from any person who is abusing you.
- Tell a parent or another trusted adult about the abuse.
- Identify three or four trusted adults whom you can ask for help.

Family Time

Cut out and hang at home

As a family, discuss how you are connected to the community. Address how you are connected to:

- Family
- Friends
- School
- Parish

Family in Action

As a family, name ways that you can live the Greatest Commandment and the Golden Rule this week.

We can live the Greatest Commandment by

....

....

We can live the Golden Rule by

....

....

Looking Ahead

In this chapter, the Holy Spirit invites you to ▶

EXPLORE one way that Catholic families act with justice.

DISCOVER how our consciences guide us in making good choices.

DECIDE to make good choices to live a holy life.

CHAPTER 19

Living a Holy LIfe

? What are some of the good choices that you have made this week?

God never leaves us alone in making good choices. We are to turn to him and listen to him. Listen to this passage from the Book of Psalms:

> How I love your law, Lord!
> I study it all day long.
> Your commandment makes me wiser than my foes,
> as it is forever with me.
> I have more insight than all my teachers,
> because I ponder your testimonies. . . .
> Your word is a lamp for my feet,
> a light for my path.
>
> Psalm 119:97-99, 105

? What is one way that the light of God's Word can help your family and parish make good decisions and live holy lives?

Disciple Power

Justice

Justice is one of the four Cardinal Virtues. It is the good habit of giving to God and to all people what is rightfully due to them. It strengthens us to make decisions that build a world of peace.

THE CHURCH FOLLOWS JESUS

CRS Rice Bowl

The Church is a "light" that God has given us to guide us in making decisions. She is our mother and our teacher.

During Lent, the Church in the United States invites Catholics to take part in Catholic Relief Services Rice Bowl. It asks Catholic families to pray, fast, learn, and share their blessings with people in need.

During Lent, Catholics give up things, such as desserts, snacks, or other things we really like. The money that we save from not buying those things is put into the Rice Bowl box. At the end of Lent, each family brings the money to church. It is collected, and the Church uses it to help people.

The people of St. Rose's parish take part in CRS' Rice Bowl every year. They feel really good and blessed to learn that their money helps farmers in Bolivia receive training to improve their crops. It gives children in Afghanistan the chance to go to school, and it helps fight hunger and poverty here in the United States.

? What does your parish do to act with justice? Make a list.

Our Call to Holiness

God calls everyone to make good choices and to live holy lives. **Conscience** and the four Cardinal Virtues are some of the many gifts that God gives us to help us live holy lives.

Your conscience helps you know and judge what is right and wrong. We need to train our consciences to do a good job. We need to pray, read the Bible, learn the teachings of the Church, and ask people for good advice. It is important to train your conscience correctly. We each have an obligation to do what our conscience says is right and not do what it says is wrong.

Moral virtues are habits of doing what is good. There are four moral virtues that are the foundation of all moral virtues. They are the Cardinal Virtues of prudence, justice, fortitude, and temperance. They help us act on our feelings correctly and do what our consciences and our faith tell us is the right thing to do or say. We must remember that good habits come from practice.

? Think about making an important decision. Tell a friend how your conscience guides you.

FAITH FOCUS
How does God help us make good choices?

FAITH VOCABULARY

conscience
Conscience is the gift that God gives to every person that helps us know and judge what is right and what is wrong.

sanctifying grace
Sanctifying grace is the gift of God sharing his own life with us, the gift of holiness.

Faith-Filled People

Saint Thomas More

Thomas More was the chief lawyer for the king of England. When he was faced with choosing between the wrong that the king wanted him to do and the good that he believed and knew God wanted him to do, Thomas followed his conscience. He chose to serve God. The Church celebrates the feast day of Saint Thomas More on June 22.

Temptation and Sin

Sometimes people and things influence us away from living holy lives. These are called *temptations*. Temptations are not sins but can lead us to sin.

We sin when we knowingly and freely choose to do or say something we know is against God's will. We can also sin by choosing to not do or say something that we know God commands us to do or say. Sin always hurts our friendship with God and other people.

Mortal and Venial Sin. Mortal sin is a serious failure in our love for God, our neighbors, ourselves, or creation. Mortal sin causes us to lose the gift of holiness, or **sanctifying grace**. All other sins are venial sins. Venial sins weaken our love for God and for one another.

Vices. Believe it or not, we can train ourselves to do what we know is against God's will. We can grow in bad habits, or vices. The Church teaches us about seven main vices. These vices are pride, greed, envy, anger, lust, gluttony, and laziness. When we let these bad habits grow in our lives, we train ourselves to sin. It is then very difficult to live holy lives.

Activity How do the actions in the list below help you learn to make good choices, say no to temptation, and avoid sin? Explain to a partner.

- ☐ Read the Bible.
- ☐ Discuss my choices with my parents.
- ☐ Pray to the Holy Spirit.
- ☐ Ask my friends for help.
- ☐ Think quietly about my choices.
- ☐ Listen to my teachers.
- ☐ Talk to the priest in my parish.

Grace

Grace is a free gift from God. At Baptism, we receive the gift of sanctifying grace. The word *sanctifying* means "making holy." Sanctifying grace is the gift of God's own life that he shares with us. It is given by the Holy Spirit to heal us of sin and to make us holy.

The Holy Spirit also gives us special graces when we receive the sacraments. At Baptism, we receive the sevenfold gift of the Holy Spirit. These gifts, which are strengthened in Confirmation, help us live our friendship with God.

The Holy Spirit always gives us the grace to help us live holy lives and to do and say what we know is the right thing. These are called actual graces. If we choose to sin, the Holy Spirit helps us turn away from sin. The Holy Spirit will help us turn our hearts back toward God's love.

Catholics Believe

Lenten Practices

During the season of Lent, the Church guides us to eat less, not to eat meat on certain days, to pray, and to share our blessings with others, especially people in need. These Lenten practices of prayer, abstaining and fasting, and almsgiving are ways that the Church guides us to live holy lives.

Knowledge helps us see the truth of all that God has made known to us.

Wonder and awe, or fear of the Lord, help us praise, thank, and bless God.

Understanding helps us see the connection between knowing our faith and living it.

Wisdom helps us see the world through the eyes of faith. We are helped to see the world as God sees it.

Fortitude, or courage, gives us the strength to make decisions to live as God wants us to live.

Right judgment, or counsel, helps us make good moral choices.

Reverence, or piety, helps us call God Abba, or Father, with love and trust.

Activity

Name someone you know who is living one of the Gifts of the Holy Spirit. Write a haiku, a three-line poem, about this person. Follow the directions under each line.

____
(title)

____
(five syllables)

____
(seven syllables)

____
(five syllables)

I FOLLOW JESUS

Each year you are learning more and more about how to make good choices to live a holy life. Your family and the Church guide you to make those choices. The Holy Spirit gives you the grace to know and choose the way that God wants you to live and to act with justice as God commands.

BECOMING CLOSER TO JESUS

Who helps you learn to live a holy life as a follower of Jesus Christ? How do they help you?

People	How I Am Helped
____________________	____ ____ ____ ____
____________________	____ ____ ____ ____

MY FAITH CHOICE

This week, I will live a holy life by following my conscience and making good choices. One good choice I will make is

____

____.

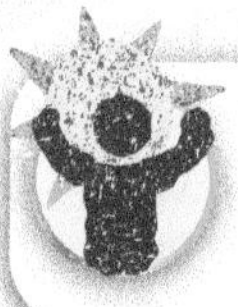

"Holy Spirit, give me the courage to act with justice and to make good choices that show my love for God and others. Amen."

Chapter Review

Write T next to the true statements. Write F next to the false statements. Make the false statements true.

______ **1.** God calls and helps every person live a holy life.

______ **2.** Conscience helps us know and judge what is right and what is wrong.

______ **3.** Moral virtues help us do what our conscience and faith tell us God wants us to do.

______ **4.** The Gifts of the Holy Spirit are prudence, justice, fortitude, and temperance.

TO HELP YOU REMEMBER

1. Conscience and moral virtues help us make choices to live holy lives.
2. Sin is freely choosing to do or say something we know is against God's will, or freely choosing not to do or say something that we know that God commands.
3. The Gifts of the Holy Spirit help us know God and choose to live as children of God and followers of Jesus.

Examination of Conscience

Examining your conscience helps you grow in living the Great Commandment to love God and your neighbor as yourself.

Leader: Let us ask the Holy Spirit to help us think about the choices that we have made. Holy Spirit, help us think about the ways we have chosen to show or not to show our love for God.

All: (*Reflect silently.*)

Leader: Holy Spirit, help us think about the ways we have chosen to show or not to show our love for other people and for ourselves.

All: (*Reflect silently.*)

Leader: God, our loving Father, you sent Jesus to teach us to live the Great Commandment. Send us the Holy Spirit to help us live holy lives as Jesus taught us to do.

All: **Amen.**

With My Family

This Week . . .

In Chapter 19, Living a Holy Life, your child learned:

- At Baptism, we receive the gift of sanctifying grace.
- Every person is born with a conscience. Conscience helps us know and judge what is and is not in agreement with God's will.
- Cardinal Virtues of prudence, justice, fortitude, and temperance and the Gifts of the Holy Spirit strengthen us to make choices that contribute to our living holy lives.
- We sometimes knowingly and freely sin. We choose to not live holy lives. When we sin, God invites us back to a life of friendship with him.
- Justice is one of the four Cardinal Virtues. It is the good habit of giving to God and to all people what is rightfully due to them.

For more about related teachings of the Church, see the *Catechism of the Catholic Church,* 1776–1794, 1803–1832, 1846–1869, and 1996–2004, and the *United States Catholic Catechism for Adults,* pages 108, 314–315, 315–317, 341.

Sharing God's Word

Read together Psalm119:97-99, 105. Emphasize that conscience, the Cardinal Virtues, and the Gifts of the Holy Spirit help us make good choices to live by God's commands.

We Live as Disciples

The Christian family is a school of discipleship. Choose one of the following activities to do as a family, or design a similar activity of your own:

- Share with each other some of the good choices you each made this past week. Explain why you made the choices and what happened after you made the choices.
- Identify someone who is living one of the Gifts of the Holy Spirit. Talk about that gift and how it might help your family live as a Christian family. Then discuss how your family can cooperate with the graces of the Holy Spirit and act with justice as God commands.

Our Spiritual Journey

Followers of Christ have the obligation and duty to form good consciences through study and prayer, such as with the Word of God and through practice. In this chapter, your child learned about and used a brief examination of conscience. Developing and using the discipline of examining one's conscience daily will enable the light of God's Word to guide you in living a holy life.

Faith-Filled People

Saint Thomas More
Feast Day: June 22
Thomas More was faced with a difficult decision. Thomas More followed his conscience and chose to serve God.

For more ideas on ways your family can live as disciples of Jesus, visit **BeMyDisciples.com**

Being Responsible

Members of a family have responsibilities toward one another—children toward parents, parents toward children, and spouse toward spouse. Family members have the rightful expectation that they can depend on one another—in good times and in bad times. Being a responsible member of the family is an expression of love and respect.

Our families depend on us. They trust that we will be responsible not only at home but in other places too. We show responsibility and dependability at school, at our friends' homes, and at church. Being responsible to our families and friends shows that they can depend on us to meet our obligations to them. We honor our parents and demonstrate our love for them by doing what they ask. When we act this way, we practice the virtue of justice.

As we grow physically, we are also growing in love. We come to see that love includes both giving and receiving. When we give of our time and of our talents for the benefit of someone else, we demonstrate self-giving love. Jesus is our model for such love.

Catholics Believe

Justice is the virtue that strengthens us to act responsibly and give to God and others what is due to them, making sure they have what they need.

Activity Talk with your family about ways you can grow in self-giving love. Write your ideas in the chart.

IN MY FAMILY	AT SCHOOL	IN MY PARISH

Family Life Connection

Cut out and hang at home

Healthy Habits @ Home

When we share with others what is due to them, we act with justice. With your family, decide on two ways you can act with justice this week.

We can act with justice by:

1. ....

2. ....

Family Time

Discuss as a family what it means to be responsible. Use the following to keep the conversation on topic:

- Brainstorm the various responsibilities of family members.
- Offer examples of people acting responsibly. Who is a good role model for responsibility?
- What characteristics does a person who is responsible demonstrate?

Faith Focus

Justice strengthens us to act responsibly.

Family in Action

Discuss, as a family, the needs of people in your community. Then make a decision to help someone in need.

- Who is someone in our community who is in need and whom we can help?

....

- What can we do to show this person that he or she can depend on us?

....

Safer Together

Families are safer together when children can turn to and depend on trusted adults. Spend time with your child identifying trusted adults. Here are a few tips to help:

- Children need to identify a few people with whom they can feel comfortable talking with about important issues.
- Trusted adults should be supporting you as a parent.
- Parents can help their children identify people outside the family yet within the community whom they can trust.

Looking Ahead

In this chapter, the Holy Spirit invites you to ▶

EXPLORE how Peter Claver sought God with all his heart.

DISCOVER that the Ten Commandments are God's Laws.

DECIDE to put the Ten Commandments into action.

CHAPTER 20

Living God's Covenant

❓ What are you learning about the great leaders and events of our nation?

The Bible is the story of the People of God listening to God and striving to know, love, and serve him. Sometimes God's people listened, but sometimes they did not. Listen to why it is important to listen to God's Word. God tells us,

> *Blessed are people who observe God's decrees,*
> *who walk by the teaching of the Lord,*
> *and who seek him with all their heart.*
> *They do no wrong, they walk in God's ways.*
>
> Based on Psalm 119:1-3

❓ What have you learned about God's decrees or Laws?

Fortitude

Fortitude is one of the four Cardinal Virtues. It is the good habit of facing difficulties with strength and courage. Fortitude strengthens us to resist temptation. Fortitude helps us overcome the things in our lives that keep us from loving God and others.

The Apostle of the Slaves

The story of the Church is filled with leaders who learned and followed God's decrees, or Laws. Each lived the words of the psalm you just prayed. They sought God with all their hearts. Peter Claver is one of those people.

Peter was the son of a farmer. More than four hundred years ago, he left his home in Spain and braved crossing the Atlantic Ocean. He traveled to Cartagena, which is now in Colombia, South America. Each year more than ten thousand enslaved people arrived by ship in Cartagena and were forced to work as slaves in the mines.

Peter boarded the ships, climbed down into the hulls, and cared for the slaves. He followed them into the mines and fed them, took care of their wounds, clothed them, and prayed with them. The slave owners and even some of the people of his parish ridiculed Peter as "the slave of the slaves." Others honored Peter with the title "the Apostle of the Slaves."

The work of Peter Claver shows us what happens when we respect the dignity and life of every person. The Church honors Peter as a saint and celebrates his feast day on March 9.

? Who do you know who has helped people by showing strength and courage? Explain.

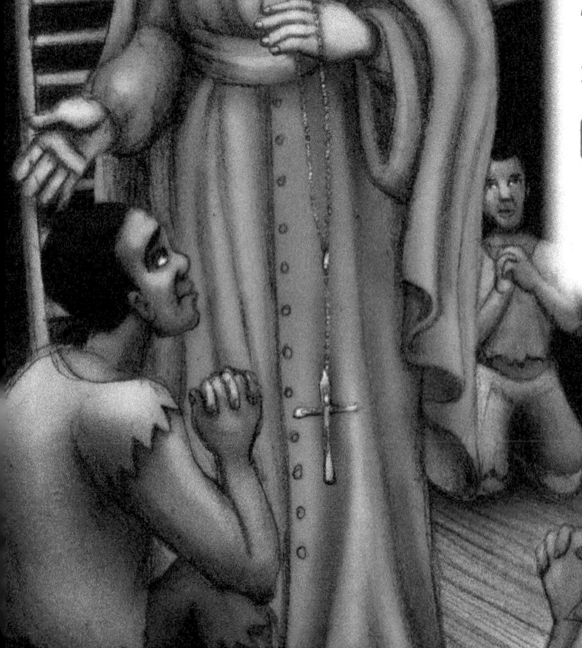

The Ten Commandments

Moses was one of the great leaders of God's people. God revealed to Moses the decrees, or Laws, that his people were to follow. These laws would guide them to live the Covenant that they entered into with God.

God chose Moses to lead the Israelites, or **Hebrews** as they were also called, out of slavery in Egypt to a new homeland. This journey from slavery to freedom is known as the Exodus. The heart of the Exodus story is the Covenant, or solemn agreement, that God and the Israelites made with each other.

God promised to be faithful and loyal to the Israelites forever. The Israelites in turn promised,

"Everything the LORD has said, we will do." Exodus 19:8

FAITH FOCUS
What does the story of the Exodus tell us about God's people?

FAITH VOCABULARY

Hebrews
Hebrews is the name given to God's people, the Israelites, when they lived in Egypt.

Ten Commandments
The Ten Commandments are the Laws of the Covenant revealed to Moses on Mount Sinai. They teach us to love God, others, and ourselves.

Activity Name the abilities that Moses would need to be a good leader of God's people. Choose one ability, and describe how it would help Moses.

____

____

____

____

____

____

____

Faith-Filled People

Saint Charles Lwanga and Companions

Charles Lwanga lived in the kingdom of Buganda, which is now part of the country of Uganda, Africa. Charles and twenty-one other young men, many of whom were teenagers, were killed on June 3, 1886. They were killed because they followed God's Laws, challenged the king's practices, and called attention to his sins. Charles and the other martyrs were proclaimed saints in 1964. The feast of the Ugandan Martyrs is celebrated on June 3.

The Lord Calls Moses

The Bible tells us that Moses saw the people's faith in God growing weak as they journeyed across the desert. So Moses went up Mount Sinai. He prayed there to learn what he should do.

When Moses came down, he told the elders of the Israelites:

> God said, "I am coming to you in a dense cloud, so that when the people hear me speaking with you, they may always have faith in you also."
>
> For three days the Israelites prepared themselves to meet God. On the morning of the third day, the Lord called Moses, and he went up to the top of Mount Sinai. God gave Moses the Ten Commandments.
>
> Based on Exodus 19:9, 14-16, 20; 20:1

The **Ten Commandments** are a sign of God's love for people. They helped the Israelites learn to live faithfully the Covenant they made with God. When we live the Ten Commandments, we faithfully live our Baptism. We live our covenant with God. We live as faithful adopted sons and daughters of God. We grow in our faith and hope in God and in our love for God.

? How is God giving us the Ten Commandments a sign of his love for us?

The Decalogue

The Decalogue is another name for the Ten Commandments. The word *decalogue* means "ten words." The Ten Commandments are God's Word to us. They are the Laws that teach us how to love God, ourselves, and other people.

Jesus, the Son of God, came to show us how to live the Ten Commandments. He said,

> "Whoever obeys and teaches these commandments will be called greatest in the kingdom of heaven."
>
> MATTHEW 5:19

The choices we make to live the Ten Commandments are signs of our faith and hope in God and of our love for God.

Catholics Believe

Social Teachings of the Catholic Church

The social teachings of the Catholic Church help us live the Ten Commandments. The Church has summarized its social teachings around themes, or main ideas. Two such themes are:

1. Every human life is sacred.
2. We have a responsibility to care for people who are treated unjustly.

Activity Design these tablets containing the Ten Commandments with words and symbols that remind you to live the Commandments.

Love God with All Your Heart

1. I am the Lord your God; you shall not have strange gods before me.
2. You shall not take the name of the Lord your God in vain.
3. Remember to keep holy the Lord's Day.

Love Yourself and Others

4. Honor your father and your mother.
5. You shall not kill.
6. You shall not commit adultery.
7. You shall not steal.
8. You shall not bear false witness against your neighbor.
9. You shall not covet your neighbor's wife.
10. You shall not covet your neighbor's goods.

I FOLLOW JESUS

Each day you learn about people who are working to free people who are slaves to drugs, food, money, and other things. The Holy Spirit helps you live the Ten Commandments and be free from these and other things that take away your freedom.

THE WAY OF FREEDOM

In the circle, write several things from which people need to be freed. In the space around the circle, write what you can do to keep yourself and others free from what you have written in the circle.

____

____

MY FAITH CHOICE

This week, I will think about my actions and put the Ten Commandments into action. I will

____

______________________________.

Pray to the Holy Spirit for the virtue of fortitude so that you will be able to face difficulties with strength and courage.

Chapter Review

Place the letter of each word in the right column in front of the phrase in the left column that best describes it.

Descriptions	Faith Words
______ **1.** Another name for the Israelites	**a.** Decalogue
______ **2.** Led God's people out of slavery in Egypt	**b.** Covenant
______ **3.** Shows us how to live the Commandments	**c.** Hebrews
______ **4.** Another name for the Ten Commandments	**d.** Moses
______ **5.** The solemn agreement that God made with the Hebrews	**e.** Jesus

TO HELP YOU REMEMBER

1. During the Exodus, God gave Moses the Ten Commandments on Mount Sinai.
2. The Ten Commandments are the Laws that teach us how to love God and our neighbors as ourselves.
3. Jesus came to show us how to live the Ten Commandments.

A Prayer of Meditation

A meditation is a prayer in which we use our imagination. We place ourselves in the Bible story and ask the Holy Spirit to teach us to live God's commands as Jesus taught.

1. Close your eyes. Remember that the Holy Spirit lives within you.
2. Recall the story of Moses leading God's people out of Egypt through the desert.
3. Imagine that you are Moses and that God is speaking to you. Read or listen as your catechist reads Exodus 19:9-20.
4. Remember that Jesus came to fulfill the Ten Commandments. Spend some quiet time in prayer and conversation with God.
5. Ask the Holy Spirit to teach you to live the Ten Commandments and be a sign of faith, hope, and love for others.

With My Family

This Week . . .

In Chapter 20, Living God's Covenant, your child learned:

- God revealed the Ten Commandments to Moses and the Israelites. The Ten Commandments are the Laws that guide all people to love God with all their hearts and to love their neighbor as themselves.
- Jesus taught that we are to obey and live the Ten Commandments.
- Fortitude, one of the four Cardinal Virtues, is the good habit of facing difficulties in living according to God's laws with strength and courage.

For more about related teachings of the Church, see the *Catechism of the Catholic Church,* 2052–2074, and the *United States Catholic Catechism for Adults,* pages 341–457.

Sharing God's Word

Read together Exodus 19:9-20, the story of Moses and the Ten Commandments, or read the adaptation of the story on page 182. Emphasize that the Ten Commandments are signs of God's love for people and that living the Ten Commandments is a sign of the love of people for God.

We Live as Disciples

The Christian family is a school of discipleship. Choose one of the following activities to do as a family, or design a similar activity of your own:

- Name the ways in which your family follows the Ten Commandments.
- Talk together about why rules and laws are necessary. Discuss the rules and laws that help your family live as a Christian family.

Our Spiritual Journey

When we practice the spiritual discipline of prayer, we are led into an ever-deepening awareness of God's presence and love. Saint Teresa of Ávila said that prayer is being on terms of friendship with God. Meditation is an ancient prayer form that deepens this friendship. In this chapter, your child prayed a meditation. Pray together the meditation on page 185.

Faith-Filled People

Saint Charles Lwanga and Companions
Feast Day: June 3
Saint Charles was martyred because he obeyed God. Charles Lwanga is the patron saint of African youth.

For more ideas on ways your family can live as disciples of Jesus, visit **BeMyDisciples.com**

Fair or Foul?

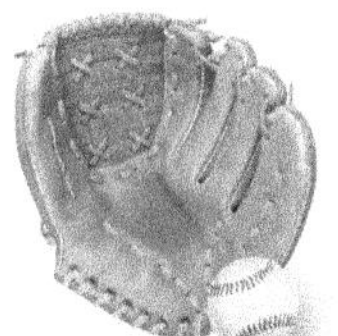

For your birthday, your family is taking you and your friends to a baseball game. You are excited! You will get to see your team play—the team that won the championship last year. You are sitting in the perfect seats for catching a foul ball. Happily, you have remembered to bring your glove.

The game starts. In between eating peanuts and cotton candy, you anxiously watch for the foul ball that might come your way. Your favorite player is up at bat. Full count: three balls, two strikes. The batter swings. It is a foul ball sailing directly above your head! It comes down ten rows above your seat. A boy reaches out to catch it. The ball bounces into his glove, and then gets knocked out as others rush in. In the mad scramble, the ball falls through the seats. It lands at your feet. Quickly grabbing it, you raise it high in the sky, triumphant. Your friends yell and scream with excitement. Looking up, you see the face of the boy in the stands who had first caught the ball.

Put yourself in the place of the boy who first caught the ball. If you were that boy, how would you like to be treated? Then decide. What is fair? What do you think is the right thing to do?

Catholics Believe

We act with love and justice toward others.

Activity Discuss the scenario with your family. What are the possible actions you could take after finding the ball at your feet? Decide which action you will take. Draw a picture of what you will do here.

Faith Focus

We show love through thoughtfulness toward others.

Healthy Habits @ Home

Putting ourselves in another person's shoes helps us choose to act with justice and fairness toward others. We can make courageous, self-giving decisions that put the other person's feelings first.

Safer Together

Use these tips to help your children feel safe when they are at large events with many people.

1. Keep the lines of communication open with your children. Set a rule that they cannot wander off or go anywhere at the venue without your permission.
2. Have your children use the buddy system. Make sure they are always accompanied by a buddy when, for example, using the restrooms or purchasing items from vendors.
3. Remind your children that, in an emergency, they should look for adults who can be trusted, such as security officers, or a parent with children.
4. Establish a simple plan that your children can follow in the event they get lost or separated from you or the adults they are with.

Family Time

Cut out and hang at home

Use the scenario as an opportunity to help your child make courageous choices.

1. Ask your child how he or she would feel to have been the boy in the stands who caught the ball and then lost it. "How would you feel?" "What would you want the boy who ended up with the ball to do?"

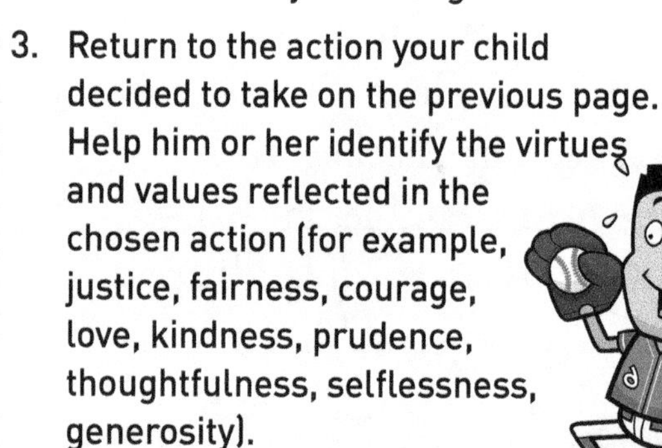

2. Invite your child to put him- or herself in the shoes of the child who found the ball but did not catch it. Ask questions to identify how the child might feel. These might include: "How would you feel?" "How hard would it be to return the ball to the boy who caught it?"
3. Return to the action your child decided to take on the previous page. Help him or her identify the virtues and values reflected in the chosen action (for example, justice, fairness, courage, love, kindness, prudence, thoughtfulness, selflessness, generosity).

Unit 5 **Review**

Name ______________________________

A. Choose the Best Word

Fill in the blanks to complete each of the sentences. Use the words from the word bank.

Decalogue	emotions	conscience
intellect	Beatitudes	sacraments

1. Our ______________ gives us the power to know God.

2. Our ______________ are gifts from God that help us make decisions to do or say something.

3. The ______________ are sayings and teachings of Jesus that describe people truly blessed by God.

4. Our ______________ helps us judge what is right or good and what is wrong or evil.

5. The ______________ is another name for the Ten Commandments.

B. Show What You Know

Match the items in Column A with those in Column B.

Column A

1. prudence

2. soul

3. generosity

4. justice

5. fortitude

Column B

____ **a.** spiritual part of every person that lives forever

____ **b.** strengthens us to give to God and others what is rightfully due to them

____ **c.** good habit of sharing our blessings with others

____ **d.** strengthens us to make good choices with courage when they are difficult to make

____ **e.** strength to know what is truly good

C. Connect with Scripture

Reread the Scripture passage on page 153.
What connection do you see between this passage and what you learned in this unit?

____

____

____

D. Be a Disciple

1. *Review the four pages in this unit titled The Church Follows Jesus. What person or ministry of the Church on these pages will inspire you to be a better disciple of Jesus? Explain your answer.*

____

____

____

2. *Work with a group. Review the four Disciple Power virtues or gifts you have learned about in this unit. After writing your own ideas, share with the group practical ways that you will live these virtues or gifts day by day.*

____

____

____

We Live

UNIT 6

Part Two

Peter and Cornelius

Cornelius was a commander of Roman soldiers who graciously welcomed Simon Peter to his home. Cornelius said, "We are all here in the presence of God to listen to all that you have been commanded by the Lord."

Peter said, "In truth, God accepts everyone who lives according to his will."

Peter proclaimed the good news of Jesus' life, death, and rising from the dead. As Peter was speaking, the holy Spirit came upon all who were listening to the word. Seeing this, Peter baptized Cornelius and his whole household in the name of Jesus Christ.

Based on Acts of the Apostles, Chapter 10:25-48

What I Have Learned

What is something you already know about these three faith terms?

worship

____

____

____

Third Commandment

____

____

____

reparation

____

____

____

Faith Terms to Know

Put an X next to the faith terms you know. Put a ? next to faith terms you need to learn more about.

_______ honor

_______ respect

_______ Lord's Day

_______ Rabbi

_______ covet

_______ Lord's Prayer

_______ Fourth Commandment

The Bible

What do you know about the Seventh Commandment?

____

____

____

The Church

What do you know about why we pray the Our Father?

____

____

____

A Question I Have

What question would you like to ask about living the Ten Commandments?

____

____

____

Popular Devotions

Our Lady of Regla

A Devotion from Cuba

The feast of Our Lady of Regla is celebrated on September 8.

Devotion to Our Lady of Regla is believed to have begun in Africa in the fourth century. Popular belief says that Saint Augustine placed an image of the Blessed Virgin Mary in his chapel. The chapel was attacked thirteen years later. The monks fled to Spain. They took the image with them. The image of Our Lady was placed in the new monastery, facing the ocean.

It is not clear when the image became known as Our Lady of Regla. The word regla means "rule." It may refer to the Augustinian rule that the monks lived by. Sailors brought the devotion from Spain to Cuba.

The shrine to Our Lady of Regla in Cuba faces the harbor. It is located in a village outside of Havana. The village is called Regla. The shrine is the first thing sailors see when ships arrive at the Port of Havana. Sailors believe it is a sign of the Virgin Mary's protection. Our Lady of Regla was declared Patroness of the Bay of Havana in 1714.

Devotion to Our Lady of Regla has been spread from Spain to Cuba by monks, lay people, and sailors who consider her their protectress. Those who leave Cuba often continue the devotion in the places where they have settled. The feast of Our Lady of Regla is celebrated on September 8. This is also the feast of the birth of Mary.

? Sailors believe Our Lady of Regla keeps watch over them. In what ways does Mary watch over you?

Popular Devotions

Our Lady of Regla

The monks and the sailors believe that Our Lady of Regla protects them from harm. Design a prayer card for Our Lady of Regla. Draw an image of Our Lady in one box. In the other box, write a prayer asking her to keep you safe.

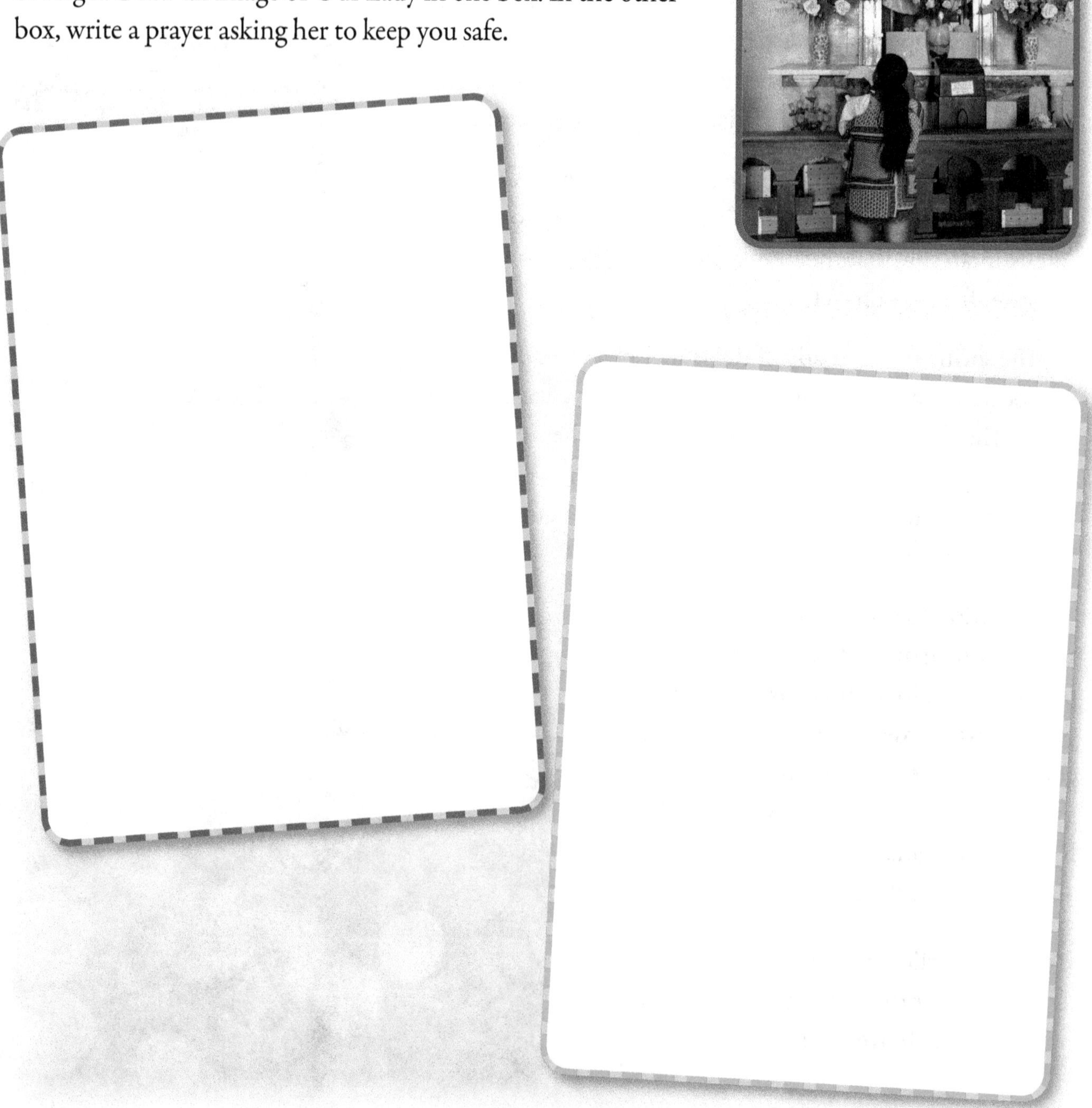

Looking Ahead

In this chapter, the Holy Spirit invites you to ▶

EXPLORE how Saint Joan of Arc stayed true to loving God.

DISCOVER what the first three Commandments teach.

DECIDE how to keep God first in your life.

CHAPTER 21

Love God with All Your Heart

? Who is someone you consider to be the best at doing something?

One day, a Pharisee wanted to quiz Jesus. He wanted to see what Jesus would say about the Ten Commandments. He asked him, "Teacher, which commandment is the greatest?" Listen to what Jesus tells him:

> "You shall love the Lord, your God, with all your heart, with all your soul, and with all your mind. This is the greatest and the first commandment."
>
> BASED ON MATTHEW 22:34-38

? How do you show that God is first in your life?

Diligence

Diligence is when you stick with something and have resolve. A person who practices the virtue of diligence is committed and stays true to loving God first and foremost.

THE CHURCH FOLLOWS JESUS

Saint Joan of Arc

Everyone wants to be "number 1," but almost every day the number 1 team, song, or movie changes. Jesus taught us that God is always number 1—and the only number 1—and that never changes!

Joan of Arc knew that God is first. She lived by the motto "Let God be served first." Joan grew up in a time of war between her country, France, and England. Joan believed that God was calling her to help France. Joan became a soldier and led France during the war. Joan's decision changed her life and the life of the French people.

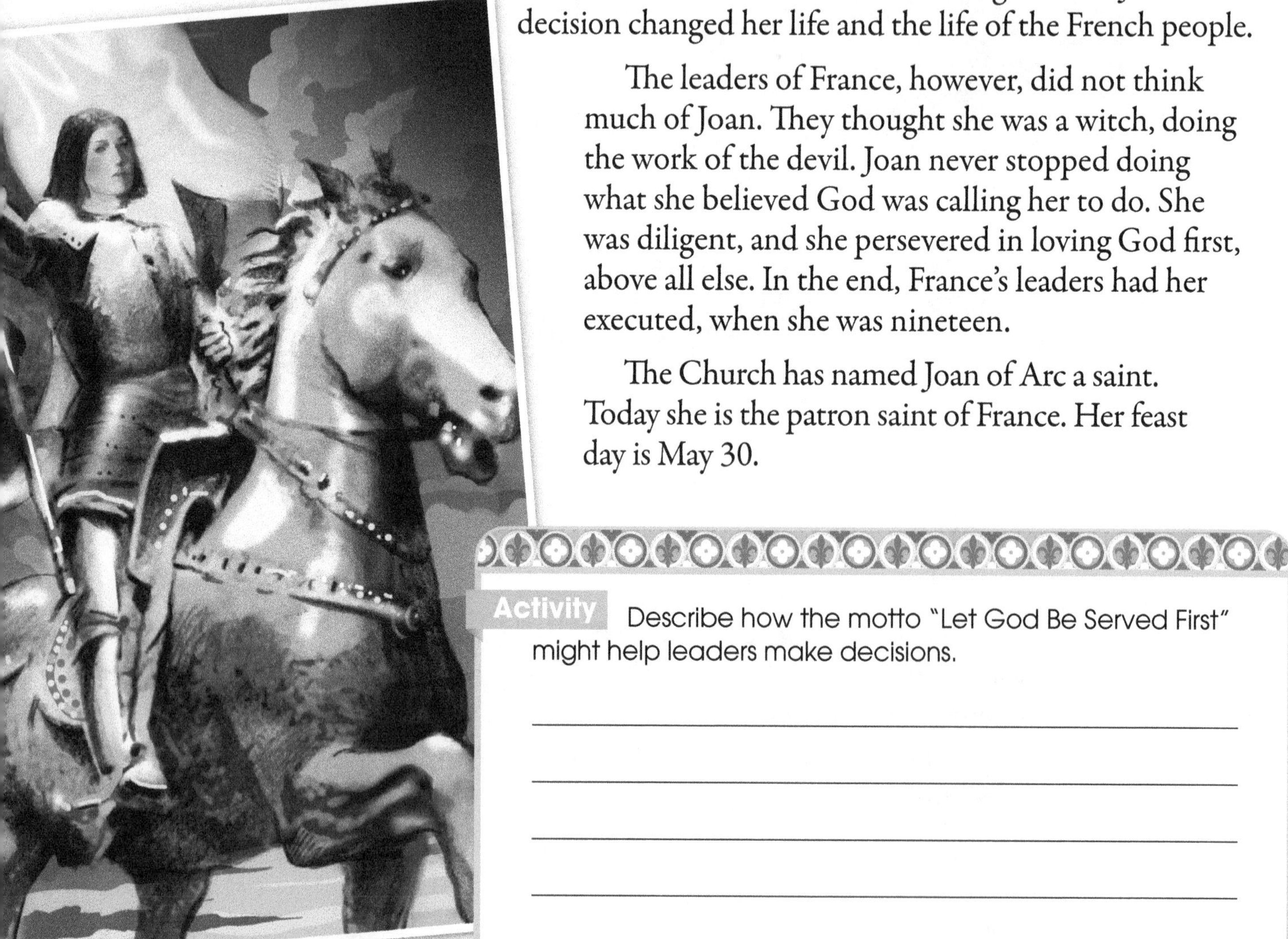

The leaders of France, however, did not think much of Joan. They thought she was a witch, doing the work of the devil. Joan never stopped doing what she believed God was calling her to do. She was diligent, and she persevered in loving God first, above all else. In the end, France's leaders had her executed, when she was nineteen.

The Church has named Joan of Arc a saint. Today she is the patron saint of France. Her feast day is May 30.

Activity Describe how the motto "Let God Be Served First" might help leaders make decisions.

____

____

____

____

____

____

God, the Center of Our Lives

FAITH FOCUS

How do the first three of the Ten Commandments help us show our love for God?

FAITH VOCABULARY

worship
To worship is to honor and respect above all else, to give adoration and praise to God.

Lord's Day
The Lord's Day is the name given to Sunday by Christians because Sunday is the day of the Lord's Resurrection.

The First, Second, and Third Commandments teach us that we are to love God with all our heart, with our whole mind, and with our whole soul. The First Commandment calls for our faith:

> I am the Lord your God: you shall not have strange gods before me. BASED ON EXODUS 20:2-3

The First Commandment teaches that God is first in our lives and that this should never change. Only God is worthy of our **worship**. To worship someone or something means that the person or thing is the center of our lives. We honor and love God above all else.

Jesus taught that no person or thing can ever take the place of God in our lives. We are not to allow any person or any thing to weaken or break our friendship with God.

> The LORD alone is God.
> BASED ON DEUTERONOMY 6:4

? What are some ways fourth graders can show that God is "number 1" in their lives? Share your ideas with the whole group.

Old Testament Prophets

The prophets were people God chose to speak in his name. There are eighteen prophetic books in the Old Testament. These books contain the teachings of the prophets.

The Second Commandment

One of the most important ways that we show our respect and love for someone is by the way that we speak about him or her, or use his or her name. The Second Commandment calls for respect of God:

> You shall not [take] the name of the LORD, your God, in vain. . . .
>
> EXODUS 20:7

The Second Commandment teaches that we are to use God's name with respect. Respect is a virtue that helps us honor God by everything we say or do. We especially must never use God's name to make people believe that a lie is the truth.

The Second Commandment also teaches that we must use the name *Jesus*, the name *Mary*, and the names of the saints with respect. We are to treat holy things and holy places with respect. When we live this way, we do not take God's name in vain. We show our respect and love for God.

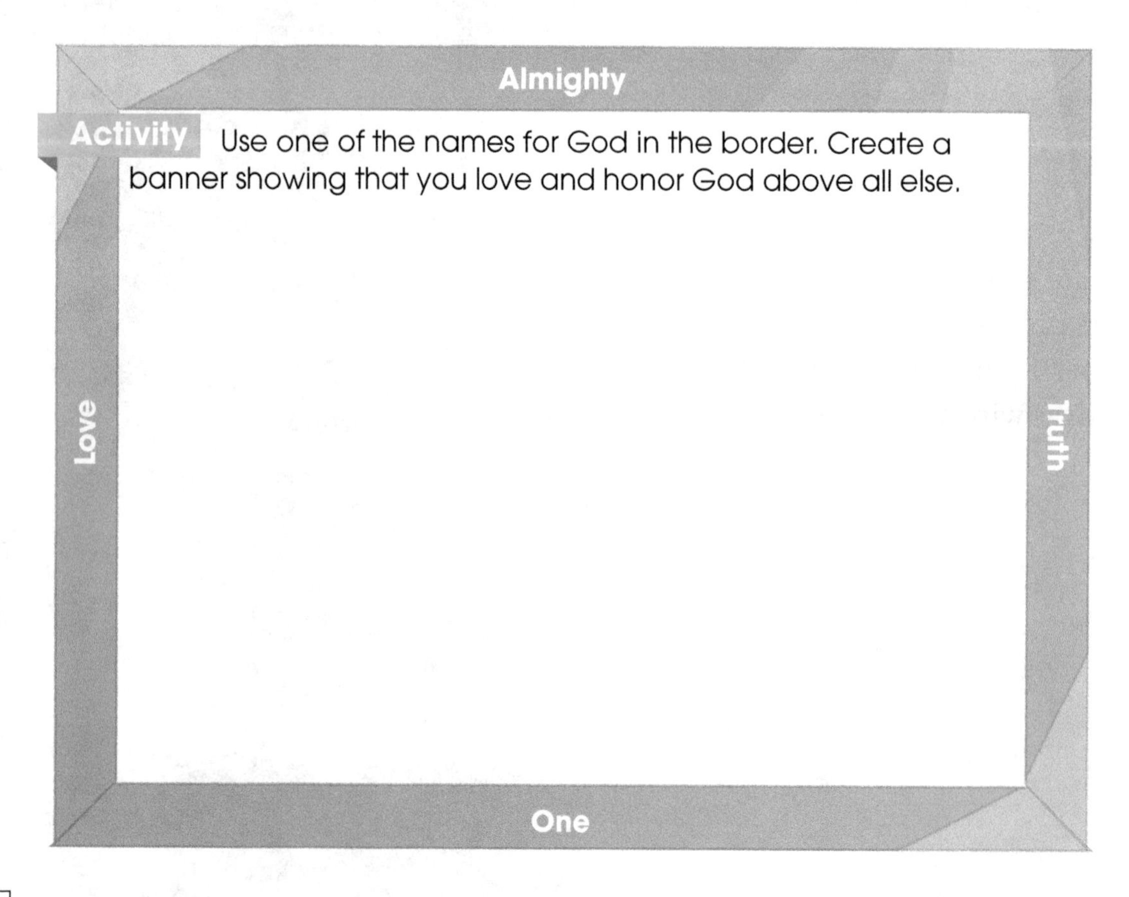

Activity Use one of the names for God in the border. Create a banner showing that you love and honor God above all else.

The Third Commandment

The Third Commandment teaches that we must set aside one day each week for the Lord God. For Christians, Sunday is the **Lord's Day**. It is the day of the Lord's Resurrection. The Third Commandment is:

Remember to keep holy the Lord's Day.

BASED ON EXODUS 20:8

Catholics live the Third Commandment by gathering for Mass on Saturday evening or Sunday to worship God. Catholics also gather for Mass on holy days of obligation.

We also live the Third Commandment by resting from unnecessary work on Sundays. On the Lord's Day, we do things that celebrate and keep God at the center of our lives all week long.

? What is one way that you might live the First, Second, or Third Commandment this week?

Catholics Believe

Precepts of the Church

The precepts of the Church are rules that the Church gives us. The precepts of the Church help us meet our responsibilities to worship God and grow in our love for God and our neighbor.

I FOLLOW JESUS

You do many things each day that show that God is first in your life. These things help others see the good things that happen when people put God first and live by his Commandments.

PUTTING GOD FIRST!

Create a bulletin board that shows why keeping God at the center of your life makes a difference. Write or draw your ideas in the space provided.

MY FAITH CHOICE

This week, I will try to remember to keep God number 1 in my life. I will

____

____.

Take a moment to thank God for his presence in your life. Pray that you will be diligent in loving God first and foremost.

Chapter Review

Match the terms in Column A with the Commandments in Column B. One of the Commandments can be used more than one time.

	Column A	Column B
____	**1.** Lord's Day	**a.** First Commandment
____	**2.** respect	**b.** Second Commandment
____	**3.** worship	**c.** Third Commandment
____	**4.** holy days of obligation	

TO HELP YOU REMEMBER

1. The First Commandment teaches that we are to worship only God.
2. The Second Commandment teaches that we are to show our love and respect for the name of God and all that belongs to God.
3. The Third Commandment teaches that we are to set aside one day each week as the Lord's Day. Christians set aside Sunday as the Lord's Day.

The Divine Praises

The Divine Praises is a prayer written to praise and honor God. Kneel and repeat each of the phrases after the leader.

Blessed be God.

Blessed be his holy name.

Blessed be Jesus Christ, true God and true man.

Blessed be the name of Jesus.

Blessed be his most Sacred Heart.

Blessed be his most precious Blood.

Blessed be Jesus in the most holy Sacrament of the altar.

Blessed be the Holy Spirit, the Paraclete.

Blessed be the great Mother of God, Mary most holy.

Blessed be her holy and Immaculate Conception.

Blessed be her glorious Assumption.

Blessed be the name of Mary, Virgin and Mother.

Blessed be Saint Joseph, her most chaste spouse.

Blessed be God in his angels and in his saints.

With My Family

This Week . . .

In Chapter 21, Love God with All Your Heart, your child learned:

- The First Commandment teaches that God is and always should be at the center of our lives. In all we do and say, we strive to give glory and honor to God.
- The Second Commandment teaches that we are to show respect for God's name and for all holy people, places, and things.
- The Third Commandment teaches that we must make one day each week the Lord's Day.
- For Christians, Sunday is the Lord's Day. On Sundays, Catholics gather to celebrate Mass. All that we do and say refreshes us and helps us keep God at the center of our lives throughout the week.
- The virtue of diligence helps us persevere in loving God first and foremost.

For more about related teachings of the Church, see the *Catechism of the Catholic Church*, 2084–2132, 2142–2159, 2168–2188, and the *United States Catholic Catechism for Adults*, pages 339–371.

Sharing God's Word

Read together the first part of the Great Commandment on page 191 or in Matthew 22:37. Emphasize that the First, Second, and Third Commandments help us keep God at the center of our lives.

We Live as Disciples

The Christian family is a school of discipleship. Choose one of the following activities to do as a family, or design a similar activity of your own:

- Look through magazines or take a walk through a store as a family. Talk about how the displays might tempt people not to keep God as number 1 in their lives.
- Talk about the ways that your family keeps Sunday holy. Choose one thing that you will do this week to keep Sunday holy.

Our Spiritual Journey

Remembering is a profoundly spiritual act. We remember that God is our God, that he created us in his image, and that he is at the center of our lives. We remember that he is present in each and every moment of our day. When we remember God, we are moved to prayer. The Divine Praises are a series of praises that Catholics have prayed for generations. We can recite this beautiful prayer any time and anywhere, to remember and to give glory and honor to God. In this chapter, your child prayed the Divine Praises. Read and pray together the prayer on page 197.

Faith-Filled People

Old Testament Prophets

The Old Testament prophets were the people God chose to speak in his name. There are eighteen prophetic books in the Old Testament.

For more ideas on ways your family can live as disciples of Jesus, visit **BeMyDisciples.com**

Welcoming Differences

Sometimes people are wrongfully excluded from groups because they look different or act differently. When this happens, they are treated with prejudice. Treating a person with prejudice does not respect the dignity of a person.

Sometimes people are excluded from a group through teasing. Teasing can hurt the heart of another person. When teasing someone becomes mean and hurtful, we are deliberately choosing to tell that person that we do not want him or her in our group. This is an act of disrespect.

Jesus often welcomed those whom others excluded from their groups. He made friends with people who were less fortunate than others. By welcoming others with respect, you act the same way Jesus did.

When people become friends, or form a community of friends, they often have things in common. But friends also enjoy learning about their differences. We welcome those who have things in common with us as well as those who are different from us. Our words and actions show that each person belongs in the community.

Catholics Believe

Love of neighbor is inseparable from love for God. Every community, with the aid of God's grace, is to support each person within that community by living the virtues.

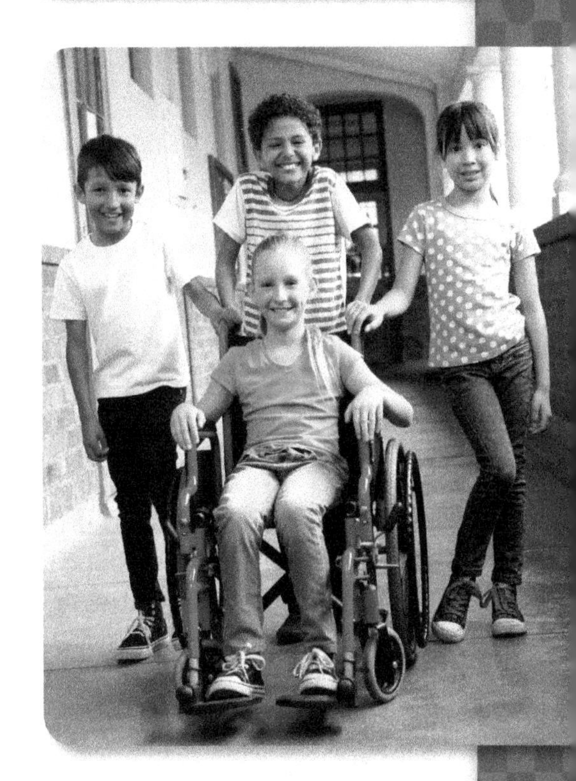

Activity Complete the chart with your family.

Ways that I am similar to other people:	Ways that I am different from other people:

Family Life Connection

Healthy Habits @ Home

As a family, brainstorm ways you can support each other when practicing the virtues.

1. Prudence

2. Temperance

3. Fortitude

4. Justice

Family Time

Cut out and hang at home

As a family, identify ways that you can be accepting of people who seem different.

Ways we can accept others:

Faith Focus

Love of God and love of neighbor are inseparable.

Family in Action

During family prayer, give attention to those who are excluded in the world. Provide an opportunity for each family member to share a name. Write the names here:

- [ ]
- [ ]
- [ ]
- [ ]

Safer Together

Share with your child these strategies about how to deal with prejudice or bullying:

- Take a breath to calm yourself, look the other person in the eye, and tell him or her that your feelings have been hurt. Then turn and walk away.
- Talk with a parent or a trusted adult.
- Recognize that you are not responsible for another person's behavior.
- Be willing to forgive.
- Pray to God for the strength to forgive.

Looking Ahead

In this chapter, the Holy Spirit invites you to ▶

EXPLORE a community that demonstrates that human life is sacred.

DISCOVER how the other Commandments teach us to respect others.

DECIDE how you will honor and respect others, as Jesus did.

CHAPTER 22

Love Your Neighbor as Yourself

❓ How did you treat each person you met today?

Remember the Pharisee had asked Jesus about the Ten Commandments. Jesus said to love God above all else. Then he said:

> "The second is like it: You shall love your neighbor as yourself. All of God's law comes from these two commandments." BASED ON MATTHEW 22:39-40

❓ What are some ways that you show respect for yourself and for other people?

Disciple Power

Respect

Respect means to give someone or something the honor that is deserved. People who are respectful treat others with dignity in the way they act and in what they say.

THE CHURCH FOLLOWS JESUS

L'Arche Communities

We see people treated in many ways. The second part of Jesus' reply to the Pharisee teaches us to show respect for ourselves and for other people. We are to honor and respect other people. We do not pick and choose those whom we respect. We respect everyone.

If you were to visit a L'Arche community, you would see Jesus' response to the Pharisee being put into action. L'Arche communities are communities of faith. The word *l'arche* means "the ark" or "the covenant." L'Arche communities live the covenant that we have with God and with one another.

L'Arche communities believe in the dignity and value of every person. They bring together Catholics and other Christians to form a family with people who have severe disabilities. All of the members of a L'Arche community live and work together. Everyone shares the blessings God has given them with everyone else.

Every day, all over the world, L'Arche communities show that all human life is sacred. Everyone is loved and valued as a child of God.

? What do the members of your parish do to show that they respect human life as sacred? What do you do?

Honor and Respect One Another

FAITH FOCUS
How do the Fourth, Fifth, Sixth, and Ninth Commandments help us live as Jesus taught?

FAITH VOCABULARY
honor
To have special respect for someone, or to hold someone in high regard, is to honor him or her.

The Fourth Commandment teaches about being good family members, neighbors, and citizens. The Fourth Commandment calls for respect:

Honor your father and your mother.

EXODUS 20:12

We are to **honor** and respect our parents. We are to care about them and think of them with love. We are to obey them and show our thanks to them for all they do to help us grow.

Parents share their faith with us. They help us come to know Jesus, and they teach us ways to live as his followers. In our families, we first come to know and trust in the love that God the Father, Son, and Holy Spirit has for us. That is what we mean when we say that the family is a sign of the Holy Trinity.

The Fourth Commandment also teaches that we are to respect other family members and other people who have the responsibility to care for us. We are to respect our teachers and all legitimate authority in our community. We are to be good and responsible citizens.

Activity Draw or write one way that you show you are living the Fourth Commandment.

Sister Helen Prejean

Sister Helen Prejean lives as a follower of Jesus by visiting and caring for prisoners, prisoners' families, and the families of victims of violent crimes.

The Fifth Commandment

God creates every person in his image and likeness. All life belongs to God and is a gift from God. That means that the life of every person is sacred, or holy. The Fifth Commandment teaches that we must treat all human life as sacred. The Fifth Commandment is

You shall not kill. EXODUS 20:13

We live the Fifth Commandment when we

- care for and respect all human life;
- respect our own lives and bodies and the lives and bodies of the other people;
- care for our own health and the health of others;
- use food and medicine wisely; and
- act safely.

The Fifth Commandment also tells us that we must not deliberately hurt or kill innocent people or misuse alcohol, drugs, or food. We are not to bully others, commit acts of terrorism, or harm ourselves or end our own lives by suicide.

Jesus taught his followers how to live the Fifth Commandment. We are to make peace with those who hurt us. We are not to take revenge or get even with people who hurt us. We are to be careful not to let our feelings of anger turn into acts of hatred. We are to love our enemies.

? How do each of these headlines show people living according to the Fifth Commandment? Share what you think with a friend.

Youth Serve as Mentors, Teaching Children to Read

Local Church Helps Build Hospital in Uganda

Parish Families Build Homes in Flood-Ravaged Neighborhood

The Sixth and Ninth Commandments

Friendship is a gift from God. Marriage is a special kind of friendship between a man and a woman. At their wedding, a man and a woman promise to love and honor each other their whole lives. The Sixth and Ninth Commandments teach us about what a husband and wife and others must do to honor the love between a husband and a wife. The Sixth Commandment honors marriage:

> You shall not commit adultery.
>
> Exodus 20:14

This Commandment teaches that a husband and a wife must honor and not betray the love that they promised to share only with each other.

The Ninth Commandment also honors marriage:

> You shall not covet your neighbor's wife.
>
> Exodus 20:17

The word *covet* means "to want or desire wrongfully what belongs to someone else." This Commandment teaches that family, friends, and neighbors are to help a husband and a wife grow in their love. No one should ever break up, or even want to break up, the love that a husband and a wife share.

We prepare to live this kind of married love when we are young. We respect our body and the bodies of others. We demand that others treat our bodies with respect. We keep the promises that we make. We work at being loyal friends.

Catholics Believe

Respect Life Sunday

Each year on the first Sunday of October, Catholics in the United States celebrate Respect Life Sunday. We celebrate that every human life is sacred. We make decisions to work for programs that respect the dignity of every person, born and unborn.

Activity Create a collage of words using qualities of a good and true friend. Using the space below, design your collage.

I FOLLOW JESUS

Every day, you can show that you honor and respect people. When you do, you build a caring school, family, and community. You build a world that respects the dignity of every person. You are living the Ten Commandments as Jesus taught.

A FRIENDSHIP COVENANT

Describe a covenant on which you and your friends build your friendship. Tell what each of you promise to do to keep your friendship strong.

MY FAITH CHOICE

This week, I will look for opportunities to show my respect for people as Jesus taught. I will

____

____.

Say a prayer asking for God's blessing as you strive to love and respect your family, teachers, classmates, and friends.

Chapter Review

Read each story. On the lines, write the number of the Commandment that each of these people is living.

1. Jane has a decision to make. Should she eat another candy bar or should she eat some fruit? She decides on the fruit. ______

2. Tom has a habit of teasing his friends. One of his friends tells him to stop and reminds him that they need to respect each other. ______

3. The teacher asks John to stop talking and bothering the class. He immediately stops and apologizes to her.
______

TO HELP YOU REMEMBER

1. The Fourth Commandment teaches about our responsibilities as family members, neighbors, and citizens.

2. The Fifth Commandment teaches that we are to respect and honor all human life, born and unborn, as a sacred gift from God.

3. The Sixth and Ninth Commandments teach that we must express and share our friendships and love in appropriate ways.

A Prayer For All People

Leader: God, Creator and Father, all life is your gift to us. Hear our prayers as we pray (pause). . .
For all people that they value the gift of life as a sacred gift from you,

All: **God of life, hear our prayer.**

Leader: For all children who suffer from abuse, from lack of food and a place to call their home,

All: **God of life, hear our prayer.**

Leader: For all unborn children, that they are taken care of so that they are born healthy,

All: **God of life, hear our prayer.**

Leader: For all people who suffer from acts of injustice, terror, and violence,

All: **God of life, hear our prayer.**

Leader: Let us pray together as Jesus taught us.

All: **Our Father . . .**

With My Family

This Week . . .

In Chapter 22, Love Your Neighbor as Yourself, your child learned:

- The Fourth through Tenth Commandments teach us to live the second part of the Great Commandment, "You shall love your neighbor as yourself" (Matthew 22:37).
- The Fourth Commandment teaches that we honor and respect our parents and live as good family members, neighbors, and citizens.
- The Fifth Commandment teaches that all human life is sacred and a gift from God. We are to respect and care for all life to the best of our ability.
- The Sixth and Ninth Commandments teach that we respect and honor marriage as a faithful lifelong commitment between a man and a woman.
- People who practice the virtue of respect treat others with dignity in the way they act and in what they say.

For more about related teachings of the Church, see the *Catechism of the Catholic Church,* 2196–2246, 2258–2317, 2331–2391, and 2514–2527, and the *United States Catholic Catechism for Adults,* pages 373–416 and 439–446.

Sharing God's Word

Read together the second part of the Great Commandment in Matthew 22:37 or on page 199. Emphasize that the Fourth through Tenth Commandments teach us to respect and love our neighbors as ourselves.

We Live as Disciples

The Christian family is a school of discipleship. Choose one of the following activities to do as a family, or design a similar activity of your own:

- Ask family members to share an experience when they felt they were treated disrespectfully. Discuss how important it is for you to treat all people with respect.
- Ask each person to share two situations in the past week when he or she followed the Ten Commandments when making a choice.
- What does your parish do to show respect for all human life? Look in your parish bulletin or on your parish website for ideas.

Our Spiritual Journey

Every kind of prayer is an expression of faith in God, hope in God, and love of God. It is also an expression of love for our neighbor. When we pray prayers of intercession, we ask God to help others. We pray that all people may know God's love for them. In this chapter, your child prayed a prayer of intercession. Read and pray together the prayer on page 205.

Faith-Filled People

Sister Helen Prejean
Sister Helen Prejean lives as a follower of Jesus by visiting and caring for prisoners, prisoners' families, and the families of victims of violent crimes. Sister Helen speaks and writes about abolishing the death penalty.

For more ideas on ways your family can live as disciples of Jesus, visit **BeMyDisciples.com**

Showing Respect to All

Two very important actions we do every day are giving and receiving affection. We show affection with our words and our actions. We might say, "I like you," to a friend. We might give a friend a hug. Our words and actions should always be right for our age and proper between people. We show respect when our expressions of affection are right and proper.

Sometimes someone may show affection in an inappropriate way. This person may say things or try to touch a person in ways that we know are wrong. These are not ways God wants affection shown. If this happens to you, you must make a courageous decision to say, "No!" You should immediately get help from a family member or an adult whom you trust. In doing so, you show confidence in yourself and in trusting others to help you.

To love as Jesus loves means to show respect for all people, not just the people who are easy to like. Showing respect means that we honor all people because they have been created in the image and likeness of God. We should love others because God loves them! When we respect a person, we treat that person as we want to be treated.

Catholics Believe

Confidence helps us make good decisions and do the right thing. With confidence we can try new things or ask for help when we need it. We can act with confidence because we know that God is there to help us.

Activity

Write an action that would show respect and love to each of the people listed. Share with your family.

Person	Action
Parents	
Siblings	
Grandparents	
Friends	
Teachers	
Neighbors	

Family Life Connection

Healthy Habits @ Home

Having confidence involves knowing our strengths and weaknesses. As a family, decide on ways to help each other practice confidence.

1. We can welcome new experiences and new learning.
2. We can face our fears.
3. We can ask the Holy Spirit for help.
4. ....

Family Time

Cut out and hang at home

Thinking ahead about situations can help us grow in confidence. As a family, talk about how these steps can help us grow in confidence:

1. Imagine the situation in advance.
2. Anticipate responses.
3. Know how to respond (what to do).

Faith Focus

Confidence helps us make good decisions and do the right thing.

Family in Action

Building up one's confidence and courage takes practice.

As a family, identify situations in which family members need to make courageous decisions.

....

....

....

....

Safer Together

Review with your child the following indicators on how to show our feelings in appropriate ways:

- We do not harm others or ourselves.
- We demonstrate respect and love for others and ourselves.
- Our words are kind and loving.
- Our actions are never aggressive or harsh.
- Our decisions follow the teachings of the Church.

Looking Ahead

In this chapter, the Holy Spirit invites you to ▶

EXPLORE how a group of people shows their love for God.

DISCOVER how the Ten Commandments help us live as Jesus taught.

DECIDE how you will be kind and merciful.

CHAPTER 23

Love One Another

❓ What is one way you show that you love others?

In the Gospels, Jesus taught his disciples what love is. He taught them about love through his words and his actions. He told them that if they loved him, they would keep his Commandments. Listen to what Jesus told his disciples:

> "This is my commandment: love one another as I love you." JOHN 15:12

❓ How do you try to live this Commandment of Jesus?

Disciple Power

Mercy

Mercy is the habit of living with kindness, compassion, and goodness. A person who lives the virtue of mercy is kindhearted and generous. A person who practices mercy looks for ways to help those who are hurting.

Love by the Truckload

People show their love for their family and friends in many ways. Each year, Christians and people of other religions join together for the Society of St. Andrew's Potato and Produce Project. They collect about twenty million pounds of potatoes and other vegetables that businesses are going to throw away. Businesses do not want the produce because they are the wrong size or shape or have marks on their skins.

The Potato and Produce Project volunteers save food from being thrown away and wasted. They make sure that the good food that God has blessed our farms with is shared by all. The volunteers bring the vegetables to food pantries, churches, and other places where people who are hungry come to get food. They feed many who are hungry because of their acts of kindness and mercy.

? How do you see the goodness in the people around you? How do you see people unselfishly sharing their blessings with others?

God's Many Blessings

The Seventh, Eighth, and Tenth Commandments help us show our love for people. They guide us in using the things we have and respecting the belongings of others.

The Seventh Commandment calls for respect of other people's property:

> You shall not steal. EXODUS 20:15

This Commandment teaches that we are to respect the gifts that God gives to others. We must justly use the things with which God has blessed us.

We must not steal, cheat, or damage what belongs to someone else. When we borrow things, we are to use them carefully and return them in good condition.

If we steal something or damage or lose something that someone has let us use, we must make **reparation**. We have the responsibility to give back what we have stolen, repair what we have damaged, or replace what we have lost.

FAITH FOCUS
How do the Seventh, Eighth, and Tenth Commandments help us live as Jesus taught?

FAITH VOCABULARY

reparation
Reparation is the work of repairing or making up for harm that we have wrongfully caused.

perjury
Perjury is lying under oath.

Activity Describe how the child in this photo can live the Seventh Commandment.

____

____

____

____

____

____

Faith-Filled People

Saint Stephen the Deacon

Saint Stephen was one of the first followers of Jesus. He was a deacon who helped widows and orphans and other Christians in need. When an angry crowd asked Stephen about Jesus, he was honest and told the truth about Jesus. The crowd put Stephen to death. The Church celebrates the feast day of Saint Stephen on December 26.

The Eighth Commandment

Jesus said, "I am the truth" (see John 14:6). Disciples of Jesus are to be honest and truthful. The Eighth Commandment helps us live this way. The Eighth Commandment reminds us to do right:

> *You shall not bear false witness against your neighbor.* EXODUS 20:16

This Commandment teaches that we must speak the truth and take responsibility for all our words and actions. We must not lie about ourselves or damage the good name or reputation of others by lying about them. We are not to gossip and put other people down or blame others for the wrong that we have done.

We are not honest or truthful when we bear false witness, or tell lies, about others. Lying under oath, or committing **perjury**, is especially serious. We must make reparation for all of these things. We need to tell the truth and repair the damage that we have wrongfully caused.

Activity Read this situation. Write your own ending.

Juan, Chelsea, and you are playing basketball at recess. Juan gets angry and kicks the ball against the wall. The ball begins to lose air. At the end of recess, Juan returns the ball to the teacher and says, "There is something wrong with this ball."

____

____

____

____

____

____

The Tenth Commandment

Jesus taught about our desire to want things. He taught,

"Your father wants you to live in the kingdom of God. Do not want things too much. They can get in the way of your getting to heaven. For your heart will always be where your treasure is."

BASED ON LUKE 12:32-34

The Tenth Commandment talks about our heart and what it wants. The Tenth Commandment forbids envy and greed:

You shall not covet your neighbor's goods.

BASED ON EXODUS 20:17

This Commandment teaches that we are to have generous, kind, and grateful hearts. We must try to be as generous and kind to other people as God is to us. We are to thank God for all the blessings that he gives to us and others.

The Tenth Commandment warns against selfishness, greed, and envy. We are selfish when we want and keep things only for ourselves. Greed is our wanting more things for ourselves than we really need. Envy is being sad and jealous over the good things that other people have. Selfishness, greed, and envy keep us from having kind, generous, and grateful hearts.

? What is one of your favorite possessions? Tell how you can share it with someone else.

Catholics Believe

The Collection at Mass

In the first days of the Church when Christians gathered for Eucharist, they brought food to church. The food was collected and given to people in need. Today some of the money that we give in the collection at Mass is used to help people in need.

I FOLLOW JESUS

Each day you make choices to live the Ten Commandments. You can be honest and truthful. You can be kind and generous. Through your actions, you can practice the virtue of mercy. You can reach out to help those who are hurting. You can continue the work of Jesus.

BEING KIND AND MERCIFUL

Describe one person who is kind and merciful to you.

Name ______________________________

What He or She Shares ______________________________

____

____

____

____

What Difference This Makes in My Life ______________________________

____

____

____

____

____

MY FAITH CHOICE

When I am honest and truthful, kind and merciful, I am following the way of Jesus. This week, I will be especially kind and merciful. I will

____

______________________________.

Pause and remember God's kindness and mercy toward you and your family. Thank him for his loving care.

Chapter Review

Match the virtues in the left column with the Commandments in the right column.

Virtues	Commandments
______ **1.** respect	**a.** Seventh Commandment
______ **2.** generosity	**b.** Eighth Commandment
______ **3.** kindness	**c.** Tenth Commandment
______ **4.** truthfulness	

TO HELP YOU REMEMBER

1. The Seventh Commandment teaches that we are to respect the property of others.
2. The Eighth Commandment teaches that we are to be honest and truthful.
3. The Tenth Commandment teaches that we are to be kind, grateful, and generous.

Signs of Mercy

Learn to sign this prayer. Teach it to your friends and your family. Pray it often each day.

God, you always show us mercy.

God,

you

always

show

us

mercy.

With My Family

This Week . . .

In Chapter 23, Love One Another, your child learned that:

- God has given the world and all the good in it to all people. We are to respect the world, use it wisely, and generously share our blessings with grateful hearts.
- The Seventh Commandment teaches that we are to respect the gifts of others.
- The Eighth Commandment teaches us to be honest and truthful. We are to respect the good name of other people.
- The Tenth Commandment teaches us to have kind, generous, and grateful hearts. Living all of the Ten Commandments helps us love God and one another as Jesus taught.
- The virtue of mercy leads us to reach out and help those who are hurting with acts of compassion and love.

For more about related teachings of the Church, see the *Catechism of the Catholic Church,* 2401–2449, 2464–2503, and 2534–2550, and the *United States Catholic Catechism for Adults,* pages 417–438, 447-457.

Sharing God's Word

Read the teaching of Jesus in Luke 12:32-34 about gathering possessions, or read the adaptation of the story on page 211. Emphasize the importance of being honest and truthful, kind, generous, and just.

We Live as Disciples

The Christian family is a school of discipleship. Choose one of the following activities to do as a family, or design a similar activity of your own:

- Talk about the people you know who unselfishly share their blessings with others. Then choose one thing that you can do this week to share your blessings with others.
- Look up the Corporal Works of Mercy and the Spiritual Works of Mercy on page 261. Talk about the ways that the Works of Mercy help you to be generous and kind.

Our Spiritual Journey

"Blessed are the merciful, for they will be shown mercy" (Matthew 5:7). There is no adequate English word for the Hebrew word that is translated as "mercy." God's mercy is the infinite and undeserved kindness, goodness, and generosity that God shares with his creation. Such mercy is nonquantifiable. As Christ "emptied himself" on the cross of humanity, so too are we to "empty ourselves" as we strive to live the Great Commandment. In this chapter, your child learned to sign a prayer of mercy. Read, sign, and pray together the prayer on page 213.

Faith-Filled People

Saint Stephen the Deacon
Feast Day: December 26
Saint Stephen helped the Apostles as a deacon. Stephen used the gift of courage to tell people about Jesus.

For more ideas on ways your family can live as disciples of Jesus, visit **www.BeMyDisciples.com**

Little Ways to Love

Thérèse Martin was an ordinary girl from a small town in France called Lisieux. Her life was not easy. She suffered from bad headaches and fevers, and she had difficulty sleeping. Thérèse did not let these things stop her from doing God's work. She realized that she did not have to do great things to serve God, the nuns in her community, and other people. Doing simple, ordinary things was Thérèse's way of doing God's work.

God invites us to love the way Thérèse Martin did. He invites us to love even in the littlest of ways. We can love in simple ways by using the gifts he has given us. We have the responsibility to discover our talents and gifts. If they include telling stories, we could share our stories with those who are lonely. Maybe our talents include doing well in school, and we could help tutor another student. We are to be good stewards of our gifts by using them to serve others. Our faith in God gives us the confidence to use our gifts well.

Catholics Believe

God calls us to love others, even in the littlest of ways. We use our gifts and talents to love others and to love God.

Activity

What are some of the little ways you can show your love for God? Write about them here. Then share what you have written with your family.

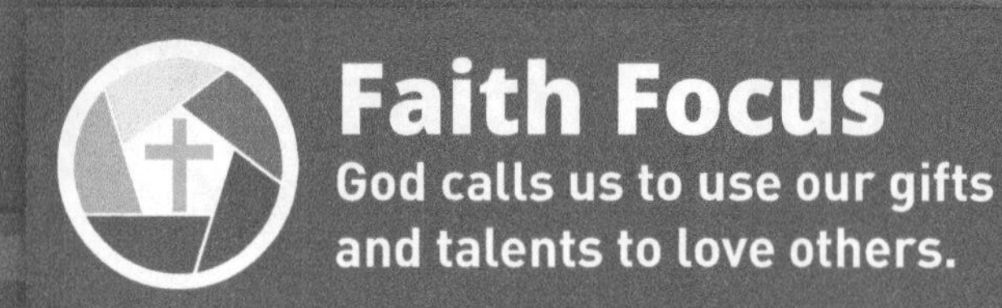

Faith Focus

God calls us to use our gifts and talents to love others.

Healthy Habits @ Home

As a family, reflect on the gifts God has given each member of your family. How do you use the gifts God has given you?

Gifts	How We Use God's Gifts

Safer Together

You can help your child stay safe by reviewing these tips:

- Remind your child that God never asks anything of him or her that would cause harm.
- If your child is ever asked to do something harmful or secret "because God wills it," he or she should say "No," get away, and tell you or another trusted adult.

Family Time

Cut out and hang at home

As a family, identify ways that God has been speaking to you this week to use your gifts and talents to help others.

Ways God speaks in our family:

- [ ] ....
- [ ] ....
- [ ] ....
- [ ] ....

Family in Action

As a family, celebrate the various gifts and talents of each family member. Invite family members to share their gifts and talents with the rest of the family through a talent show. Make an action plan here:

Member	Talent

Looking Ahead

In this chapter, the Holy Spirit invites you to ▶

EXPLORE how a parish teaches that Jesus' love is alive today.

DISCOVER how the Our Father teaches us to be disciples of Jesus.

DECIDE to pray the Our Father every day.

CHAPTER 24

The Prayer of Disciples

? How do your parents and teachers help you learn?

One day Jesus was spending time with his disciples. He was teaching them about what it means to be a disciple, and he was praying. Listen to what one of his disciples asked him when he had finished praying:

> *"Lord, teach us to pray as John the Baptist taught his disciples to pray."* Based on Luke 11:1

? Do you remember how Jesus answered the disciple?

Disciple Power

Charity

Charity is one of the three Theological Virtues. Another word for charity is love. We practice the virtue of charity by loving God above all things and by loving our neighbor as ourselves.

THE CHURCH FOLLOWS JESUS

A Gift of Hope and Love

Every day we can live the Lord's Prayer, or Our Father, by the things that we do or say. We can choose to live as Jesus' disciples.

The children of Blessed Sacrament Church accepted Jesus' invitation to be his disciples. They learned that more than one billion people go to bed hungry every night. They decided to raise money for Heifer International.

Through Heifer, people buy animals that are given to families around the world. These families raise the animals and give the offspring to other families in need.

The children of Blessed Sacrament Church decided to earn enough money to buy two flocks of chicks for a family. They were living their prayer, "Give us this day our daily bread." They were giving a family the gift of food and the gift of hope and love.

The children of Blessed Sacrament Church were teaching everyone that God is at work in the world. He is at work building the Kingdom that Jesus taught will one day come. Everyone then will really know that God is the Father of all people.

? Can you describe some of the people or organizations you know who practice the virtue of charity and share the gift of hope with others?

Kenyan child with goats provided through Heifer International

The Summary of the Gospel

In Jesus' time, some people were honored with the title of **rabbi**, or teacher. People gathered around such a teacher to understand and live God's Law. These people were disciples of that teacher. A disciple is a person who learns from and follows the teachings of another person.

Jesus was honored with the title of rabbi. The disciples of Jesus traveled with him. They went to the Temple and synagogue with him. All the time, they listened and watched. They asked question after question, seeking his advice. They trusted him to help them understand and live faithfully the laws and customs of their religion.

When Jesus taught his disciples the Our Father, he was helping them understand God's Law and how to live God's Law. The disciples of Jesus came to believe that Jesus was the One sent by God to be the Messiah. He was the One who fulfilled the Law and everything that God had promised to his people.

FAITH FOCUS
What does Jesus teach us in the Our Father?

FAITH VOCABULARY

rabbi
Rabbi is a Hebrew word meaning "teacher," a title of honor and respect in the Bible given to someone whom people trusted to help them understand and live the Law of God.

Lord's Prayer
The Lord's Prayer is another name for the Our Father, the prayer that Jesus, our Lord, taught his disciples to pray.

A Jewish rabbi teaching Hebrew to a young boy

Activity Name two things you have learned about God from Jesus.

God is ______________________________

____

______________________________.

God is ______________________________

____

______________________________.

Faith-Filled People

Martha and Mary

Martha and Mary were sisters who were close friends of Jesus. They were his disciples. When their brother Lazarus died, Jesus wept with Martha and Mary. The sisters had great faith in Jesus. Martha said, "I believe you are the Messiah, the Son of God, the one who is coming into the world." Jesus then went to the tomb and cried, "Lazarus, come out!" Jesus raised Lazarus from the dead (based on John 11:1-44).

Lord, Teach Us to Pray

Recall the Scripture verse that you read on the first page of this lesson. Listen now to the answer that Jesus gave to the disciple:

> *"When you pray, say:*
> *Father, hallowed be your name,*
> *your kingdom come.*
> *Give us each day our daily bread*
> *and forgive us our sins*
> *for we ourselves forgive everyone in debt to us,*
> *and do not subject us to the final test."*
>
> LUKE 11:2-4

When the disciples and the first Christians gathered, they prayed as Jesus had taught them. This prayer became known as the **Lord's Prayer** or the Our Father.

Activity Underline the words in the Scripture quotation that are similar to the words we pray in the Our Father.

The Our Father

When we pray the Our Father, we tell God that he is the center of our lives. We place our trust in him above everyone and everything else. Each time we pray the Our Father:

- We worship God by honoring and respecting his name as holy.
- We petition, or ask, God to continue to build his Kingdom. We promise God that we want to live as Jesus taught us.
- We petition God for our "daily bread." We ask for all that we and others need to live as children of God.
- We petition God to forgive our sins and to help us forgive others as he forgives us. We remember that Jesus' dying and being raised from the dead are the greatest signs of God's forgiving love for us.
- We petition God to help us do good and to avoid sin. We ask God to help us follow Jesus' way of serving others.

The Our Father is the prayer of all Christians. Its words teach us both how to pray and how to live as disciples of Jesus. That is why it is called the perfect prayer for Christians. It is the summary of the Gospel.

? When have you done one thing that the Our Father teaches you to do?

Catholics Believe

The Doxology

We pray the Our Father at every Mass. At Mass, we conclude the Our Father by singing or saying aloud, "For the kingdom, the power, and the glory are yours, now and forever." These words are called a *doxology*. A doxology is a prayer of praise. The Church has prayed this doxology from the early days of the Church.

I FOLLOW JESUS

The Holy Spirit helps you understand, pray, and live the Our Father.

LIVING THE OUR FATHER

Choose one of the lines of the Our Father. Describe how it could help you live as a better follower of Jesus.

____

____

____

____

____

____

____

____

____

____

MY FAITH CHOICE

This week, I will pray the Our Father every day. When I do, I will

____

____.

Pray, "Our Father who art in heaven. Hallowed be your name."

Chapter Review

Match the words from the Our Father in Column A with their meanings in Column B.

	Column A	Column B
______	**1.** Hallowed be thy name.	**a.** The Holy Spirit works with us to prepare for the coming of the Kingdom that Jesus began.
______	**2.** Thy kingdom come.	**b.** We give glory to God who is All-holy.
______	**3.** Give us this day our daily bread.	**c.** We trust that God will give us all that we need to live as his children.
______	**4.** Forgive us our trespasses.	**d.** We ask God to help us do good and avoid doing wrong. We ask him to help us follow Jesus' way of serving others.
______	**5.** Deliver us from evil.	**e.** We trust that God will forgive our sins.

TO HELP YOU REMEMBER

1. Jesus is our Teacher, who helps us best understand and live as children of God.
2. Jesus taught us to call God, our Father, in prayer.
3. When we pray the Our Father, we tell God that he is the center of our lives.

The Our Father

The Church prays the Our Father every day. Join together as members of the Church. Pray as Jesus taught us:

Leader: O God, by the grace of the Holy Spirit, we call you Father and live as your children. We pray as Jesus taught us.

All: **Our Father . . .**

Leader: Let us conclude by praising God.

All: **For the kingdom, the power, and the glory are yours, now and forever. Amen.**

With My Family

This Week . . .

In Chapter 24, The Prayer of Disciples, your child learned that:

- From the earliest days of the Church, Christians have prayed the Our Father, or Lord's Prayer, when they gathered for prayer.
- When we pray the Our Father, we acknowledge that God is the center of our lives.
- The Our Father is the summary of the Gospel.
- The Our Father not only teaches us how to pray but also shows us how to live as the children of God, who is the Father of all people.
- We practice the virtue of charity by loving God above all things and by loving our neighbor as ourselves.

For more about related teachings of the Church, see the *Catechism of the Catholic Church*, 2759–2856, and the *United States Catholic Catechism for Adults*, pages 481–495.

Sharing God's Word

Read together the Bible story in Luke 11:2-4 about Jesus teaching his disciples to pray, or read the adaptation of the story on page 218. Emphasize that Jesus gave us the Our Father to pray.

We Live as Disciples

The Christian family is a school of discipleship. Choose one of the following activities to do as a family, or design a similar activity of your own:

- The first Christian communities prayed the Our Father three times a day. Follow the example of the first Christians and do the same this week.
- The Our Father is the prayer of all Christians. Learn the words of the Our Father in a language other than the language that you usually use to pray.

Our Spiritual Journey

Praying the Lord's Prayer often during the day is an ancient tradition. This Christian practice gives a basic outline and vision for the Christian life. Develop the habit of pausing and reflectively praying the Our Father several times a day. Praying it when you wake up, in the morning, mid-morning, noon, mid-afternoon, and evening is one way to join with Christians who pray the Liturgy of the Hours. In this chapter, your child prayed the Our Father. Pray it together every day.

Faith-Filled People

Martha and Mary

Martha and Mary were sisters and disciples of Jesus in the New Testament. The story of Martha and Mary teaches us that we must listen to God and learn from him.

For more ideas on ways your family can live as disciples of Jesus, visit **BeMyDisciples.com**

Growing Together

A member of your church has moved away. She owns a small plot of land next to the parish. She has used the land as a garden. Much of the food she grew was given to the local food bank. Some was given to families who lacked food.

The woman gave the land to the parish. Her only request is that the parish use it as a community garden. The parish is organizing teams of families to care for the garden and distribute the food to those in need.

The parish is committed to the hard work it will take to grow an abundant harvest. The work of kind and generous people will make a difference in the lives of others. What might your family do to contribute to the community effort?

Catholics Believe

By working together and using our gifts and talents, we can make a difference for good in the world.

Activity

Share ideas about how your family can help with the community garden. Decide on three things you can do. List them here.

1

2

3

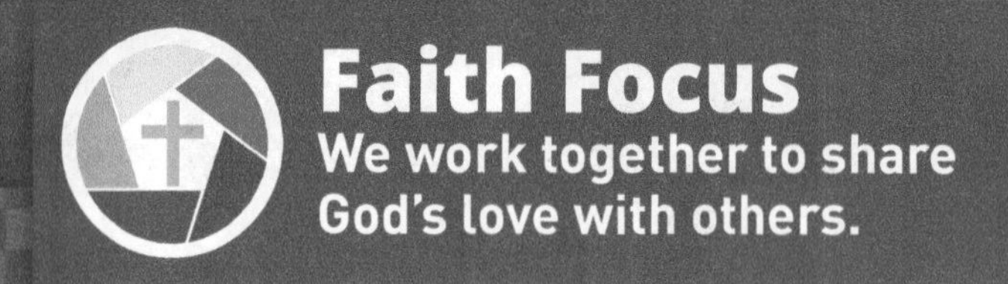

Faith Focus

We work together to share God's love with others.

Safer Together

Cut out and hang at home

Help your children be safe by reinforcing the 3 R's of Safety: **Recognize**, **Respond**, and **Report** dangerous situations.

- **Recognize:** Tell your children that feeling unsafe or uncomfortable (or distressed in any way) is a sign that something is not right.
- **Respond:** Your children do not have to suffer in silence. They can speak to the person who is making them feel uncomfortable, to a trusted adult, and hopefully to both.
- **Report:** If your children reach out to you, listen to them, help them sort out what is happening, and respond in a helpful manner.

Healthy Habits @ Home

We help our children identify their interests and strengths and build on them when we encourage them to experience and try new things. Express your confidence in their ability to take on new and challenging tasks.

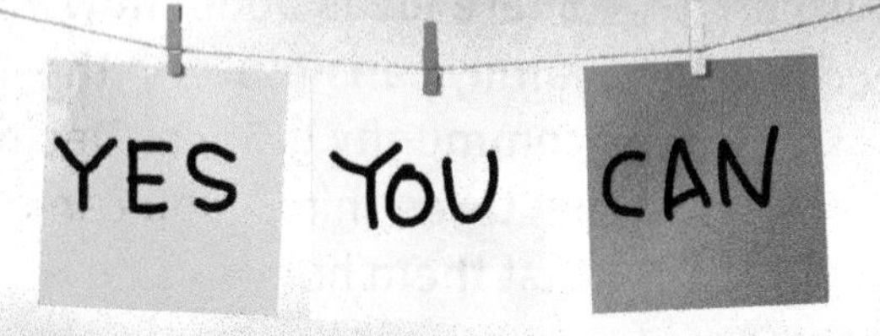

Family Time

The woman who gave the land to the parish had the gift and talent of gardening. She used her gift and talent to help others. Use the story to talk with your children about the gifts and talents of family members and ways these can be used to make a difference for good in your community.

Our Gifts and Talents	Who Can We Help?	How Can We Help?

Unit 6 **Review**

Name ____________________

A. Choose the Best Word

Use the words in the word bank to complete the sentences.

Our Father	**honor**	**selfishness**
truth	**worship**	**perjury**

1. The Fourth Commandment calls us to ____________ and obey our parents.

2. The Eighth Commandment teaches us to speak the ____________.

3. The First Commandment says that only God is worthy of ____________.

4. The Tenth Commandment warns against ____________ and greed.

5. ____________ is lying under oath.

B. Show What You Know

Match the items in Column A with those in Column B.

Column A

____ **1.** "You shall not kill."

____ **2.** "You shall not commit adultery."

____ **3.** "Give us this day our daily bread."

____ **4.** "Thy kingdom come."

____ **5.** Only God is worthy of our worship.

Column B

a. The Holy Spirit works with us to prepare for the coming of the Kingdom Jesus began.

b. We trust that God will give us all we need to live as his children.

c. Fifth Commandment

d. Sixth Commandment

e. First Commandment

C. Connect with Scripture

Reread the Scripture passage on page 189. What connection do you see between this passage and what you learned in this unit?

____

____

____

D. Be a Disciple

1. *Review the four pages in this unit titled The Church Follows Jesus. What person or ministry of the Church on these pages will inspire you to be a better disciple of Jesus? Explain your answer.*

____

____

____

2. *Work with a group. Review the four Disciple Power virtues, or gifts, you have learned about in this unit. After writing your own ideas, share with the group practical ways that you will live these virtues day by day.*

____

____

____

The Year of Grace

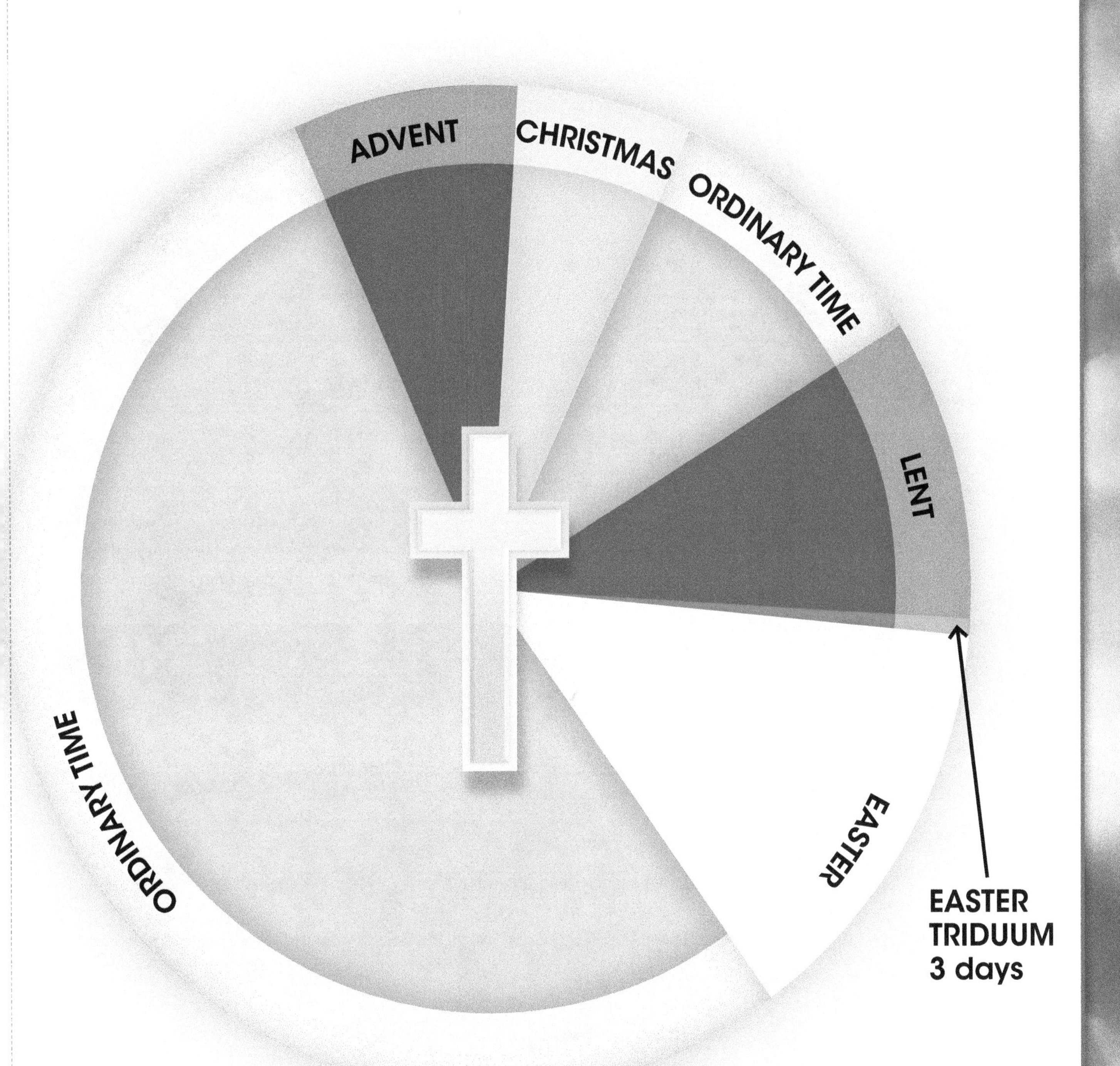

The Liturgical Year

While many things you see and hear at Mass are always the same, other things change. The readings change, as do the colors of banners and vestments. All of the changes help us know what part of the Church year we are celebrating. Each year is a year of grace because we celebrate the saving presence of Christ in the world.

Advent

We begin the liturgical year by anticipating the birth of Jesus Christ during the season of Advent. It is a time to prepare ourselves through prayer and sacrifice. In these ways, we make room in our hearts for the birth of the Lord.

Christmas

We celebrate the Incarnation of Jesus Christ through his birth to the Virgin Mary. During the Christmas season, we also celebrate the Solemnity of Mary, the Holy Mother of God; Epiphany; and the Baptism of the Lord.

Lent

During the forty days of Lent, we pray and make personal sacrifices so that we can turn our hearts more completely toward God. We are preparing for the greatest celebration of the Church year—the Resurrection of the Lord.

The Triduum

The Easter Triduum is at the center of our year of worship. Beginning on the evening of Holy Thursday and ending on Easter Sunday evening, the Triduum is our three-day solemn celebration of the Paschal Mystery.

Easter

On each of the fifty days of Easter, we celebrate our new life in the Risen Christ. At the Easter Vigil, we light the Paschal candle in the midst of darkness to remind us that Jesus is the light of the world. Our celebration continues until Pentecost.

Ordinary Time

The rest of the Church year is called Ordinary Time. We celebrate many events in the life and ministry of Jesus. We also celebrate other great feasts and solemnities honoring Jesus, Mary, and the saints.

Faith Focus
Why do we celebrate the Solemnity of All Saints?

The Word of the Lord
These are the readings for the Solemnity of All Saints. Choose one, and ask your family to read it with you. Talk about the reading with them.

First reading
Revelation 7:2-4, 9-14

Second reading
1 John 3:1-3

Gospel
Matthew 5:1-12a

Solemnity of All Saints

Throughout her history, the Church has named certain women and men to be saints. Their lives are holy examples of God's love. They are the kind of heroes and heroines that God wants us to model. The Blessed Virgin Mary, Mother of Jesus, is the greatest of these saints. We pray to Mary and the saints, asking them to pray for us.

The members of the Church who are named as saints come from all nations and all times. During their lives on Earth, they loved God more than anyone or anything else. Some saints were teachers, some were farmers, others were writers, and still others were parents. While on Earth, the saints now in Heaven were different people doing different work, but in everything they did they devoted their lives to doing the will of God. Now these saints live in Heaven with Jesus in the presence of God the Father. There are also many unknown saints who are now in Heaven.

The Church celebrates the feast of all of the saints in Heaven on November 1. This is called the Solemnity of All Saints. On this holy day of obligation, we go to Mass. We thank God for the faith of the saints who are models for us. Together with the saints in Heaven and the souls in Purgatory, members of the Church on Earth make up the Communion of Saints. Through the Communion of Saints we help one another become holy.

Saint Teresa of Calcutta, Saint Peter Claver, Saint Augustine

Saints as Friends

In the left column, write the names of three favorite saints. In the right column, tell how they help you to be a good disciple of Jesus.

Saints to Guide Me

Saints	How They Help Me
1. ______________________	______________________
	______________________
2. ______________________	______________________
	______________________
3. ______________________	______________________
	______________________

This week, I will learn about one of God's saints. With an adult's help, I will (circle one):

- Sign out a library book about the saints and learn about a new saint.
- Go to **SaintsResource.com** and read about a saint whom I do not know.

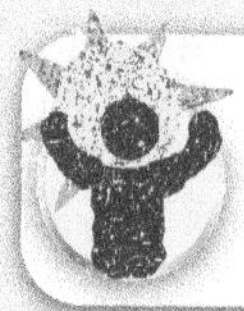

Pray, "Dear Father in Heaven, thank you for the saints who help us be signs of your love for others. Amen."

Faith Focus

What do we prepare for during Advent?

The Word of the Lord

These are the Gospel readings for the First Sunday of Advent. Choose this year's reading and look it up in the Bible. Read and discuss the reading with your family.

Year A:
Matthew 24:37-44

Year B:
Mark 13:33-37

Year C:
Luke 21:25-28, 34-36

Advent

During the month of December, we make or buy gifts and wrap them. We decorate a tree. Families get ready for Christmas, and so does the Church.

Advent is the time we remember God's promise to send the Messiah. During the Masses of Advent, we listen to stories from the Old Testament about this promise. In one of the Advent readings, we read in the book of the prophet Isaiah:

> The wilderness and parched land will exult;
> the [steppes] will rejoice and bloom.
> Like the crocus it shall bloom abundantly,
> and rejoice with joyful song.
>
> Isaiah 35:1-2a

On each of the four Sundays of Advent, we light a candle on our Advent wreath. The candles help us count the weeks until Christmas. They also remind us that Jesus lights our world as the sun lights the Earth.

We prepare for Christmas by being lights for others. We find ways to help others. We offer gifts of service. We may delight in finding ways to be secret givers. Our gifts light up the lives of others.

Be a Light in the World!

Fill in the dates for Christmas and the four Sundays of Advent that precede it. For each week of Advent, write in at least one thing you could do to prepare for the coming of Jesus, alone or with your family. Decorate your calender with symbols of Advent.

M	T	W	Th	F	S	S

MY FAITH CHOICE

For the season of Advent, I will be a light for others. I will

____

____

____

Pray, "Jesus, you are the Light of the world."

The Immaculate Conception

Faith Focus
Why is Mary the greatest saint?

The Word of the Lord
This is the second reading for the Solemnity of the Immaculate Conception of the Blessed Virgin Mary. Ask your family to read it with you. Talk about the reading with them.

Ephesians 1:3-6, 11-12

Mary is the greatest saint. She is Mary, Most Holy. She always lived as a child of God. All that Mary did and said showed her love for God.

Each year on December 8th, the Church honors Mary, Most Holy. We celebrate the Solemnity of the Immaculate Conception of the Blessed Virgin Mary. The Immaculate Conception is a celebration of our faith. The Church uses the word *immaculate* to tell us that Mary was always free from sin.

God the Father chose Mary to be the Mother of the Son of God. The Holy Spirit prepared her for this great privilege by keeping her soul free of sin from the first moment of her life. This is called the Immaculate Conception. With God's grace, Mary remained sinless her entire life until her Assumption into Heaven.

Saint Joachim, Saint Anne, and the Child Mary by Tracy L. Christianson

Mary, Model of Holiness

When the angel Gabriel announced to Mary that God had chosen her to be the Mother of the Son of God, he told her to name her baby Jesus. Mary did not understand what the angel was saying. "How could this be?" she asked. But Mary said, "May it be done to me according to your word" (Luke 1:38). Mary said yes to God because of her great faith and love of God.

Mary is our model of holiness. Mary shows us what it means to live as a child of God. She shows us to follow the will of God always. Our Blessed Mother, Mary, hears our prayers and prays for us. She helps us understand what God wants us to do. Her prayers for us help us to live holy lives.

Models of Faith

According to Catholic tradition, Saint Anne and Saint Joachim were the parents of Mary. They handed on to her their strong faith and helped prepare her to be the Mother of the Savior.

How has Mary been a model of faith for you? Write her a note thanking her for her example. Decorate your note.

Dear Mary:

____

____

____

____

____

____

____

____

MY FAITH CHOICE

This week, I will follow the example of Mary, Most Holy. I will

____

____

______________________________.

Pray, "Mary, blessed are you among all women!"

Faith Focus

Why do we honor Mary as Our Lady of Guadalupe?

The Word of the Lord

These are the three readings for the Feast of Our Lady of Guadalupe. Choose one of the readings and find it in a Bible. Read and discuss the reading with your family.

Isaiah 7:10-14
Galatians 2:4-7
Luke 1:39-48

Our Lady of Guadalupe

December 12 is a special feast day of the Church in the Americas. On this day, we honor the Blessed Virgin Mary with the title of Our Lady of Guadalupe.

On that day, in the year 1531, the Virgin Mary appeared to Juan Diego at Tepeyac. Tepeyac is a hill near present-day Mexico City. Mary told Juan to ask the bishop to build a shrine on the hill. When the bishop wanted a sign from Mary, she told Juan to gather roses to give to the bishop.

Juan wrapped the roses in his *tilma*, which is a cloak made of cactus cloth. When Juan unwrapped it, there was an image of Mary on the cloth. The image shows Mary, the Mother of Jesus, as "a woman clothed with the sun, with the moon under her feet" (Revelation 12:1). Juan's *tilma* and the image of the Virgin Mary have survived for almost five hundred years.

Since 1886, people in Mexico have made pilgrimage to the Basilica of Guadalupe. Some people walk many miles from their homes; many others ride bicycles. Some enter the basilica walking on their knees. Many people visit the basilica to worship God, pray to Mary, and ask her to pray for them.

When we take part in Mass on the feast of Our Lady of Guadalupe, the Patroness of the Americas, we pray that Mary will help all people to accept each other as brothers and sisters. We pray for the gift of peace that her Son, Jesus, gave to the world.

The Peace of Christ

On December 12, we honor Mary as Our Lady of Guadalupe, Patroness of the Americas. In the space below, write a slogan or short prayer for peace. Ask Mary to ask her Son, Jesus, to help all people live in peace.

MY FAITH CHOICE

This week, I will honor Mary by showing respect for others. I will

____

____

____.

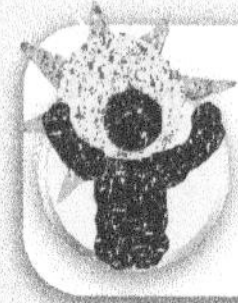

Pray, "Our Lady of Guadalupe, help me to see all people as brothers and sisters."

Christmas

Faith Focus

What did the shepherds do when they heard the angels' message about Jesus?

The Word of the Lord

These are the Gospel readings for Mass on Christmas Day. Choose one reading and find it in the Bible. Read and discuss the reading with your family.

Years A, B, and C:
John 1:1-18 or
John 1:1-5, 9-14

When you were born, your whole family rejoiced! Many rejoiced when Jesus was born too.

The Gospel tells us that the glory of the Lord shone in the dark night over the place where shepherds were watching their sheep. The shepherds were afraid, but the angels brought this Good News:

> [T]oday in the city of David a savior has been born for you who is Messiah and Lord. LUKE 2:11

Jesus was born in Bethlehem, which is called the "city of David." Many years before, Israel's greatest king, David, had been born in Bethlehem.

The angels did not announce the birth of Jesus, the Savior, to great kings. The angels announced his birth to shepherds, who then left their sheep and went to see the Child born in Bethlehem. Then the shepherds went about

> glorifying and praising God for all they had heard and seen, just as it had been told to them. LUKE 2:20

Shepherds See the Star
by Steve Bridger

Glory and Praise to God

When we pray the Gloria at Mass, we are praising God just as the shepherds did. Give glory to God by praying part of the Gloria together as a class.

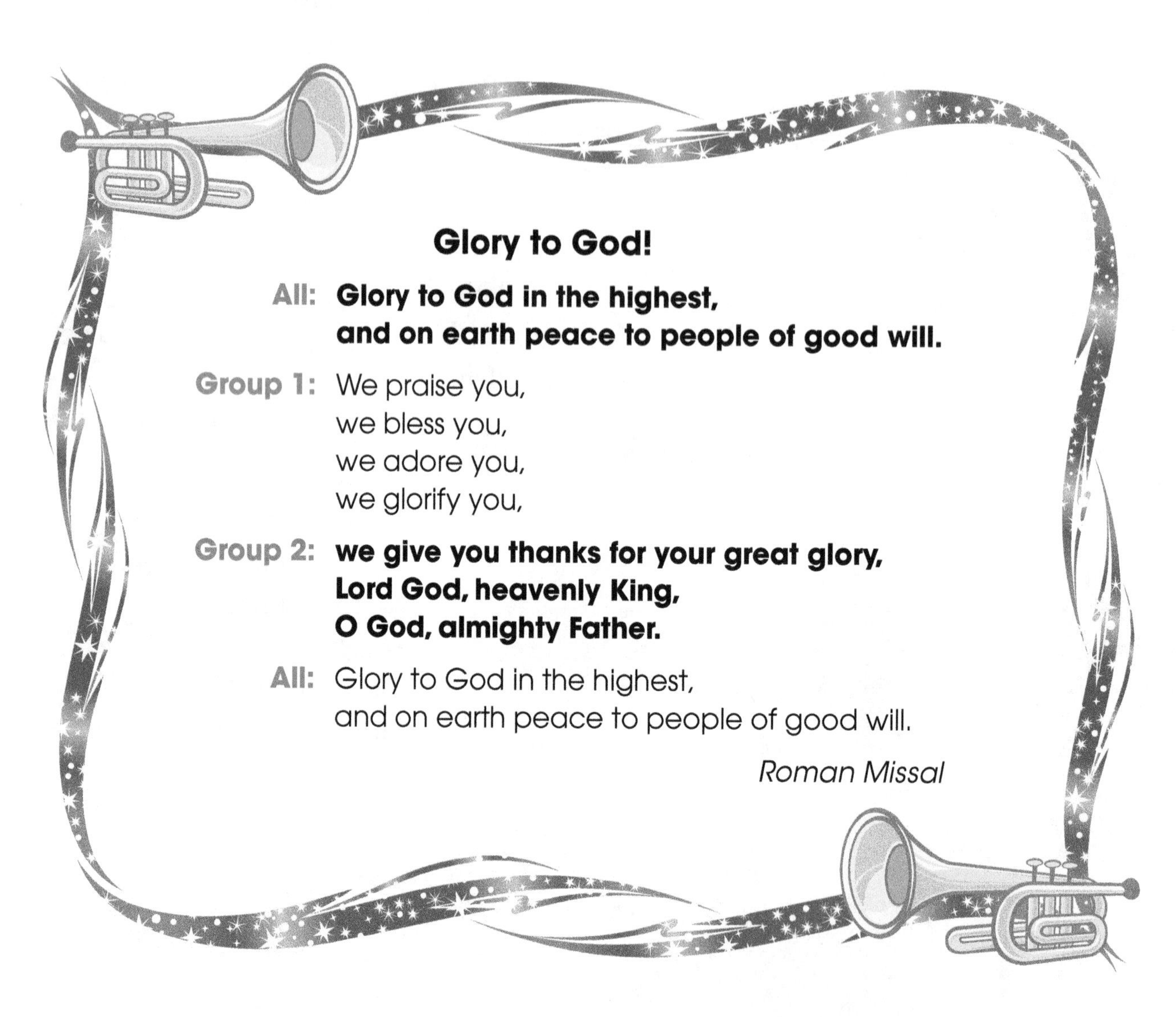

Glory to God!

All: **Glory to God in the highest,**
and on earth peace to people of good will.

Group 1: We praise you,
we bless you,
we adore you,
we glorify you,

Group 2: **we give you thanks for your great glory,**
Lord God, heavenly King,
O God, almighty Father.

All: Glory to God in the highest,
and on earth peace to people of good will.

Roman Missal

MY FAITH CHOICE

This week, I will follow the example of the shepherds. I will

____

____

____.

Pray, "Jesus, you are Messiah and Lord!"

Faith Focus

How does Mary, our mother, lead us to peace?

The Word of the Lord

This is the Gospel reading for the Solemnity of Mary, the Holy Mother of God. Read and discuss it with your family.

Gospel:
Luke 2:16-21

Mary, the Holy Mother of God

On Christmas Day, we celebrate the birth of Jesus Christ, the Son of God and the Son of Mary. The Church continues to celebrate the birth of Jesus, the Savior of the world, for two weeks. We call this the Christmas season. The celebration of the Christmas season lasts until the Feast of the Baptism of the Lord.

On January 1, the Church celebrates the Solemnity of Mary, the Holy Mother of God. Because Mary is the Mother of Jesus, who is truly God, Mary is truly the Mother of God. This day is a holy day of obligation. During the liturgy, we pray:

> Hail, Holy Mother, who gave birth
> to the King who rules heaven and earth
> for ever.
>
> Entrance Antiphon, Solemnity of Mary, the Holy Mother of God, *Roman Missal*

In 1967 Pope Paul VI named January 1 World Day of Prayer for Peace. Since then, Christians have been asked to begin the New Year with prayers for peace. When we celebrate the Solemnity of Mary, the Holy Mother of God, we ask Mary to take our prayers for peace to her Son, Jesus, the Prince of Peace.

The Coronation of Virgin Mary
by Rudolf Max Pirner
Prague, Czech Republic

Mother of Jesus

Read one of the Bible passages below. Under it, write what new thing Mary learned about her Son, Jesus, in the event described in the story.

Luke 2:22-33 (The Presentation of Jesus in the Temple)

____

____

Luke 2:41-52 (The Boy Jesus in the Temple)

____

____

John 2:1-11 (The Wedding at Cana)

____

____

MY FAITH CHOICE

This week, I will work for peace as Mary asks. I will

____

____

____.

Pray, "Holy Mother of God, bring peace to our world."

Epiphany

Faith Focus

Who were the Magi?

The Word of the Lord

This is the second reading for the Solemnity of the Epiphany of the Lord. Find it in the Bible and read and discuss it with your family.

Years A, B, and C:
Ephesians 3:2-3, 5-6

Name a leader for whom you have great respect. Why do you respect this leader? How do you show your respect for this person?

At the time Jesus was born, some wise men, called Magi, studied the stars to find signs of the birth of a great and holy leader. One night the Magi saw a great star in the sky. They believed the star would lead them to this great leader.

The Magi set out on a long journey and followed the star. It led them to Bethlehem. There they found Jesus, Mary, and Joseph. They offered gifts of gold, frankincense, and myrrh to Jesus to honor him as a king and show their great respect for him.

The precious metal, gold, signified that Jesus would be our king. Frankincense was burned by ancient people, who believed it carried their prayers to Heaven. Today, we burn incense to symbolize that our High Priest, Jesus, carries our prayers to Heaven too. Myrrh was used in the burial of the dead. It was an ointment used later in the burial of Jesus.

God's Salvation is for all people—the poor shepherds, the royal Magi, us, and everyone.

Gifts of Service

The Magi honored and respected Jesus with gifts. In each of the gift boxes, write a gift of service that you will do to honor Jesus and help build his KIngdom.

MY FAITH CHOICE

This week, I will help others come to know Jesus. I will

____

____

____.

Pray, "Lord, help me to follow you always."

Faith Focus
Why does the Church bless us with ashes on Ash Wednesday?

The Word of the Lord
This is the first reading for Ash Wednesday. Read and discuss it with your family.

First reading
Joel 2:12-18

Ash Wednesday

Every journey has a beginning. Ash Wednesday is the first day of our Lenten journey toward Easter. Lent begins on Ash Wednesday and ends on Holy Thursday.

During the season of Lent, we prepare for Easter through fasting, prayer, and acts of charity. We make sacrifices remembering the great sacrifice of Jesus on the Cross.

On Ash Wednesday, we join with Catholics all over the world. We go to church and listen to the Word of God. Our foreheads are marked with ashes in the form of a cross. These ashes are made from the palm branches blessed on Palm Sunday of the Passion of the Lord. This ritual is a sign that we desire to change our hearts. We want to turn away from sin and change our lives. We want to live as loving children of God.

As the priest blesses the ashes, he prays,

> "O God, . . . pour out the grace of your blessing on your servants who are marked with these ashes, that . . . they may be worthy to come with minds made pure to celebrate the Paschal Mystery of your Son."
>
> BLESSING AND GIVING OF ASHES, *ROMAN MISSAL*

Gifts of Sacrifice and Giving

On Ash Wednesday, we remember how much God loves us. We remember that the Son of God became one of us. He showed us how much God loves us. He showed us how we are to show our love for God.

During Lent, we give up or sacrifice something special in honor of Jesus. We also give to others to share our love for God. For each week in Lent, write one sacrifice and one act of giving that you will do. Be sure to write when you will do it.

Weeks In Lent	Giving Up . . .		Giving To . . .	
	What	**When**	**Who**	**When**
1				
2				
3				
4				
5				
6				
EASTER!				

MY FAITH CHOICE

This week, I will do a special work of charity, or love, for someone in my family. I will

____

____

____

Pray, "Lord, help me to turn away from sin and live with love."

Lent

Faith Focus
Why does the Church celebrate Lent?

The Word of the Lord
These are the Gospel readings for the First Week of Lent. Choose this year's reading and look it up in a Bible. Read and discuss the reading with your family.

Year A:
Matthew 4:1-11

Year B:
Mark 1:12-15

Year C:
Luke 4:1-13

What You Hear
The word *alleluia* is not used during Lent. Before the reading of the Gospel, only a psalm verse is read.

When spring comes, we put on lighter and more comfortable clothing. We often do spring cleaning around our homes. Spring is a time to enjoy a fresh, new, colorful season of the year.

Lent is the Church's springtime. It is the time of the Church year that we spend preparing for our Easter celebration of Jesus' Resurrection to new life.

Lent begins on Ash Wednesday. On Ash Wednesday, as a cross is traced on our foreheads with ashes, we hear the words,

"Repent, and believe in the Gospel." Roman Missal

Lent is a time to remember the new life of Christ given to us through Baptism. We are reminded that we are in need of God's forgiveness. We remember our needs for daily prayer. We often look for ways to share our blessings with others. We renew our efforts to live the Gospel by loving God and one another.

Live the Gospel

The Fruits of the Holy Spirit help us live the Gospel. Look at the list of some of the Fruits of the Holy Spirit. In each of the spaces below, draw or write a scene showing someone living one of the Fruits of the Holy Spirit. Write the fruit at the top of each picture.

Fruits of the Holy Spirit

gentleness	self-control	love	joy
kindness	peace	faithfulness	generosity
patience			

MY FAITH CHOICE

This week, I will live the Gospel by practicing a virtue. I will

____

____

______________________________.

Pray, "Jesus, help me to renew my efforts to love God and others."

Faith Focus
What does the Church remember and celebrate on the Sunday that begins Holy Week?

The Word of the Lord
These are the Gospel readings for Palm Sunday of the Passion of the Lord. Choose this year's reading and find it in a Bible. Read and discuss the reading with your family.

Year A:
Matthew 26:14–27:66
or Matthew 27:11-54

Year B:
Mark 14:1–15:47
or Mark 15:1-39

Year C:
Luke 22:14–23:56
or Luke 23:1-49

Palm Sunday of the Passion of the Lord

When you have a birthday party, you need to prepare for it in many ways. You have to decide on a time to have the party and who to invite. Will a cake be baked or ordered?

Once when it was time to celebrate Passover, Jesus sent his disciples to Jerusalem to prepare for the celebration. They went to Jerusalem ahead of Jesus and made all the preparations.

Today on Palm Sunday of the Passion of the Lord, we gather near the entrance of the church to prepare for our celebration. We are given palm branches to use in the celebration.

The priest, wearing red vestments, and the other ministers join us. The palm branches are blessed. Holding them in our hands, we walk in procession into the church while singing,

"Hosanna to the Son of David;
blessed is he who comes in the name of the Lord."

Matthew 21:9

Palm Sunday is the beginning of Holy Week. It is the day on which the Church celebrates Jesus' entry into Jerusalem to celebrate Passover. Our celebration of Palm Sunday prepares us for our celebration of the Easter Triduum, the last three days of Holy Week.

Giving Praise to God

This hymn often is sung during the procession at the beginning of the liturgy on Palm Sunday. Pray the words of this hymn reverently.

All Glory, Laud, and Honor

All: **All glory, laud, and honor**
To you, Redeemer King!
To whom the lips of children
Made sweet hosannas ring.

Group 1: You are the King of Israel,
And David's royal Son,
Now in the Lord's Name coming,
Our King and Blessed One.

All: **All glory, laud, and honor**
To you, Redeemer King!
To whom the lips of children
Made sweet hosannas ring.

Group 2: The people of the Hebrews
With palms before you went:
Our praise and prayers and anthems
Before you we present.

All: **All glory, laud, and honor**
To you, Redeemer King!
To whom the lips of children
Made sweet hosannas ring.

Traditional Hymn

MY FAITH CHOICE

This week, I will honor Jesus as my King. I will

____

____

____.

Pray, "We praise and welcome you, Lord."

Triduum/ Holy Thursday

We all have favorite memories of events and celebrations. Triduum is a word the Church uses for the last three days of Holy Week. The three celebrations of the Triduum are Holy Thursday, Good Friday, and Easter Vigil/Easter.

On Holy Thursday, we remember the last time Jesus shared a meal with his disciples. Together they celebrated Passover.

During the Passover meal, bread and wine were shared. When Jesus shared the bread and wine at the Last Supper, he gave it a new meaning. He took bread, said the blessing prayer, broke the bread, and said,

"This is my body, which will be given for you." LUKE 22:19

After the meal, he shared the cup of wine and said,

"This cup is the new covenant in my blood,
which will be shed for you." LUKE 22:20

Jesus commanded the Apostles to share this meal with one another. He said,

"[Do] this in memory of me." LUKE 22:19

The Church follows Jesus' command each time we celebrate the Eucharist.

Faith Focus
What do we remember on Holy Thursday?

The Word of the Lord
These are the three Scripture readings for Mass on Holy Thursday evening. Choose one of the readings and find it in a Bible. Read and discuss the reading with your family.

First Reading:
Exodus 12:1-8, 11-14

Second Reading:
1 Corinthians 11:23-26

Gospel:
John 13:1-15

What You See
Members representing the assembly come forth. The priest pours water over their feet and dries them. This reminds us that Jesus washed the disciples' feet at the Last Supper. By doing this, Jesus taught us to serve others too.

Mosaic of the Institution of the Eucharist at the Last Supper
Medugorje, Federation of Bosnia and Herzegovina

In Memory of Me

Write a cinquain about either the bread or the wine and the new meaning Jesus gave it. Follow the pattern to write your cinquain.

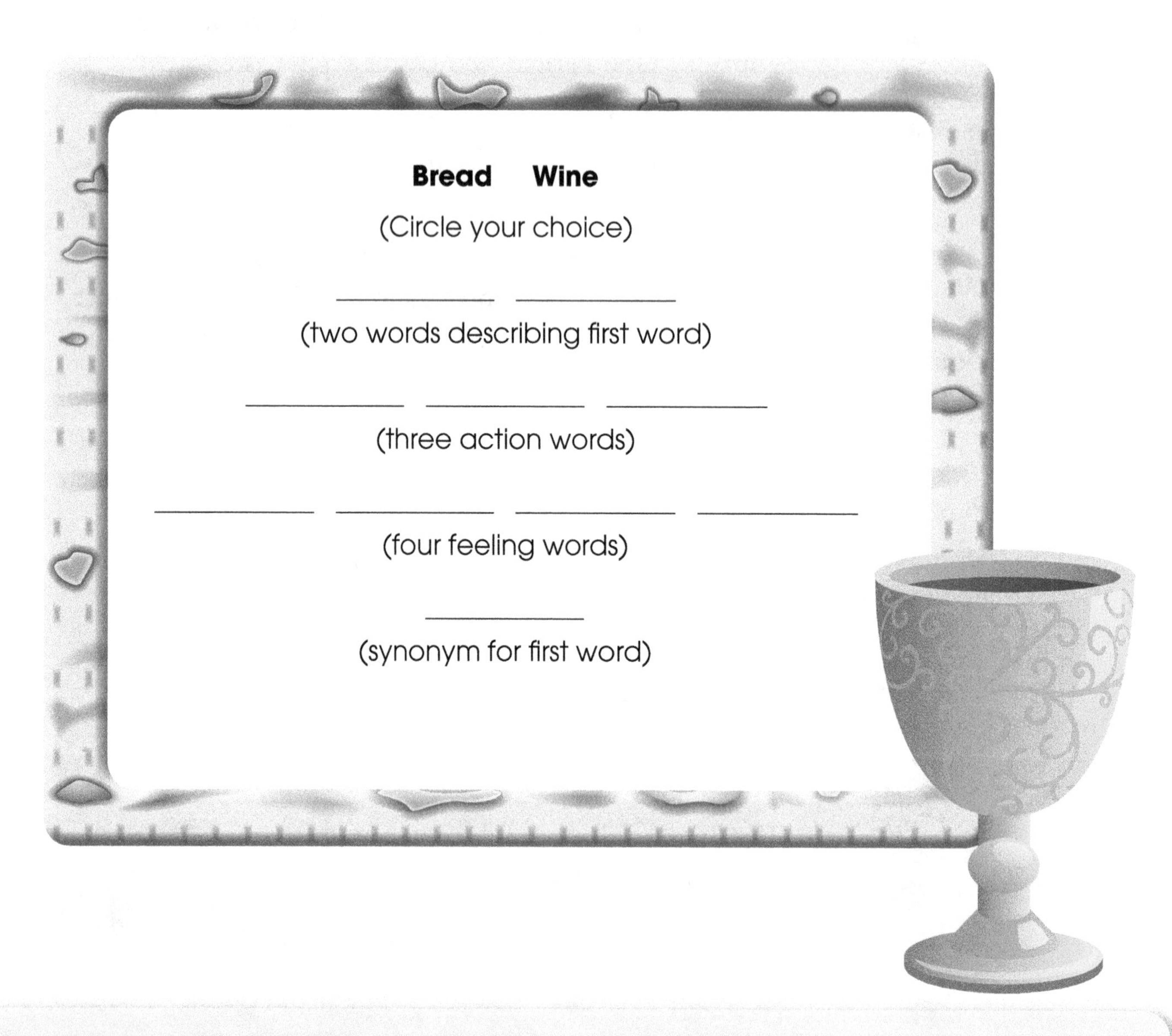

MY FAITH CHOICE

I will serve others in Jesus' name. I will

____

____

____.

Pray, "Whoever eats the bread and drinks from the cup will live forever."

Triduum/Good Friday

Faith Focus
What does the Church remember and celebrate on Good Friday?

The Word of the Lord
These are the three Scripture readings for Good Friday. Choose one of the readings and find it in the Bible. Read and discuss the reading with your family.

First Reading:
Isaiah 52:13–53:12

Second Reading:
Hebrews 4:14-16, 5:7-9

Gospel:
John 18:1-19:42

On Good Friday we celebrate the Passion and Death of Jesus. No Mass is celebrated anywhere. Our celebration on Good Friday is made up of three parts: the Liturgy of the Word, the Adoration of the Holy Cross, and Holy Communion.

The priest begins with a prayer asking God to watch over us and make us holy. Next we listen to the readings from the Old Testament and the New Testament. Then the Passion of Jesus is read from the Gospel according to John.

Next we join the priest in praying for the Church and its leaders, the people who are preparing for Baptism, and for all people who need our prayers.

After the Liturgy of the Word, the deacon or priest enters the church holding the cross up high. Three times he sings out loud, "Behold the wood of the Cross, / on which hung the salvation of the world." We answer, "Come, let us adore." Then we are invited to walk up to the cross and show our reverence for it.

Now the altar is prepared and we are invited to receive Holy Communion. When our celebration ends, we leave the church in silence. We thank God for his great love for us.

The Wood of the Cross

On the sides and bottom of the cross, write the three parts of the celebration on Good Friday. Below the cross, write a prayer of thanksgiving to God for his great love for us. Pray it quietly by yourself.

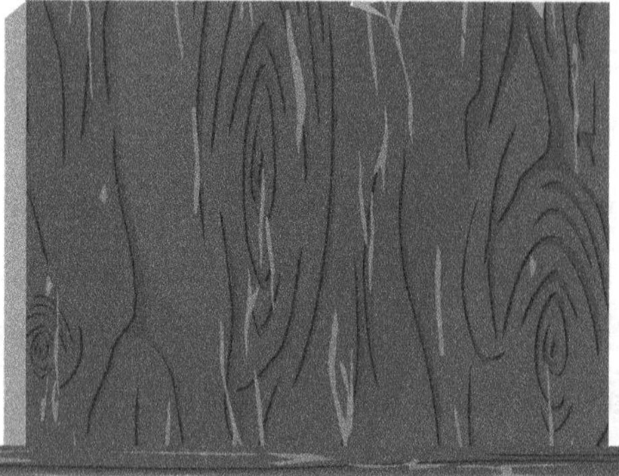

Part 1 ______________________

Part 2 ______________________

Part 3 ______________________

____

____

____

MY FAITH CHOICE

I will remember the Passion and Death of Christ. I will

____

____

______________________.

Honor the suffering of Christ. Pray, "You are the Savior of the world!"

Faith Focus

What do we remember and celebrate at the Easter Vigil and on Easter Sunday?

The Word of the Lord

These are the Gospel readings for Mass on Easter Sunday. Choose this year's reading and find it in a Bible. Read and discuss the reading with your family.

Years A, B, and C:
John 20:1-9 or
Matthew 28:1-10 or
Luke 24:13-35

Triduum/ Easter

Easter is a special day for Christians. Some families decorate their homes with flowers. Christians around the world celebrate Easter in a special way! It is the most important season of the Church year.

The Church invites us to celebrate joyfully the seven Sundays of the Easter season. The Church celebrates Easter for fifty days. Each of its seven Sundays recalls the new life Jesus won for us.

Throughout the Easter season, we sing and proclaim "Alleluia" out loud for all to hear. *Alleluia* means "Praise the Lord!" We also remember Easter Sunday as a special day. To celebrate our joy, we may sing, "This is the day the Lord has made; let us rejoice and be glad" (RESPONSORIAL PSALM, EASTER SUNDAY).

He Is Risen

Pray the end of this hymn that we sing at the Easter Vigil Mass. It is from the Easter Proclamation, also called the Exsultet.

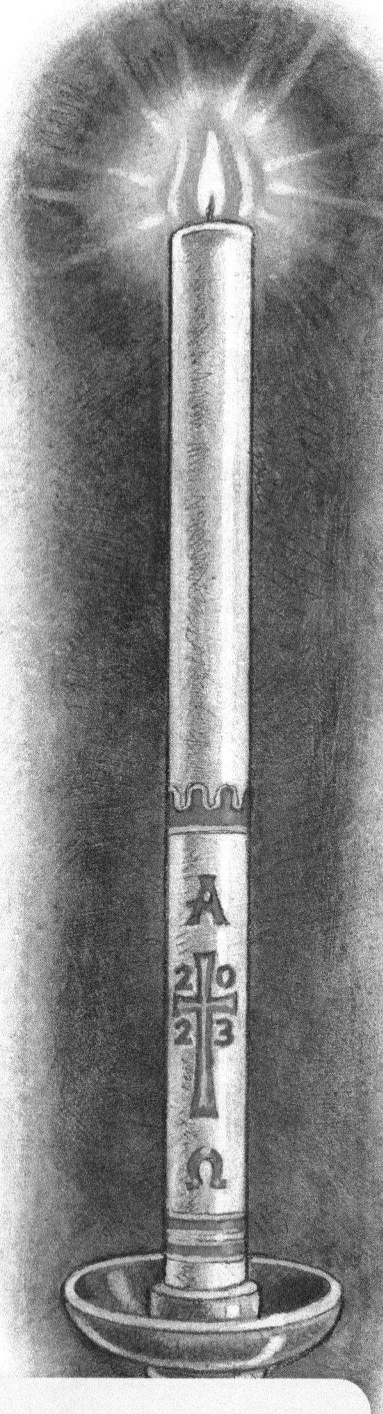

Exsultet

Leader: **On this, your night of grace, O holy Father,**
accept this candle, a solemn offering,
the work of bees and of your servants' hands,
an evening sacrifice of praise,
this gift from your most holy Church.

All: **Therefore, O Lord,**
we pray you that this candle,
hallowed to the honor of your name,
may persevere undimmed,
to overcome the darkness of this night.
Receive it as a pleasing fragrance,
and let it mingle with the lights of heaven.
May this flame be found still burning
by the Morning Star:
the one Morning Star who never sets,
Christ your Son,
who, coming back from death's domain,
has shed his peaceful light on humanity,
and lives and reigns for ever and ever.
Amen.

ROMAN MISSAL

MY FAITH CHOICE

This week, I will be grateful for new life in Christ. I will

____

____

____.

Honor the Resurrected Christ. Pray "Alleluia, Alleluia, Jesus Christ is risen today, Alleluia, Alleluia!"

Faith Focus
What do we believe about the Ascension of the Lord?

The Word of the Lord
These are the Gospel readings for the Ascension of the Lord. Ask your family to read the Gospel for this year with you. Talk about the reading with them.

Year A:
Matthew 28:16-20

Year B:
Mark 16:15-20

Year C:
Luke 24:46-53

Ascension

During the forty days after Easter, the Risen Jesus appeared to the Apostles. They ate and drank together, and Jesus continued to teach them about the Kingdom of God. One day, as they were gathered together on a hillside, Jesus reminded them that God would send the Holy Spirit to help them teach others about God's kingdom.

Jesus told them that through the power of the Holy Spirit, the Apostles would

> "make disciples of all nations, baptizing them in the name of the Father, and of the Son, and of the holy Spirit."
>
> Matthew 28:19

Jesus promised to be with them always until the end of the world. Then Jesus

> "was taken up into heaven and took his seat at the right hand of God."
>
> Mark 16:19

We call this the Ascension of the Lord. Jesus ascended into Heaven and returned to his Father.

The Church celebrates the Ascension of the Lord forty days after Easter (or on the Seventh Sunday of Easter). The Ascension gives all of Jesus' disciples hope. Jesus promised his followers that he was going to Heaven to prepare a place for us. We believe that, one day, we too will share everlasting life with God if we have tried to live as faithful followers of Jesus.

Thank You, Lord

Imagine you are one of the Apostles after the Ascension of Jesus into Heaven. As an Apostle, you are grateful for the time you spent with Jesus and all that you learned from him. In the space below, write a letter thanking Jesus, and share with him how you will continue to live as his faithful follower.

MY FAITH CHOICE

This week, I will show my hope in Jesus' promise of everlasting life. I will

____

____

____.

Pray, "Bless us, Lord, and prepare a place for us in your Kingdom."

Pentecost Sunday

Faith Focus
What do Christians remember and celebrate on Pentecost Sunday?

The Word of the Lord
These are the Gospel readings for Pentecost Sunday. Choose this year's reading and find it in a Bible. Read and discuss the reading with your family.

Year A:
John 7:37-39
John 20:19-23

Year B:
John 7:37-39 or
John 15:26-27, 16:12-15

Year C:
John 7:37-39 or
John 14:15-16, 23-26

Sometimes we hear a person speak a language we do not know. We wish we could understand.

On Pentecost, fifty days after Jesus' Resurrection, people from many places and who spoke many languages were in Jerusalem. On that day, Mary and the disciples were praying together in an upstairs room in the city of Jerusalem. Suddenly, a great wind roared through the room. Tongues of fire rested over their heads. They were filled with the Holy Spirit.

Then Peter, filled with courage, went out and addressed the crowds in the streets. He proclaimed the Good News of Jesus' Death and Resurrection. Everyone heard Peter in his or her own language and understood his message! When they asked Peter what they should do, Peter told them to change their ways and be baptized.

On Pentecost Sunday, we remember that we too are filled with the Holy Spirit. We proclaim the Good News of Jesus' Death and Resurrection. We do this by our good, helpful, loving acts toward others.

Pentecost
by Navarro Perez Dolz
Santuario Nuestra Senora del Sagrado Corazon, Barcelona

The Work of the Holy Spirit

Look at each of the pictures. The last frame is blank. Draw or write how you will help do the work of the Holy Spirit as one of Jesus' disciples.

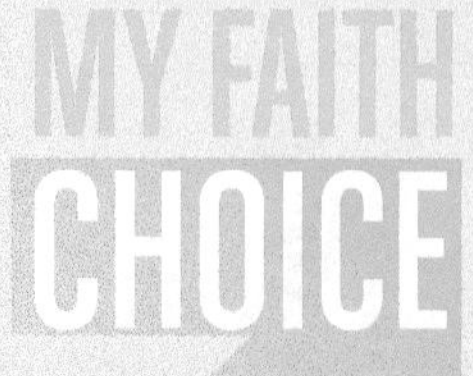

MY FAITH CHOICE

This week, I will ask the Holy Spirit to guide me. I will

____

____

____

Each day I will pray, "Come, Holy Spirit, come!"

Catholic Prayers and Practices

Sign of the Cross

In the name of the Father,
and of the Son,
and of the Holy Spirit. Amen.

Signum Crucis

In nómine Patris,
et Fílii,
et Spíritus Sancti. Amen.

Our Father

Our Father, who art in heaven,
hallowed be thy name;
thy kingdom come,
thy will be done
on earth as it is in heaven.
Give us this day our daily bread,
and forgive us our trespasses,
as we forgive those who trespass
against us;
and lead us not into temptation,
but deliver us from evil.
Amen.

Pater Noster

Pater noster, qui es in cælis:
sanctificétur nomen tuum;
advéniat regnum tuum;
fiat volúntas tua, sicut
in cælo, et in terra.
Panem nostrum cotidiánum
da nobis hódie;
et dimítte nobis débita nostra,
sicut et nos dimíttimus debitóribus
nostris;
et ne nos indúcas in tentatiónem;
sed líbera nos a malo. Amen.

Glory Be (Doxology)

Glory be to the Father
and to the Son
and to the Holy Spirit,
as it was in the beginning
is now, and ever shall be
world without end. Amen.

Gloria Patri

Glória Patri
et Fílio
et Spirítui Sancto.
Sicut erat in princípio,
et nunc et semper
et in sæcula sæculórum. Amen.

The Hail Mary

Hail, Mary, full of grace,
the Lord is with thee.
Blessed art thou among women
and blessed is the fruit
of thy womb, Jesus.
Holy Mary, Mother of God,
pray for us sinners,
now and at the hour of our death.
Amen.

Ave, Maria

Ave, María, grátia plena,
Dóminus tecum.
Benedícta tu in muliéribus,
et benedíctus fructus ventris tui, Iesus.
Sancta María, Mater Dei,
ora pro nobis peccatóribus,
nunc et in hora mortis nostræ.
Amen.

Apostles' Creed

(from the *Roman Missal*)

I believe in God,
the Father almighty,
Creator of heaven and earth,
and in Jesus Christ, his only Son,
our Lord,

(At the words that follow, up to and including the Virgin Mary, *all bow.)*

who was conceived by the Holy Spirit,
born of the Virgin Mary,
suffered under Pontius Pilate,
was crucified, died and was buried;
he descended into hell;
on the third day he rose again
from the dead;
he ascended into heaven,
and is seated at the right hand of God
the Father almighty;
from there he will come to judge
the living and the dead.

I believe in the Holy Spirit,
the holy catholic Church,
the communion of saints,
the forgiveness of sins,
the resurrection of the body,
and life everlasting. Amen.

Nicene Creed

(from the *Roman Missal*)

I believe in one God,
the Father almighty,
maker of heaven and earth,
of all things visible and invisible.

I believe in one Lord Jesus Christ,
the Only Begotten Son of God,
born of the Father before all ages.
God from God, Light from Light,
true God from true God,
begotten, not made, consubstantial
with the Father;
through him all things were made.
For us men and for our salvation
he came down from heaven,

(At the words that follow, up to and including and became man, *all bow.)*

and by the Holy Spirit was incarnate
of the Virgin Mary,
and became man.

For our sake he was crucified under
Pontius Pilate,
he suffered death and was buried,
and rose again on the third day
in accordance with the Scriptures.
He ascended into heaven
and is seated at the right hand
of the Father.
He will come again in glory
to judge the living and the dead
and his kingdom will have no end.

I believe in the Holy Spirit, the Lord,
the giver of life,
who proceeds from the Father and
the Son,
who with the Father and the Son is
adored and glorified,
who has spoken through the prophets.

I believe in one, holy, catholic and
apostolic Church.
I confess one Baptism for the
forgiveness of sins
and I look forward to the resurrection
of the dead
and the life of the world to come.
Amen.

Morning Prayer

Dear God,
as I begin this day,
keep me in your love and care.
Help me to live as your child today.
Bless me, my family, and my friends
in all we do.
Keep us all close to you. Amen.

Grace Before Meals

Bless us, O Lord,
and these thy gifts,
which we are about to receive
from thy bounty,
through Christ our Lord.
Amen.

Grace After Meals

We give thee thanks,
for all thy benefits, almighty God,
who lives and reigns forever.
Amen.

Evening Prayer

Dear God,
I thank you for today.
Keep me safe throughout the night.
Thank you for all the good I did today.
I am sorry for what I have chosen
to do wrong.
Bless my family and friends. Amen.

A Vocation Prayer

God, I know you will call me
for special work in my life.
Help me follow Jesus each day
and be ready to answer your call. Amen.

Prayer to the Holy Spirit

Come, Holy Spirit, fill the hearts
of your faithful.
And kindle in them the
fire of your love.
Send forth your Spirit and
they shall be created.
And you will renew the
face of the earth. Amen.

Act of Contrition

My God,
I am sorry for my sins
with all my heart.
In choosing to do wrong
and failing to do good,
I have sinned against you,
whom I should love above all things.
I firmly intend, with your help,
to do penance,
to sin no more,
and to avoid whatever leads me to sin.
Our Savior Jesus Christ
suffered and died for us.
In his name, my God, have mercy. Amen.

The Beatitudes

"Blessed are the poor in spirit,
for theirs is the kingdom of heaven.
Blessed are they who mourn,
for they will be comforted.
Blessed are the meek,
for they will inherit the land.
Blessed are they who hunger
and thirst for righteousness,
for they will be satisfied.
Blessed are the merciful,
for they will be shown mercy.
Blessed are the clean of heart,
for they will see God.
Blessed are the peacemakers,
for they will be called children
of God.
Blessed are they who are persecuted for
the sake of righteousness,
for theirs is the kingdom of heaven."

MATTHEW 5:3-10

The Angelus

Leader: The Angel of the Lord declared unto Mary,

Response: And she conceived of the Holy Spirit.

All: **Hail, Mary . . .**

Leader: Behold the handmaid of the Lord,

Response: Be it done unto me according to your Word.

All: **Hail, Mary . . .**

Leader: And the Word was made flesh,

Response: And dwelt among us.

All: **Hail, Mary . . .**

Leader: Pray for us, O Holy Mother of God,

Response: That we may be made worthy of the promises of Christ.

Leader: Let us pray.

All: **Pour forth, we beseech you, O Lord, your grace into our hearts; that we, to whom the Incarnation of Christ your Son was made known by the message of an Angel, may by his Passion and Cross be brought to the glory of his Resurrection. Through the same Christ our Lord. Amen.**

The Ten Commandments

1. I am the LORD your God: you shall not have strange gods before me.
2. You shall not take the name of the LORD your God in vain.
3. Remember to keep holy the LORD's Day.
4. Honor your father and your mother.
5. You shall not kill.
6. You shall not commit adultery.
7. You shall not steal.
8. You shall not lie.
9. You shall not covet your neighbor's wife.
10. You shall not covet your neighbor's goods.

BASED ON EXODUS 20:2-3, 7-17

Precepts of the Church

1. Participate in Mass on Sundays and holy days of obligation, and rest from unnecessary work.
2. Confess sins at least once a year.
3. Receive Holy Communion at least during the Easter season.
4. Observe the prescribed days of fasting and abstinence.
5. Provide for the material needs of the Church, according to one's abilities.

The Great Commandment

"You shall love the Lord,
your God, with all your
heart, with all your soul,
and with all your mind. . . .
You shall love your neighbor as yourself."

MATTHEW 22:37, 39

The Law of Love

"This is my commandment:
love one another as I love you."

JOHN 15:12

Corporal Works of Mercy

Feed people who are hungry.
Give drink to people who are thirsty.
Clothe people who need clothes.
Visit people who are in prison.
Shelter people who are homeless.
Visit people who are sick.
Bury people who have died.

Spiritual Works of Mercy

Help people who sin.
Teach people who are ignorant.
Give advice to people who have doubts.
Comfort people who suffer.
Be patient with other people.
Forgive people who hurt you.
Pray for people who are alive and for those who have died.

Rosary

Catholics pray the Rosary to honor Mary and remember the important events in the lives of Jesus and Mary.There are twenty mysteries of the Rosary. Follow the steps from 1 to 5.

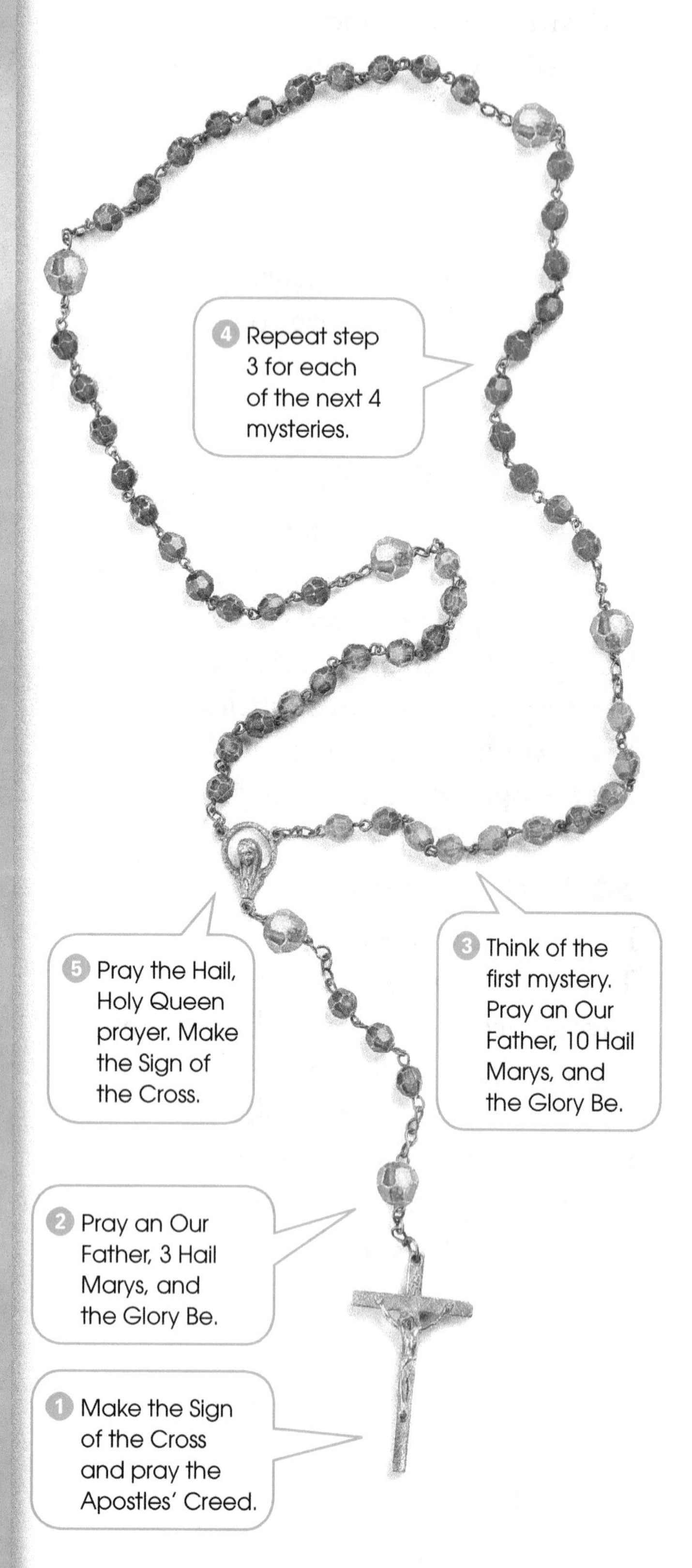

Joyful Mysteries

1. The Annunciation
2. The Visitation
3. The Nativity
4. The Presentation in the Temple
5. The Finding of the Child Jesus After Three Days in the Temple

Luminous Mysteries

1. The Baptism at the Jordan
2. The Miracle at Cana
3. The Proclamation of the Kingdom and the Call to Conversion
4. The Transfiguration
5. The Institution of the Eucharist

Sorrowful Mysteries

1. The Agony in the Garden
2. The Scourging at the Pillar
3. The Crowning with Thorns
4. The Carrying of the Cross
5. The Crucifixion and Death

Glorious Mysteries

1. The Resurrection
2. The Ascension
3. The Descent of the Holy Spirit at Pentecost
4. The Assumption of Mary
5. The Crowning of the Blessed Virgin as Queen of Heaven and Earth

Hail, Holy Queen

Hail, holy Queen, Mother of mercy:
Hail, our life, our sweetness, and our hope.
To you do we cry, poor banished children of Eve. To you do we send up our sighs, mourning and weeping in this valley of tears. Turn then, most gracious advocate, your eyes of mercy toward us; and after this our exile show unto us the blessed fruit of your womb, Jesus. O clement, O loving, O sweet Virgin Mary.

Stations of the Cross

1. Jesus is condemned to death.

2. Jesus accepts his Cross.

3. Jesus falls the first time.

4. Jesus meets his mother.

5. Simon helps Jesus carry the Cross.

6. Veronica wipes the face of Jesus.

7. Jesus falls the second time.

8. Jesus meets the women.

9. Jesus falls the third time.

10. Jesus is stripped of his clothes.

11. Jesus is nailed to the Cross.

12. Jesus dies on the Cross.

13. Jesus is taken down from the Cross.

14. Jesus is buried in the tomb.

(Some parishes conclude the Stations by reflecting on the Resurrection of Jesus.)

The Seven Sacraments

Jesus gave the Church the Seven Sacraments. The sacraments are the main liturgical signs of the Church. They make the Paschal Mystery of Jesus, who is always the main celebrant of each sacrament, present to us. They make us sharers in the saving work of Christ and in the life of the Holy Trinity.

Sacraments of Christian Initiation

Baptism

Through Baptism, we are joined to Christ and become members of the Body of Christ, the Church. We are reborn as adopted children of God and receive the gift of the Holy Spirit. Original Sin and all personal sins are forgiven.

Confirmation

Confirmation completes Baptism. In this sacrament, the gift of the Holy Spirit strengthens us to live our Baptism.

Eucharist

Sharing in the Eucharist joins us most fully to Christ and to the Church. We share in the one sacrifice of Christ. The bread and wine become the Body and Blood of Christ through the power of the Holy Spirit and the words of the priest. We receive the Body and Blood of Christ.

Sacraments of Healing

Penance and Reconciliation

Through the ministry of the priest, we receive forgiveness of sins committed fter our Baptism. We need to confess all mortal sins.

Anointing of the Sick

Anointing of the Sick strengthens our faith and trust in God when we are seriously ill, dying, or weak because of old age.

Sacraments at the Service of Communion

Holy Orders

Through Holy Orders, a baptized man is consecrated to serve the whole Church as a bishop, priest, or deacon in the name of Christ. Bishops, who are the successors of the Apostles, receive this sacrament most fully. They are consecrated to teach the Gospel, to lead the Church in the worship of God, and to guide the Church to live holy lives. Bishops are helped in their work by priests, their coworkers, and by deacons.

Matrimony

Matrimony unites a baptized man and a baptized woman in a lifelong bond of faithful love to honor each other always and to accept the gift of children from God. In this sacrament, the married couple is consecrated to be a sign of God's love for the Church.

We Celebrate the Mass

The Introductory Rites

We remember that we are the community of the Church.
We prepare to listen to the Word of God and to celebrate the Eucharist.

The Entrance

We stand as the priest, deacon, and other ministers enter the assembly. We sing a gathering song. The priest and deacon kiss the altar. The priest then goes to the chair where he presides over the celebration.

Sign of the Cross and Greeting

The priest leads us in praying the Sign of the Cross. The priest greets us, and we say, **"And with your spirit."**

The Penitential Act

We admit our wrong doings.
We bless God for his mercy.

The Gloria

We praise God for all the good that he has done for us.

The Collect

The priest leads us in praying the Collect. We respond, **"Amen."**

The Liturgy of the Word

God speaks to us today. We listen and respond to God's Word.

The First Reading from Scripture

We sit and listen as the reader reads from the Old Testament or from the Acts of the Apostles. The reader concludes, "The word of the Lord." We respond,

"Thanks be to God."

The Responsorial Psalm

The song leader leads us in singing a psalm.

The Second Reading from Scripture

The reader reads from the New Testament, but not from the four Gospels. The reader concludes, "The word of the Lord." We respond,

"Thanks be to God."

The Acclamation

We stand to honor Christ, present with us in the Gospel. The song leader leads us in singing **"Alleluia, Alleluia, Alleluia"** or another chant during Lent.

The Gospel

The deacon or priest proclaims,
"A reading from the holy Gospel according to (name of Gospel writer)."
We respond,

"Glory to you, O Lord."

He proclaims the Gospel. At the end he says, "The Gospel of the Lord."
We respond,

"Praise to you, Lord Jesus Christ."

The Homily

We sit. The priest or deacon preaches the homily. He helps the people gathered to understand the Word of God spoken to us in the readings.

The Profession of Faith

We stand and profess our faith.
We pray the Nicene Creed together.

The Prayer of the Faithful

The priest leads us in praying for our Church and her leaders, for our country and its leaders, for ourselves and others, for those who are sick and those who have died. We can respond to each prayer in several ways. One way that we respond is

"Lord, hear our prayer."

The Liturgy of the Eucharist

We join with Jesus and the Holy Spirit to give thanks and praise to God the Father.

The Preparation of the Gifts

We sit as the altar is prepared and the collection is taken up. We share our blessings with the community of the Church and especially with those in need. The song leader may lead us in singing a song. The gifts of bread and wine are brought to the altar.

The priest lifts up the bread and blesses God for all our gifts. He prays, "Blessed are you, Lord God of all creation. . . ." We respond,

"Blessed be God for ever."

The priest lifts up the cup of wine and prays, "Blessed are you, Lord God of all creation. . . . " We respond,

"Blessed be God for ever."

The priest invites us,

"Pray, brothers and sisters, that my sacrifice and yours may be acceptable to God, the almighty Father."

We stand and respond,

"May the Lord accept the sacrifice at your hands for the praise and glory of his name, for our good, and the good of all his holy Church."

The Prayer over the Offerings

The priest leads us in praying the Prayer over the Offerings.
We respond, **"Amen."**

Preface

The priest invites us to join in praying the Church's great prayer of praise and thanksgiving to God the Father.

Priest: "The Lord be with you."

Assembly: **"And with your spirit."**

Priest: "Lift up your hearts."

Assembly: **"We lift them up to the Lord."**

Priest: "Let us give thanks to the Lord our God."

Assembly: **"It is right and just."**

After the priest sings or prays aloud the preface, we join in acclaiming,

"Holy, Holy, Holy Lord God of hosts.
Heaven and earth are full of your glory.
Hosanna in the highest.
Blessed is he who comes in the name of the Lord.
Hosanna in the highest."

The Eucharistic Prayer

The priest leads the assembly in praying the Eucharistic Prayer. We call on the Holy Spirit to make our gifts of bread and wine holy so that they become the Body and Blood of Jesus. We recall what happened at the Last Supper. The bread and wine become the Body and Blood of the Lord. Jesus is truly and really present under the appearances of bread and wine.

The priest sings or says aloud, "The mystery of faith." We respond using this or another acclamation used by the Church,

"We proclaim your Death, O Lord, and profess your Resurrection until you come again."

The priest then prays for the Church. He prays for the living and the dead.

Doxology

The priest concludes the praying of the Eucharistic Prayer. He sings or prays aloud,

"Through him, and with him,
and in him,
O God, almighty Father,
in the unity of the Holy Spirit,
all glory and honor is yours,
for ever and ever."

We respond by singing **"Amen."**

The Communion Rite

The Lord's Prayer

We pray the Lord's Prayer together.

The Sign of Peace

The priest invites us to share a sign of peace, saying, "The peace of the Lord be with you always." We respond,

"And with your spirit."

We share a sign of peace.

The Fraction, or the Breaking of the Bread

The priest breaks the host, the consecrated bread. We sing or pray aloud,

"Lamb of God, you take away
the sins of the world,
have mercy on us.
Lamb of God, you take away
the sins of the world,
have mercy on us.
Lamb of God, you take away the sins of the world,
grant us peace."

Communion

The priest raises the host and says aloud,

"Behold the Lamb of God,
behold him who takes away the sins of the world.
Blessed are those called to the supper of the Lamb."

We join with him and say,

"Lord, I am not worthy that
you should enter under my roof,
but only say the word
and my soul shall be healed."

The priest receives Communion. Next, the deacon, the extraordinary ministers of Holy Communion, and the members of the assembly receive Communion.

The priest, deacon, or extraordinary minister of Holy Communion holds up the host. We bow, and the priest, deacon, or extraordinary minister of Holy Communion says, "The Body of Christ." We respond, **"Amen."** We then receive the host in our hands or on our tongues.

If we are to receive the Blood of Christ, the priest, deacon, or extraordinary minister of Holy Communion holds up the cup containing the wine. We bow, and the priest, deacon, or extraordinary minister of Holy Communion says, "The Blood of Christ." We respond, **"Amen."** We take the cup in our hands and drink from it.

The Prayer After Communion

We stand as the priest invites us to pray, saying, "Let us pray." He prays the Prayer After Communion. We respond, **"Amen."**

The Concluding Rites

We are sent forth to do good works, praising and blessing the Lord.

Greeting

We stand. The priest greets us as we prepare to leave. He says, "The Lord be with you." We respond,

"And with your spirit."

Final Blessing

The priest or deacon may invite us,

"Bow down for the blessing."

The priest blesses us, saying,

"May almighty God bless you,
the Father, and the Son,
and the Holy Spirit."

We respond, **"Amen."**

Dismissal of the People

The priest or deacon sends us forth, using these or similar words,

"Go in peace, glorifying the Lord by your life."

We respond,

"Thanks be to God."

We sing a hymn. The priest and the deacon kiss the altar. The priest, deacon, and other ministers bow to the altar and leave in procession.

The Sacrament of Reconciliation

Individual Rite

Greeting

"When the penitent comes to confess [his or her] sins, the priest welcomes [him or her] warmly and greets [the penitent] with kindness" (*Rite of Penance* 41).

Scripture Reading

"[T]hrough the word of God Christians receive light to recognize their sins and are called to conversion and to confidence in God's mercy" (*Rite of Penance* 17).

Confession of Sins and Acceptance of Penance

"[The priest] urges [the penitent] to be sorry for [his or her] faults, reminding [him or her] that through the sacrament of penance the Christian dies and rises with Christ and is renewed in the paschal mystery" (*Rite of Penance* 44).

Act of Contrition

"The most important act of the penitent is contrition . . .The genuineness of penance depends on [a] heartfelt contrition" (*Rite of Penance* 6a).

Absolution

"The form of absolution indicates that the reconciliation of the penitent comes from the mercy of the Father" (*Rite of Penance* 19).

Closing Prayer

"After receiving pardon for sin, the penitent praises the mercy of God and gives him thanks . . . Then the priest bids the penitent to go in peace" (*Rite of Penance* 20).

Communal Rite

Greeting

"When the faithful have assembled, they may sing a psalm, antiphon, or other appropriate song while the priest is entering the church" (*Rite of Penance* 48).

Scripture Reading

"[T]hrough his word God calls his people to repentance and leads them to a true conversion of heart" (*Rite of Penance* 24).

Homily

"The homily . . . should lead the penitents to examine their consciences and renew their lives" (*Rite of Penance* 52).

Examination of Conscience

"A period of time may be spent in making an examination of conscience and in arousing true sorrow for sins" (*Rite of Penance* 53).

Litany of Contrition, and the Lord's Prayer

"The deacon or another minister invites all to kneel or bow, and to join in saying a general formula for confession" (*Rite of Penance* 54).

Individual Confession and Absolution

"[T]he penitents go to the priests designated for individual confession, and confess their sins. Each one receives and accepts a fitting act of satisfaction and is absolved" (*Rite of Penance* 55).

Closing Prayer

"After the song of praise or the litany [for God's mercy], the priest concludes the common prayer" (*Rite of Penance* 57).

The Mystery of God

Divine Revelation

Who am I?

Every human person was created by God to live in friendship with him both here on Earth and forever in Heaven.

How do we know this about ourselves?

We know this because every person wants to know and love God and wants God to know and love them. We also know this because God told us this about ourselves and about him.

How did God tell us?

First of all, God tells us this through all he has created. Creation reflects God's goodness and beauty and tells us about him. Second, God came to us and told us about himself. He revealed this most fully by sending his Son, Jesus Christ, who became one of us and lived among us.

What is faith?

Faith is a supernatural gift from God. It allows us to come to know God and all that he has revealed. It also allows us to respond to God with our whole hearts and minds.

What is a mystery of faith?

The words *mystery of faith* mean that we can never fully understand God and his loving plan for us. We only know who God is and his plan for us because he has told us about himself.

What is Divine Revelation?

Divine Revelation is God's free gift of making himself known to us. God has told us about himself and his divine plan for us gradually. He has done this so that we can live in friendship with him and with one another forever.

What is Sacred Tradition?

The word *tradition* means "to pass on." Sacred Tradition is the passing on of all that God has revealed through the Church by the power and guidance of the Holy Spirit.

Sacred Scripture

What is Sacred Scripture?

The words *sacred scripture* come from two Latin words meaning "holy writings." Sacred Scripture is the collection of all of the writings that God has inspired authors to write in his name.

What is the Bible?

The word *bible* comes from a Greek word meaning "book." The Bible includes the forty-six books of the Old Testament and the twenty-seven books of the New Testament. These are the books named by the Church as all of the writings that God has inspired human authors to write in his name.

What does it mean to say that the Bible is inspired?

When we say the Bible is inspired, we mean that the Holy Spirit guided the human authors of Sacred Scripture to record, faithfully and accurately, what God wants to tell us about himself.

What is the Old Testament?

The Old Testament is the first main part of the Bible, the forty-six books inspired by the Holy Spirit, which were written before the birth of Jesus. These books tell us about the Covenant between God and the people of Israel, and God's promise of the Messiah, or Savior. The Old Testament includes the story of creation and of Adam and Eve. It tells the story of the Hebrew people. It includes their holy writings, including the writings of the prophets.

What is the Covenant?

The Covenant is the solemn agreement of faithfulness that God and his people freely made. It was renewed and fulfilled in Jesus Christ. The Church calls Jesus the new and everlasting Covenant.

What are the writings of the prophets?

The word *prophet* comes from a Greek word meaning "those who speak before others." The prophets in the Bible were people whom God chose to speak in his name. There are eighteen books of the writings of the prophets. They tell the message of the prophets to God's people. They remind God's people of his unending faithfulness to them and of their responsibility to be faithful to the Covenant.

What is the New Testament?

The New Testament is the second main part of the Bible, the twenty-seven books inspired by the Holy Spirit and written during the time of the Apostles. These books focus on Jesus Christ and his saving work among us.

What are the Gospels?

The word *gospel* means "good news." The Gospels tell the Good News of God's loving plan of Salvation. There are four Gospels: Matthew, Mark, Luke, and John. The four Gospels are the heart of the Bible because they tell the story of Jesus Christ.

What are letters of Saint Paul?

There are twenty-one documents in the New Testament that are called letters. Fourteen of these letters are traditionally attributed to Saint Paul. The letters appear between the Acts of the Apostles and the Book of Revelation. The letters usually include a greeting, a prayer of thanksgiving, Church teaching, and practical advice about Christian living. Many of the letters of Paul were written before the four Gospels, and so they are among the earliest writings in the New Testament era.

The Holy Trinity

Who is the Mystery of the Holy Trinity?

The Holy Trinity is the mystery of One God in Three Divine Persons—God the Father, God the Son, and God the Holy Spirit. The Holy Trinity is the central mystery of the Christian faith.

Who is God the Father?

God the Father is the First Person of the Holy Trinity.

Who is God the Son?

God the Son is Jesus Christ, the Second Person of the Holy Trinity. He is the only Son of the Father, who became one of us while still remaining God.

Who is God the Holy Spirit?

God the Holy Spirit is the Third Person of the Holy Trinity, who proceeds from the Father and Son. He is the Advocate, or Helper, sent to us by the Father in the name of his Son, Jesus.

What are the works of the Holy Trinity?

God works as One; however, we connect certain activities to each of the Divine Persons of the Trinity. The work of creation is connected mostly to the Father, the work of Salvation is connected to the Son, and the work of holiness is connected to the Holy Spirit.

Divine Work of Creation

What does it mean to call God the Creator?

Creation means that God brings into existence everything and everyone, both visible and invisible. God does this out of love and without any help.

Who are angels?

Angels are spiritual beings who do not have bodies as humans do. Angels give glory to God at all times. They sometimes serve God by bringing his message to people.

Why are human beings special?

Every human being is created in the image and likeness of God. God calls each of us to a life of happiness with him.

What is the soul?

The soul is the spiritual part of who a person is that will never die. It is your very center and bears the image of God.

What is free will?

Free will is the power given to each of us by God to choose between good and evil and turn toward God.

What is Original Sin?

Original Sin is the sin of Adam and Eve. They chose evil over obedience to God. As a result of Original Sin, death, sin, and suffering came into the world.

Jesus Christ, Son of God, Son of Mary

What is the Annunciation?

The Annunciation is the announcement by the angel Gabriel to Mary. The angel told her that God had chosen her to become the Mother of his Son, Jesus, by the power of the Holy Spirit.

What is the Incarnation?

Incarnation means that the Son of God, the Second Person of the Holy Trinity, truly became human while remaining truly God. Jesus Christ is true God and true man.

What does it mean that Jesus is Lord?

The word *lord* means "master or ruler." When we call Jesus "the Lord," we mean that Jesus is truly God.

What is the Paschal Mystery?

The Paschal Mystery is the saving events of the Passion, Death, Resurrection, and glorious Ascension of Jesus Christ. It is the passing over of Jesus from death into a new and glorious life. It is the name that we give to God's plan of Salvation in Jesus Christ.

What is Salvation?

The word *salvation* means "to save." It is the saving of all people from the power of sin and death through Jesus Christ.

What is the Resurrection?

The Resurrection means that Jesus was raised from the dead to new life after his Death on the Cross and burial in the tomb.

What is the Ascension?

The Ascension is the return of the Risen Christ in glory to his Father in Heaven.

What is the Second Coming of Christ?

The Second Coming of Christ means that Christ will come again in glory at the end of time to judge the living and the dead. This is the fulfillment of God's plan.

What does it mean that Jesus is the Messiah?

The word *messiah* means "anointed one." Jesus Christ is the Anointed One, the Messiah, whom God promised to send to save all people. Jesus is the Savior of the world.

The Mystery of The Church

What is the Church?

The word *church* means "those who are called together." The Church is the Body of Christ on Earth, the people whom God the Father has called together in Jesus Christ through the power of the Holy Spirit.

What does the Church do?

The Church proclaims the Gospel, or Good News, of Jesus Christ. She invites all people to come to know and believe in him and to follow him.

What is the Body of Christ?

When we call the Church the Body of Christ, we mean that all of the members of the Church are one in Christ, who is the Head of the Church. Each member of the Church has a unique and important part to play to continue the work of Jesus in the world.

Who are the People of God?

The People of God are those whom God the Father has chosen and gathered in Christ in the Church. All people are invited to belong to the People of God and to live as one family of God.

What is the Communion of Saints?

The Communion of Saints is all of the holy people that make up the Church. It includes those living on Earth, those who have died who are still becoming holier, and those who are enjoying everlasting life and happiness with God.

What are the Marks of the Church?

There are four Marks, or main characteristics, of the Church. The Church is one, holy, catholic, and apostolic.

Who are the Apostles?

The Apostles were those disciples chosen and sent by Jesus to preach the Gospel and to make disciples of all people. Their names are Simon called Peter; his brother Andrew; James, the son of Zebedee; his brother John; Philip and Bartholomew; Thomas; Matthew the tax collector; James, the son of Alphaeus; Thaddaeus; Simon from Cana; and Judas Iscariot, who betrayed Jesus. The Apostle Matthias was chosen after Jesus' Ascension.

What is Pentecost?

Pentecost is the day that the Holy Spirit came to the Church as promised by Jesus. This is the day on which the work of the Church began.

Who are the clergy?

The clergy are bishops, priests, and deacons. They have received the Sacrament of Holy Orders to serve the whole Church.

What is the work of the pope?

Jesus Christ is the true Head of the Church. The pope and all the bishops govern the Church in his name. The pope is the bishop of Rome and the successor of Saint Peter the Apostle. The pope is the sign of unity for the whole Church. When the pope speaks officially to the entire Church on a serious matter of faith or morals, the Holy Spirit guides him to speak without error.

What is the work of the bishops?

The other bishops are the successors of the Apostles. They teach and lead the Church in their own dioceses. When all of the bishops gather together with the pope and decide a serious matter of faith or morals, the Holy Spirit also guides them to speak without error.

What is religious life?

This is a way of life chosen by some men and women who dedicate their whole lives to following Jesus in a special way. They promise not to marry and to dedicate their whole lives to continuing Jesus' work. They make promises, called vows, that they will live holy lives. They promise to live very simply, sharing what they have with one another. They live in communities of men or women rather than with their families. They promise to obey the rules of their communities and to obey the community leaders. They may lead quiet lives of prayer, teach, or take care of sick or poor people.

Who are laypeople?

Laypeople are all baptized people who have not received the Sacrament of Holy Orders and are not members of a religious community. They are called to be witnesses for Christ in their everyday lives.

The Blessed Virgin Mary

Who is Mary?

Mary is the woman whom God chose to be the Mother of his only Son, Jesus. Mary has a unique role in God's plan of Salvation for humanity. Because Jesus Christ is truly God and truly man, the Church teaches that Mary is the Mother of God, the Mother of Christ, and the Mother of the Church. She is the greatest saint of the Church.

What is the Immaculate Conception?

The Immaculate Conception means that from the first moment of her existence, Mary was preserved from the stain of all sin. This special grace continued throughout her life.

What is the Assumption of Mary?

At the end of her life on Earth, the Blessed Virgin Mary was taken body and soul into Heaven. Mary the Mother of the Church, hears our prayers and tells her Son. She reminds us of the life that we all hope to share when Christ, her Son, comes again in glory.

Life Everlasting

What is eternal life?

Eternal life is life after death. At death, the soul is separated from the body and passes into eternal life.

What is Heaven?

Heaven is eternal life and communion with the Holy Trinity. It is the happiness of living with God forever, for which he created us.

What is the Kingdom of God?

The Kingdom of God, or Kingdom of Heaven, is the image used by Jesus to describe all people and creation living in harmony with God. The Kingdom of God will be fully realized when Christ comes again in glory at the end of time.

What is Purgatory?

Purgatory is the opportunity after death to purify and strengthen our love for God before we enter Heaven.

What is Hell?

Hell is the immediate and everlasting separation from God and the saints.

Celebration of the Christian Life and Mystery

Liturgy and Worship

What is worship?

Worship is the adoration and honor given to God. The Church worships God publicly in the celebration of the liturgy.

What is liturgy?

The liturgy is the Church's worship of God. It is the work of the whole Christ, Head and Body. In the liturgy, Christ is made present by the power of the Holy Spirit.

What is the liturgical year?

The liturgical year is the cycle of seasons and great feasts that make up the Church year of worship. The main seasons of the Church year are Advent, Christmas, Lent, and Easter. The Easter Triduum is the three high holy days. The rest of the liturgical year is called Ordinary Time.

The Sacraments

What are the sacraments?

The sacraments are seven signs of God's love and the main liturgical actions of the Church. They make us sharers in the Paschal Mystery of Christ. The sacraments were instituted by Christ and entrusted to the Church. Through the sacraments, the divine life of grace is shared with us.

What are the Sacraments of Christian Initiation?

The Sacraments of Christian Initiation are Baptism, Confirmation, and the Eucharist. These three sacraments are the foundation of every Christian life.

What is the Sacrament of Baptism?

Through Baptism we are reborn into new life in Christ. We are joined to Jesus Christ, become members of the Church, and are reborn as God's children. We receive the gift of the Holy Spirit, and Original Sin and our personal sins are forgiven. Baptism marks us indelibly and forever as belonging to Christ. Because of this, Baptism can be received only once.

What is the Sacrament of Confirmation?

Confirmation strengthens the graces of Baptism and celebrates the special gift of the Holy Spirit that empowers us in a fuller way to share the Good News of Jesus Christ with others.

What is the Sacrament of the Eucharist?

In the Eucharist, the faithful join with Christ to give thanksgiving, honor, and glory to the Father through the power of the Holy Spirit.

Through the power of the Holy Spirit and the words of the priest, the bread and wine become the Body and Blood of Christ.

What is our obligation to participate in the Eucharist?

Catholics have the obligation to participate in the Eucharist on Sundays and holy days of obligation. Sunday is the Lord's Day. Sunday, the day of the Lord's Resurrection, is the heart of the whole liturgical year. Regular participation in the Eucharist and receiving Holy Communion are necessary to the Christian life. In the Eucharist we receive the Body and Blood of Christ.

What is the Mass?

The Mass is the main celebration of the Church. The Mass has two parts. In the first part, the Liturgy of the Word, we gather to listen to the Word of God. In the second part, the Liturgy of the Eucharist, we are made sharers in the saving Death and Resurrection of Christ and give praise and thanksgiving to the Father.

What are the Sacraments of Healing?

The two Sacraments of Healing are the Sacrament of Penance and Reconciliation and the Sacrament of the Anointing of the Sick. Through the power of the Holy Spirit, Christ's work of Salvation and of healing the members of the Church is continued.

What is the Sacrament of Penance and Reconciliation?

The Sacrament of Penance is one of the two Sacraments of Healing through which we receive God's forgiveness for the sins that we have committed after Baptism.

What is confession?

Confession is the telling of sins to a priest in the Sacrament of Penance and Reconcilition. Confession is another name for the sacrament.

What is contrition?

Contrition is sorrow for sins. It includes the desire and commitment to make up for the harm our sins have caused. It also includes our firm intention not to sin again. Contrition is a necessary part of the Sacrament of Penance and Reconciliation.

What is a penance?

A penance is a prayer or act of kindness that shows that we are truly sorry for our sins. The penance given to us by the priest helps to repair the damage caused by our sins. Accepting and doing our penance are necessary parts of the Sacrament of Penance and Reconciliation.

What is absolution?

Absolution is the forgiveness of sins by God through the ministry of the priest.

What is the Sacrament of the Anointing of the Sick?

The Sacrament of the Anointing of the Sick is one of the two Sacraments of Healing. The grace of this sacrament strengthens our faith and trust in God when we are seriously ill, weakened by old age, or dying. Catholics may receive this sacrament each time that they are seriously ill or when an illness gets worse.

What are the Sacraments at the Service of Communion?

Holy Orders and Matrimony are the two Sacraments at the Service of Communion. These sacraments give those who receive them a particular work, or mission, to serve and build up the People of God.

What is the Sacrament of Holy Orders?

The Sacrament of Holy Orders is one of the two Sacraments at the Service of Communion. It is the sacrament in which baptized men are consecrated as bishops, priests, or deacons to serve the whole Church in the name and person of Christ.

Who is a bishop?

A bishop is a priest who receives the fullness of the Sacrament of Holy Orders. He is a successor of the Apostles who leads and serves a particular diocese entrusted to him. He teaches, leads worship, and governs the Church as Jesus did.

Who is a priest?

A priest is a baptized man who has received the Sacrament of Holy Orders. Priests are co-workers with their bishops. The priest teaches the faith; celebrates liturgy, above all the Eucharist; and helps to guide the Church.

Who is a deacon?

A deacon is ordained to assist bishops and priests. He is not ordained to the priesthood but to a ministry of service to the Church.

What is the Sacrament of Matrimony?

The Sacrament of Matrimony is one of the two Sacraments at the Service of Communion. In the Sacrament of Matrimony, a baptized man and a baptized woman dedicate their lives to the Church and to one another in a lifelong bond of faithful, life-giving love. In this sacrament, they receive the grace to be a living sign of Christ's love for the Church.

What are the sacramentals of the Church?

Sacramentals are sacred signs instituted by the Church. They include blessings, prayers, and certain objects that prepare us to participate in the sacraments. They also make us aware of and help us respond to God's loving presence in our lives.

Life in the Spirit

The Moral Life

Why did God create us?

We were created to give honor and glory to God and to live a life of blessing with God here on Earth and forever in Heaven.

What does it mean to live a moral life?

Baptized Christians have new life in Christ in the Holy Spirit. God places in us the desire to be happy with him. We respond to this gift by accepting the grace of the Holy Spirit and living the Gospel. The liturgy and sacraments nourish us to live the moral life more fully.

What is the Great Commandment?

The Great Commandment is Jesus' teaching to love God above all else and our neighbor as ourselves. It is the path to happiness. It is the summary and heart of the Commandments and all of God's Law.

What are the Ten Commandments?

The Ten Commandments are the Laws of the Covenant that God revealed to Moses and the Israelites on Mount Sinai. They teach us how to love God, others, and ourselves. The Bible tells us that the Commandments are written on the hearts of all people.

What are the Beatitudes?

The Beatitudes are the teachings of Jesus that summarize the path to true happiness. They explain the meaning of the Kingdom of God, which is living in communion and friendship with God, with Mary, and with all of the saints. The Beatitudes guide us in living as disciples of Christ by keeping our lives centered on God.

What are the Works of Mercy?

The word *mercy* refers to God's unconditional love and kindness at work in the world. Human works of mercy are acts of loving kindness by which we reach out to people in their physical and spiritual needs.

What are the Corporal Works of Mercy?

Some of the Works of Mercy are called the Corporal Works of Mercy. They are seven ways that we live Jesus' command to help people care for their bodily, or corporal, needs.

What are the precepts of the Church?

The precepts of the Church are five rules of the Church that help us as Catholics meet our responsibilities to worship God and grow in love of God and of our neighbor.

Holiness of Life and Grace

What is holiness?

Holiness is living in communion with God. It is the characteristic of a person who is in right relationship with God, with people, and with all of creation.

What is grace?

Grace is the gift of God's sharing his life and love with us.

What is sanctifying grace?

The word *sanctifying* comes from a Latin word meaning "to make holy." Sanctifying grace is a free gift of God, given by the Holy Spirit.

What are the Gifts of the Holy Spirit?

The seven Gifts of the Holy Spirit are graces that strengthen us to live our Baptism, our new life in Christ. They are wisdom, understanding, right judgment (counsel), courage (fortitude), knowledge, reverence (piety), and wonder and awe (fear of the Lord).

The Virtues

What are the virtues?

The virtues are spiritual powers or habits that help us to do what is good.

What are the Theological Virtues?

The Theological Virtues are the three virtues of faith, hope, and charity (love). These virtues are gifts and powers from God that help us to keep him at the center of our lives.

What are the Cardinal Virtues?

Moral Virtues are those attitudes and habits that help make it possible for us to live a moral life. The Cardinal Virtues are the four Moral Virtues of prudence, justice, fortitude, and temperance. They are called the *Cardinal*, or *hinge*, Virtues because all of the Moral Virtues are related to and grouped around them.

What is conscience?

Conscience is that part of every human person that helps us to judge whether a moral act is in harmony with God's Law. Our conscience moves us to do good and avoid evil.

Evil And Sin

What is evil?

Evil is the harm that we willingly inflict on one another and on God's good creation.

What is temptation?

Temptation is everything, either within us or outside us, that tries to move us from doing something good and to do or say something that we know is wrong. Temptation moves us away from living a holy life.

What is sin?

Sin is freely and knowingly doing or saying what we know is against the will of God. Sin turns our hearts away from God's love.

What is mortal sin?

A mortal sin is knowingly and willingly choosing to do something that is gravely contrary to the Law of God. The effect of mortal sin is the loss of sanctifying grace.

What are venial sins?

Venial sins are sins that are less serious than a mortal sin. They weaken our love for God and for one another and make us less holy.

Christian Prayer

What is prayer?

Prayer is conversation with God. It is talking and listening to him, raising our minds and hearts to God the Father, Son, and Holy Spirit.

What is the Our Father?

The Lord's Prayer, or Our Father, is the prayer of all Christians. It is the prayer that Jesus taught his disciples and gave to the Church. Praying the Lord's Prayer brings us closer to God and to his Son, Jesus Christ. It helps us to become like Jesus and to place our trust in God the Father.

What is vocal prayer?

Vocal prayer is spoken prayer, or prayer using words said aloud or in the quiet of one's heart.

What is the prayer of meditation?

Meditation is a form of prayer in which we use our minds, hearts, imaginations, emotions, and desires. Meditation helps us to understand and follow what the Lord is asking us to do.

What is the prayer of contemplation?

Contemplation is a form of prayer that is simply being with God.

Glossary

A-B

Almighty *page 29*
God's power to do everything and anything good.

Beatitudes *page 165*
The Beatitudes are the sayings or teachings of Jesus that describe real happiness, the happiness that God created people to have.

Bible *page 13*
The Bible is the Word of God. It was written by human writers who were inspired by the Holy Spirit.

Body of Christ *page 73*
The Body of Christ is a New Testament image for the Church that teaches that the members of the Church are made one in Christ, the Head of the Church.

charity *page 216*
Charity is one of the three Theological Virtues. Another word for charity is love. We practice the virtue of charity by loving God above all things and by loving our neighbor as ourselves.

compassion *page 136*
A person who has compassion feels the suffering someone else is having and reaches out to help that person. The parable of the Good Samaritan (Luke 10:29-37) is a good example of what Jesus teaches us about a person who has compassion.

conscience *page 173*
Conscience is the gift that God gives to every person that helps us know and judge what is right and what is wrong.

courage *page 56*
Courage, or fortitude, helps us do or say what is right even when it is hard or scary. Following Jesus means having courage as he did. Courage helps a person to be brave even when he or she is very afraid. People with courage know that God is always with them.

Creator *page 29*
God, who created everything and everyone, seen and unseen, out of love and without help.

diligence *page 192*
Diligence is when you stick with something and have resolve. A person who practices the virtue of diligence is committed and stays true to loving God first and foremost.

Divine Providence *page 29*
God's caring love for us.

Divine Revelation *page 21*
God making known both himself and his plan of creation and Salvation for the world and all people.

domestic church *page 145*
The domestic church is the church of the home.

E-F-G-H

Exodus *page 121*
The journey of the Israelites, under the leadership of Moses, from slavery in Egypt to freedom in the land God promised them.

faith *page 20*
Faith is a gift from God. It is the Theological Virtue that helps us know God and believe in him and in all that he has revealed.

forgiveness *page 128*
Forgiveness is an act of kindness or mercy. It is an action of the Beatitude, "Blessed are the merciful." People who generously practice forgiveness are peacemakers. They do not hold grudges.

fortitude *page 180*
Fortitude is one of the four Cardinal Virtues. It is the good habit of facing difficulties with strength and courage. Fortitude strengthens us to resist temptation. Fortitude helps us overcome the things in our lives that keep us from loving God and others.

free will *page 157*
Free will is the part of every person that gives him or her the ability to choose to love and serve God and others as he has created us to do, or to choose not to love and serve God and others.

generosity *page 164*
Generous people freely share what they have. They share because of their love for God and for people. Generous people truly believe that we are all members of the family of God.

Hebrews *page 181*
Hebrews is the name given to God's people, the Israelites, when they lived in Egypt.

holiness *page 144*
Holiness is living in communion with God. People who are holy are living signs of God's love in the world. Every person has the vocation to grow in holiness.

honor *page 201*
To have special respect for someone or to hold someone in high regard is to honor him or her.

hope *page 36*
Hope is a gift from God. The Theological Virtue of hope enables us to trust in God and in his promises. It helps us trust that God is always with us, in good times and difficult times.

I-J-K-L

Incarnation *page 49*
The Incarnation is the mystery of the Son of God, the Second Divine Person of the Trinity, becoming truly human while not giving up being God.

intellect *page 157*
Intellect is the part of every person that gives him or her the ability to know God, oneself, and other people, and how God wants us to live.

joy *page 108*
Joy is one of the Fruits of the Holy Spirit. It is a sign that we are living our Baptism. Joy comes from knowing that we are deeply loved by God. The gift of joy helps us be aware that life is a gift from God.

justice *page 172*
Justice is one of the four Cardinal Virtues. It is the good habit of giving to God and to all people what is rightfully due to them. It strengthens us to make decisions that build a world of peace.

kindness *page 120*
A kind person is loving and caring toward others. A kind person always treats people with respect. We live the virtue of kindness by treating others as we want to be treated.

knowledge *page 100*
Knowledge is one of the seven Gifts of the Holy Spirit. It helps us to see the truth of everything that God has made known to us. A person who uses this gift tries to learn more about God and what it means to be a child of God.

Last Supper *page 57*
The Last Supper is the last meal that Jesus celebrated with the disciples. At this meal, he gave the Church the gift of his Body and Blood, the Eucharist.

liturgy *page 93*
The liturgy is the work of the Church, the Body of Christ, as we worship God.

Liturgy of the Hours *page 85*
The daily, public, and communal prayer of the Church is called the Liturgy of the Hours.

Lord's Day *page 193*
The Lord's Day is the name given to Sunday by Christians because Sunday is the day of the Lord's Resurrection.

Lord's Prayer *page 217*
The Lord's Prayer is another name for the Our Father, the prayer that Jesus, our Lord, taught his disciples to pray.

love *page 48*
Love is the greatest of all the virtues. Jesus commanded his disciples, "Love one another as I love you" (John 15:12). Jesus loves us so much that he died on the Cross for us.

M-N-O

manna *page 121*
The bread-like food the Israelites ate in the desert during the Exodus is called manna.

mercy *page 208*
Mercy is the habit of living with kindness, compassion, and goodness. A person who lives the virtue of mercy is kindhearted and generous. A person who practices mercy looks for ways to help those who are hurting.

Messiah *page 37*
The Messiah is the person whom God promised to send to save people from sin. Jesus Christ is the Messiah.

Original Sin *page 37*
The sin committed by the first humans, who lost original holiness not only for themselves but for all human beings.

P-Q

Paschal Mystery *page 93*
The Paschal Mystery is Jesus' passing over from suffering and death to new and glorious life; Christ's work of Salvation accomplished by his Passion (his suffering and Death), Resurrection, and Ascension.

Passover *page 57*
Passover is the Jewish feast celebrating God freeing the Israelites from suffering and slavery in Egypt and leading them to freedom in the land that he had promised them.

Pentecost *page 65*
Pentecost is the day, fifty days after the Resurrection, that the Holy Spirit came to the disciples as Jesus had promised.

People of God *page 73*
A New Testament image for the Church that teaches that God has called together all people in Jesus Christ to be his people

perjury *page 209*
Perjury is lying under oath.

piety *page 92*
Piety, also called reverence, is one of the seven Gifts of the Holy Spirit. Piety is a deep respect for God and for the Church. A person who practices piety gives reverence and honor to God.

pray *page 85*
To pray is to raise our minds and hearts to God, who is Father, Son, and Holy Spirit; it is to talk and listen to God.

prudence *page 156*
One of the four Cardinal Virtues, prudence is a virtue that helps us know what is truly good for us. It also helps us know how to choose what is right and good.

public ministry of Jesus *page 49*
This is the saving work that God the Father sent his Son, Jesus, to do, beginning with the baptism of Jesus and his announcement of that work in the synagogue in Nazareth.

R–S

rabbi *page 217*
Rabbi is a Hebrew word meaning "teacher," a title of honor and respect in the Bible given to someone whom people trusted to help them understand and live the Law of God.

reparation *page 209*
Reparation is the work of repairing or making up for harm that we have wrongfully caused.

respect *page 200*
Respect means to give someone or something the honor that they deserve. People who are respectful treat others with dignity in the way they act and in what they say.

sacraments *page 101*
The sacraments are the seven main liturgical signs of the Church, given to us by Jesus Christ. They make us sharers in the saving work of Christ and in the life of the Holy Trinity through the power of the Holy Spirit.

Sacraments at the Service of Communion *page 145*
Holy Orders and Matrimony are called the Sacraments at the Service of Communion.

Sacraments of Christian Initiation *page 101*
Baptism, Confirmation, and Eucharist, which are the foundation of the Christian life, are called the Sacraments of Christian Initiation.

Sacraments of Healing *page 129*
The Sacrament of Penance and Reconciliation and the Sacrament of the Anointing of the Sick

Sacred Scripture *page 13*
The holy writings of the People of God, inspired by the Holy Spirit, and collected in the Bible

sanctifying grace *page 173*
Sanctifying grace is the gift of God sharing his own life with us, the gift of holiness.

sin *page 129*
Freely choosing to turn away from God's love and weakening or breaking one's friendship with God and the Church

suffering *page 137*
In the Sacrament of the Anointing of the Sick, our suffering is united with the saving work of Jesus.

synagogue *page 137*
The place in which Jewish people gather to pray, read, and study the Scriptures and the Law of God and other teachings of the Jewish religion

T–Z

Ten Commandments *page 181*
The Ten Commandments are the Laws of the Covenant revealed to Moses on Mount Sinai. They teach us to love God, others, and ourselves.

trust *page 28*
To trust in someone is to count on them to care for our well-being and respect us. To say "I trust in God" means that we know that we can count on him to be true to his word.

truthfulness *page 12*
God is the source of all truth. His word is truth. God wants us to live in the truth. We do this when we let God's Word guide our words and actions. A person who is truthful does not tell lies. A truthful person admits mistakes. Love and trust grow when we practice truthfulness.

understanding *page 72*
Understanding is one of the seven Gifts of the Holy Spirit. Understanding helps us find the truth about God and about ourselves. It helps us discover what it means to be disciples of Jesus, the Son of God.

vocation *page 109*
A vocation is the work that we do as members of the Church. We are called to use our talents to carry on Christ's mission in the world.

wisdom *page 64*
Wisdom is one of the seven Gifts of the Holy Spirit. This gift helps us see the world as God does. It helps us treat people with love as God treats everyone.

wonder and awe *page 84*
Wonder and awe, also called fear of the Lord, is a gift that strengthens our awareness of God's great love for us. Wonder is a gift that we experience more and more as our friendship with God grows through prayer.

worship *page 193*
To worship is to honor and respect above all else, to give adoration and praise to God.

Index

P-Q

R-S-T-U

V-W-X-Y-Z

Credits

Cover Illustration: Marcia Adams Ho/RCL Benziger

IMAGE CREDITS

FM: pF2a: ©cyb3rking/Getty; pF2b: ©Mark Edward Atkinson/Tracey Lee/Blend Images/SuperStock; p6: ©Ridofranz/Getty, ©Shutterstock; p8: ©Marcia Adams Ho/RCL Benziger

U1: p9-10: ©Jenny Reynish/RCL Benziger; pP10a: ©colorcocktail/Getty, ©VillageOfMaryAtSubukiaShrine_NacieNacie, ©NationalShrineSubukia_TysonOmosa; pP10b: ©NationalShrineSubukia_GidizDeMwarabu, ©Oceloti/Getty

CH1: p11: ©Tom Grill/Getty Elite, ©Rembrandt van Rijn/Bridgeman Images, ©DeSpaceStudio/Shutterstock, ©len4foto/Getty; p12: ©Tom Grill/Getty Elite; p13: ©robertharding/Alamy Stock Photo, ©Christophe Testi/Shutterstock; p14: ©Rembrandt van Rijn/Bridgeman Images; p15: ©Fabio Leone/RCL Benziger, ©RCL Benziger; p16: ©dpaint/Shutterstock; p17: ©DeSpaceStudio/Shutterstock; p18: ©Design Pics / Chris Futcher/Getty Elite; pF18a: ©Visual Generation/Getty, ©Design Pics/SuperStock; pF18b: ©Andrey Kozhekiny/iStock/Getty; pF18b: ©g-stockstudio/iStock/Getty; **FLC icons:** ©Andrey Kozhekiny/iStock/Getty, ©Mykyta Dolmatov/iStock/Getty, ©Giraphics/iStock/Getty, ©Jane_Kelly/iStock/Getty, ©mamanamsai2y/iStock/Getty;

CH2: p19: ©Jupiter Images/Getty, ©Biletskiy_Evgeniy/Getty, ©Bill Wittman, ©skynesher/Getty Elite; p20: © IMAGEMORE Co., Ltd. / Alamy Stock Photo, ©vejaa/Getty; p21: ©Biletskiy_Evgeniy/Getty; p22: ©Jenny Reynish/RCL Benziger; p23: ©Bill Wittman; p26: ©Bill Wittman; pF26a: ©Alison Wright/Corbis Documentary/Getty, ©M-image/iStock/Getty, ©ajr_images/iStock/Getty, ©Milkos/iStock/Getty, ©pixelheadphoto/iStock/Getty; pF26b: ©kaz_c/iStock/Getty, ©Jose Luis Pelaez Inc/DigitalVision/ Getty

CH3: p27: ©Sue Williams/RCL Benziger, ©Gary John Norman/Getty Elite, ©Bill Wittman, ©Alan Uster/Shutterstock; p28: ©Sue Williams/RCL Benziger; p29: ©davex83/Getty Elite; p30: ©Gary John Norman/Getty Elite; p31: ©Valentina Razumova/Shutterstock, ©Foto2rich/Shutterstock, ©monkeybusinessimages/Getty, ©jackhollingsworth/Shutterstock; p33: ©Bill Wittman; p34: ©MBI/Alamy Stock Photo; pF34a: ©Comstock Images/Stockbyte/Getty; pF34b: ©Wavebreakmedia/Getty

CH4: p35: ©Tracy L. Christianson/www.portraitsofsaints.com, ©Gene Plaisted, OSC/The Crosiers, ©colematt/Getty, ©Jenny Reynish/RCL Benziger; p36: ©Tracy L. Christianson/www.portraitsofsaints.com, ©Design Pics/SW Productions/Getty Elite; p37: ©Brand X Pictures/Getty, ©SDI Productions/Getty; p38: ©Gene Plaisted, OSC/The Crosiers, ©Yasuko Aoki/amanaimagesRF/Getty Elite; p39: ©Lisa F. Young/Alamy Stock Photo, ©Tetra Images, LLC/Alamy Stock Photo; p41: ©colematt/Getty; p42: ©Hispanolistic/Getty Elite; pF42a: ©LSOphoto/Getty; pF42b: ©IconicBestiary/Getty

U2: p45-46: ©Jenny Reynish/RCL Benziger; pP46a: ©colorcocktail/Thinkstock/Getty, ©Photo Beto/GettyElite, ©Brent Hofacker/Alamy Stock Photo; pP46b: Photo by RCL Benziger, ©Nadzeya_Dzivakova/Getty

CH5: p47: © jozef sedmak / Alamy Stock Photo, ©Jupiterimages/Getty, ©Bill Wittman, ©Jupiterimages/Getty; p48: © jozef sedmak / Alamy Stock Photo; p49: ©Jupiterimages/Getty, ©Cathy Baxter /Bridgeman Images; p50: ©Jenny Reynish/RCL Benziger; p53: ©Bill Wittman; p54: ©PG Arphexad / Alamy Stock Photo; pF54a: ©Gustavo Mazali/RCL Benziger, ©lvdesign77/Getty; pF54b: ©Linda Prater/RCL Benziger, ©nicolesy/iStock/Getty

CH6: p55: ©Kristin Sorra/RCL Benziger, ©Laura James/Bridgeman Images, ©Bill Wittman, ©Jon Feingersh Photography Inc/Getty; p56: ©Kristin Sorra/RCL Benziger; p57: ©Laura James/Bridgeman Images; p58: ©Jenny Reynish/RCL Benziger (all 3 images); p59: ©Jenny Reynish/RCL Benziger; p61: ©Bill Wittman; p62: ©ULTRA.F/GettyElite; pF62a: ©monkeybusinessimages/Getty; pF62b: ©pixelliebe/iStock/Getty, ©monkeybusinessimages/Getty

CH7: p63: ©Sean Sprague/Alamy Stock Photo, ©Jenny Reynish/RCL Benziger, ©SurfUpVector/Getty, ©Jason Patrick Ross/Shutterstock; p64: ©Used with permission. Maryknoll Sisters Photo Library, ©Sean Sprague/Alamy Stock Photo; p65: ©Jenny Reynish/RCL Benziger; p66: ©Jenny Reynish/RCL Benziger; p69: ©SurfUpVector/Getty; p70: ©fizkes/Getty; pF70a: ©serkorkin/Getty, ©Flying Colours Ltd/Getty

CH8: p71: ©Q2A Media/RCL Benziger, ©solarisimages/Getty, ©PeopleImages/Getty, ©MARIO LAPORTA/Stringer/Getty Images; p72: ©Q2A Media/RCL Benziger (all 7 Martyrs); p73: ©Marmaduke St. John/Alamy Stock Photo; p75: ©solarisimages/Getty; p77: ©PeopleImages/Getty; p78: ©Fuse/GettyElite; pF78a: ©yacobchuk/Getty, ©fiorigianluigi/Getty, ©pikepicture/Getty: pF78b: ©coja1108/Getty

U3: p81-82: ©Jenny Reynish/RCL Benziger; pP82a: ©colorcocktail/Thinkstock/Getty, ©EvgeniiAnd/Getty; pP82b: ©Jeff Preston/GoodSalt

CH9: p83: ©Design Pics/Alamy Stock Photo, ©Digital Vision./Getty, ©Zvonimir Atletic/Shutterstock, ©FatCamera/Getty Elite, ©Design Pics/Alamy Stock Photo; p85: ©RubberBall Productions/Getty Elite; p86: ©Digital Vision/Getty; p87: ©Bill Wittman p89: ©Zvonimir Atletic/Shutterstock; p90: ©Tetra Images/Alamy Stock Photo; pF90a: ©3sbworld/Getty, ©Purestock/Getty; pF90b: ©Wavebreakmedia/Getty

CH10: p91: ©Nature and Science / Alamy Stock Photo, © Vibrant Image Studio/Shutterstock, ©Gene Plaisted, OSC/The Crosiers, ©Spotmatik Ltd/Shutterstock; p92: ©Nature and Science / Alamy Stock Photo, ©Gene Plaisted, OSC/The Crosiers; p94: ©Kevin Howchin/Alamy Stock Photo; p95: ©Burgandy Beam/RCL Benziger, ©Vibrant Image Studio/Shutterstock; p97: ©Gene Plaisted, OSC/The Crosiers; p98: ©BananaStock/Getty; pF98a: ©Tracy L. Christianson/www.portraitsofsaints.com; pF98b: ©Hero Images Inc./Alamy Stock Photo

CH11: p99: ©Pep Roig/Alamy Stock Photo, ©Ted Foxx / Alamy Stock Photo, ©Gene Plaisted, OSC/The Crosiers, ©Jose Luis Pelaez Inc/Getty Elite; p100: ©Pep Roig / Alamy Stock Photo; p101: ©Bill Wittman; p102: ©Ted Foxx/Alamy Stock Photo, ©Bill Wittman; p103: ©Bill Wittman; p105: ©Gene Plaisted, OSC/The Crosiers; p106: ©Bill Wittman; pF106a: ©Getty, ©Jupiterimages/Getty; pF106b: ©Pict Rider/Getty

CH12: p107: ©Bob Mullen/The Catholic Photographer/www.catholicphotographer.com, ©Bill Wittman, ©Paul Simcock/GettyElite, ©Jenny Reynish/RCL Benziger; p108: ©Bob Mullen/The Catholic Photographer/www.catholicphotographer.com, ©Bob Mullen/The Catholic Photographer/www.catholicphotographer.com, ©Bill Wittman; p109: ©Bill Wittman (both); p110: ©Jim West/Alamy Stock Photo, ©Design Pics Inc/Alamy Stock Photo; p111: ©David Grossman /Alamy Stock Photo, ©Robertharding / Alamy Stock Photo; p113: ©Paul Simcock/GettyElite; p114: ©Wavebreakmedia/Getty; pF114a: ©DragonImages/Getty; pF114b: ©yayayoyo/Getty, ©MarianVejcik/Getty, ©ilkercelik/Getty, ©kwanchaichaiudom/Getty, ©Victor_Brave/Getty

U4: p117-118: ©Jenny Reynish/RCL Benziger; pP118a: ©colorcocktail/Thinkstock/Getty, ©Photo by Jean-Michel COUREAU/Gamma-Rapho via Getty Images; pP118b: ©Dennis Cox/Alamy Stock Photo, ©Dineshkpn/Getty

CH13: p119: ©Gina Capaldi/RCL Benziger, ©Mike Kemp/Getty Elite, ©Bill Wittman, ©Lotus_studio/Shutterstock; p120: ©Gina Capaldi/RCL Benziger; p122: ©Jenny Reynish/RCL Benziger; p125: ©Bill Wittman; p126: ©Tomas Rodriguez/Corbis/GettyElite; pF126a: ©Bob Mullen/The Catholic Photographer/www.catholicphotographer.com, Courtesy of Dominican Sisters of Mary, Mother of the Eucharist, www.sistersofmary.org, ©monkeybusinessimages/Getty; pF126b: ©Rawpixel/Getty

Credits

CH14: p127: © MercurioMT/Wikimedia/Creative Commons, ©PT Images/GettyElite, ©BryanBrayley-Willmetts/Getty, ©Raul Teran Aquino/Getty; p128: © MercurioMT/Wikimedia/Creative Commons; p129: ©Jenny Reynish/RCL Benziger; p130: ©Art Directors & TRIP/Alamy Stock Photo; p131: ©PT Images/GettyElite; p133: ©BryanBrayley-Willmetts/Getty; p134: ©Nancy R. Cohen/GettyElite; pF134a: ©Arleevector/Getty, ©Christopher Robbins/Getty; pF134b: ©Victor_Brave/Getty, ©MaksimYremenko/Getty, ©Ciaran Griffin/Getty

CH15: p135: ©imtmphoto/Alamy Stock Photo, ©Design Pics Inc / Alamy Stock Photo, ©David De Lossy/Getty, ©Jenny Reynish/RCL Benziger; p136: ©imtmphoto/Alamy Stock Photo; p137: ©laflor/Getty; p138: ©Design Pics Inc / Alamy Stock Photo; p139: ©Bill Wittman; p141: ©David De Lossy/Getty; p142: ©Wealan Pollard/GettyElite; pF142a: ©Goldfaery/Getty; pF142b: ©GlobalStock/Getty

CH16: p143: ©Kristin Sorra/RCL Benziger, ©Brand X Pictures/Getty, ©Stockbyte/Getty, ©Jupiterimages/Getty; p144: ©Kristin Sorra/RCL Benziger; p145: ©Pascal Deloche/Getty Editorial RF, © Ilene MacDonald / Alamy Stock Photo, ©Brand X Pictures/Getty; p146: ©OLIVER LANG/DDP/AFP via Getty Images, © M.T.M. Images / Alamy Stock Photo, © Spencer Grant / Alamy Stock Photo; p147: ©Antonio_Diaz/Getty, ©Stockbyte/Getty, ©Choreograph/Getty, ©Stockbyte/Getty; p149: ©Stockbyte/Getty; p150: ©Ryan McVay/Getty; pF150a: ©Bob Mullen/The Catholic Photographer/www.catholicphotographer.com, ©Getty; pF150b: ©Victor_Brave/Getty, ©Elizabeth Lowry/RCL Benziger, ©Highwaystarz-Photography/Getty, ©Yobro10/Getty

U5: p153-154: ©Jenny Reynish/RCL Benziger, pP154a: ©colorcocktail/Getty, ©JUAN DE LEON/ESTUARDO VILA S, ©AP Photo/Rodrigo Abd; pF154b: ©REUTERS/Alamy Stock Photo, ©Dineshkpn/Getty, ©ekazansk/Getty

CH17: p155: ©Fabio Leone/RCL Benziger, ©beyond foto/Getty Elite, ©Compassionate Eye Foundation/Justin Pumfrey/Getty Elite, ©PeopleImages/Getty; p156: ©Fabio Leone/RCL Benziger; p157: ©Jupiterimages/Getty Elite; p158: ©Peter Muller/Getty Elite; p159: ©beyond foto/Getty Elite; p161: ©Compassionate Eye Foundation/Justin Pumfrey/Getty Elite; p162: ©LM Productions/Getty Elite; pF162a: ©monkeybusinessimages/iStock/Getty, ©monkeybusinessimages/iStock/Getty; pF162b: ©DGLimages/Getty

CH18: p163: ©Tim Graham/GettyElit, ©Jupiterimages/Getty, ©Kristo-Gothard Hunor/Shutterstock, ©Jeffrey Isaac Greenberg 8+/Alamy Stock Photo; p164: ©Tim Graham/GettyElite; p165: ©Jupiterimages/Getty; p166: ©PhotoAlto/Alamy Stock Photo; p167: ©Cavan Images/Getty Elite, ©FatCamera/Getty Elite, ©uzhursky/Getty; p169: ©Kristo-Gothard Hunor/Shutterstock; p170: ©Jose Luis Pelaez Inc/Getty Elite; pF170a: ©Tim Graham/Alamy Stock Photo; pF170b: ©kotoffei/Getty, ©Military Collection/Alamy Stock Photo

CH19: p171: ©Sean Sprague/CRS/Alamy Stock Photo, ©Jupiterimages/Getty, ©Design Pics/Alamy Stock Photo, ©Yuriy Kulik/Shutterstock; p172: ©Sean Sprague/CRS/Alamy Stock Photo, ©Jennifer Hardy/Catholic Relief Services/CRS, ©Philip Laubner/Catholic Relief Services/CRS, ©Catholic Relief Services/CRS; p173: ©Wavebreakmedia/Getty, ©Jupiterimages/Getty; p174: ©dmbaker/Getty; p177: ©Design Pics/Alamy Stock Photo; p178: ©Tetra Images/Alamy Stock Photo; pF178a: ©LuckyTD/Getty, ©Zaikina/Getty; pF178b: ©Tomwang112/Getty, ©Paul Bradbury/Getty

CH20: p179: ©Cherie Zamazing/RCL Benziger, ©DAJ/Getty Elite, ©jarenwicklund/Getty, ©Jim West/Alamy Stock Photo; p180: ©Cherie Zamazing/ RCL Benziger; p181: ©Jenny Reynish/ RCL Benziger; p182: ©DAJ/Getty Elite; p183: ©Shutterstock; p184: ©dpaint/Shutterstock; p185: ©jarenwicklund/Getty; p186: ©PHOVOIR/Alamy Stock Photo; pF186a: ©iStockPhoto/Getty; pF186b: ©monkeybusinessimages/Getty, ©cthoman/Getty, ©John Rowley/Getty

U6: p189-190: ©Jenny Reynish/RCL Benziger; pP190a: ©colorcocktail/Thinkstock/Getty, ©Ana Lorena Gamboa & Alex Mene (both); pP190b: ©YAMIL LAGE/AFP via Getty Images, ©Dineshkpn/Getty

CH21: p191: ©Val Bochkov/RCL Benziger, ©ESB Professional/Shutterstock, ©Digital Focus/Alamy Stock Photo, © Peter Adams Photography / Alamy Stock Photo; p192: ©Val Bochkov/RCL Benziger; p193: ©Bill Wittman; p196: ©ESB Professional/Shutterstock, © SW Productions/Getty Elite, ©MIXA/Getty Elite; p197: ©Digital Focus/Alamy Stock Photo; p198: ©Jon Feingersh Photography Inc/Getty Elite; pF198a: ©Lisitsa/Getty, ©Wavebreakmedia/Getty; pF198b: ©Lisitsa/Getty

CH22 p199: ©monkeybusinessimages/Getty, ©Robert Daly/Getty, ©Amorn Suriyan/Getty, ©Ricky John Molloy/Getty Elite; p200: ©monkeybusinessimages/Getty, ©Halfpoint/Getty, ©miriam-doerr/Getty; p201: ©beyond foto/Getty Elite; p202: ©Chris Amaral/Getty; p203: ©Robert Daly/Getty, ©Design Pics/Alamy Stock Photo; p205: ©Amorn Suriyan/Getty; p206: ©DigitalVision/GettyImages; pF206a: ©Drazen Zigic/Getty; pF206b: ©Stretch Photography/GettyElite, ©Pollyana Ventura/Getty

CH23: p207: ©Wavebreakmedia/Getty, ©David Madison/GettyElite, ©Cherie Zamazing/RCL Benziger, ©Robert Daly/Getty; p208: ©Wavebreakmedia/Getty, ©JackF/Getty; p209: ©Design Pics/Alamy Stock Photo; p210: ©David Madison/GettyElite; p211: ©Nick Onken/GettyElite; p213: ©Cherie Zamazing/RCL Benziger; p214: ©Jose Luis Pelaez Inc/GettyElite; pF214a:©Tracy L. Christianson/www.portraitsofsaints.com, ©Stockbyte/Getty, ©YasnaTen/Getty; pF214b: ©fizkes/Getty, ©LuckyBusiness/Getty

CH24: p215: ©Tina Manley/Alamy Stock Photo, ©Bill Wittman, ©Gene Plaisted, OSC/The Crosiers, ©Jenny Reynish/RCL Benziger; p216: ©Tina Manley/Alamy Stock Photo; p217: ©Howard Barlow/Alamy Stock Photo; p218: ©Purestock/Getty Elite; p219: ©Bill Wittman; p221: ©Gene Plaisted, OSC/The Crosiers; p222: ©Stockbyte/Getty; pF222a: ©monkeybusinessimages/Getty; pF222b: ©airdone/Getty, ©danijelala/Getty

Liturgical Seasons: p225: ©dpaint/Shutterstock; p226: ©Fotosearch/Getty Elite, ©Steve Bridger/GoodSalt, ©ZUMA Press Inc /Alamy Stock Photo, ©Bill Wittman, ©RomoloTavani/Getty, ©Bill Wittman; p227: © Tim Graham/Corbis via Getty Images, ©Gene Plaisted, OSC/The Crosiers, ©Gene Plaisted, OSC/The Crosiers; p229: ©Fotosearch/Getty Elite; p231: ©Tracy L. Christianson/www.portraitsofsaints.com; p233: ©Marc De Simone/Alamy Stock Photo; p234: ©Catharine Collingridge/RCL Benziger; p235: ©Steve Bridger/GoodSalt; p237: © jozef sedmak / Alamy Stock Photo; p239: ©Nigel Paul Monckton/Shutterstock; p241: ©Bill Wittman, ©ZUMA Press Inc/Alamy Stock Photo; p243: ©Akira Kaede/Getty Elite; p245: ©Gene Plaisted, OSC, The Crosiers; p247: © Adam Ján Figel / Alamy Stock Photo; p249: ©RomoloTavani/Getty; p251: ©RomoloTavani/Getty; p252: ©Dan Bridy/RCL Benziger p253: ©Gene Plaisted, OSC, The Crosiers; p255: ©sedmak/Getty Editorial; p256: ©Yellow Dog Productions/Getty Elite, ©M.T.M. Images/Alamy Stock Photo, ©Sean Sprague /CRS/Alamy Stock Photo; p257: ©Bill Wittman p260: ©Mary Wessel/RCL Benziger; p262: ©Zoran Vukmanov Simokov/Shuttterstock; p263: All Stations of the Cross images: ©Zvonimir Atletić/Alamy Stock Photo; p265: ©Gene Plaisted, OSC, The Crosiers; p266: ©Bill Wittman; p267: ©Bill Wittman; p268: ©Bill Wittman; p269: ©Bill Wittman; p270: ©Bill Wittman; p271: ©Gene Plaisted, OSC, The Crosiers

Notes